BUSINESS SCHOOLS AND
THE CHALLENGE OF INTERNATIONAL BUSINESS

Papers Presented at the
Conference on Education for International Business
November 30, December 1 and 2, 1967
Tulane University

EDITED BY STEPHEN A. ZEFF
GRADUATE SCHOOL OF BUSINESS ADMINISTRATION
TULANE UNIVERSITY, NEW ORLEANS, LA., 1968

USINESS SCHOOLS AND
HE CHALLENGE OF INTERNATIONAL BUSINESS

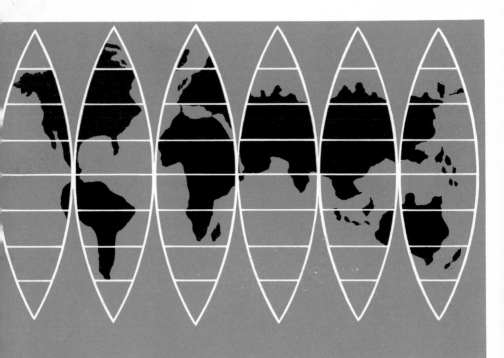

EDITED BY STEPHEN A. ZEFF
GRADUATE SCHOOL OF BUSINESS ADMINISTRATION
TULANE UNIVERSITY, NEW ORLEANS, LA.

Preface

What should business schools be doing about the international dimension of modern business enterprise? Should they participate in institution-building programs abroad, and if so, what are the caveats of which administrators should be aware? Should international business be a major or field of emphasis in bachelor's and master's programs? Should any course work in international business be offered at all? What type of research is needed in international business? Indeed, what *is* international business? Is it business conducted in foreign countries? Comparative business systems? The conduct of business across boundaries? All of these? — none of these?

These and other questions have been facing business schools in the United States for several years, and the responses have varied. Some schools have developed international business majors. Others have developed one or two courses in international business, disdaining a major. Some have chosen to rely on the student's experience abroad as the internationalizing catalyst. A number of schools have engaged in ambitious technical-assistance projects abroad. Some of these have had only partial success, while others have succeeded to a high degree.

Experience has thus been accumulated by business schools in answering the challenge of international business—in curriculum, research, continuing education, student exchange, and technical assistance. The thinking of business educators on the role of business schools in international business has begun to crystallize, though few will say they have achieved long-term solutions for their schools.

A school's decision, or strategy, depends on many factors: its objectives, its faculty interests, its funds, its size. Particularly in technical assistance abroad, much can be learned from the experience of those who have pioneered, many of the lessons falling under the head, "Adaptation to Environment."

This book endeavors to present the thinking and experience of some thirty business-school deans, professors and business executives who have been active in one or more aspects of international business. They have planned curricula, taught courses, written textbooks and articles, engaged in research, participated in significant foreign assignments, or they have engaged in the conduct of international business itself. Some of the papers discuss curriculum policy at the authors' schools, while others review their experiences abroad. They write not only as narrators but as critics of the programs in which they have been involved. Still other papers are devoted entirely to the development of hypotheses about the role of the business school in international business, drawing heavily on the authors' personal experiences.

The papers in this volume were presented at a Conference on Education for International Business, held at Tulane University on November 30, December 1 and 2, 1967. It was jointly sponsored by Education and World Affairs and the Tulane Graduate School of Business Administration. The Conference was aimed mainly at business school deans. Included in the attendance of 146 deans, professors, business executives, and others were representatives from 98 U. S. business schools and 11 Latin American business schools. In most cases, the dean himself attended. Thus, an opportunity was provided for key administrators to become involved in an exchange of ideas and experiences.

The taking-off point for the Conference was a report issued in June, 1967 by Education and World Affairs, discussing the international dimensions of education for business administration and public administration, as part of EWA's overall study of The Professional School and World Affairs. (The part of the report dealing with business administration is referred to in this book as "EWA Report.") Early in 1968, the University of New Mexico Press will publish in one volume all five of the reports which emerged from the EWA study.[1]

If one theme is dominant in most of the papers, it is that a school must plan its involvement in international business with care and thoroughness. This counsel applies with especial emphasis to prospective involvements abroad. In the area of curriculum policy, decisions on international business can have important implications for the thrust of the entire degree program. Once made, some decisions are hard to retrieve. They may set in motion a series of other, perhaps unexpected, decisions, leaving an indelible mark on the school's escutcheon.

But it is not my task to distill the essence from the papers. The papers speak for themselves, and the syntheses of the exchanges

---

[1]The other four reports deal with medicine and public health, agriculture and engineering, law, and education. The address of EWA is 522 Fifth Avenue, New York, New York 10036.

Page references in this volume to the "EWA Report" pertain to the separately-published paperback issued in June, 1967. To find the corresponding page references to the University of New Mexico Press volume, add 2 to these page numbers.

that occurred at the several discussion sessions reflect reactions to what was said in the papers.

For the reader who did not attend the Conference, the best guide to the setting in which each paper was given is the Conference program, which is reproduced, together with the list of participants, immediately prior to the first paper. A biographical note is given for each author, based on information provided prior to the Conference.

It is my duty to record an occurrence that saddened all those who attended the Conference. On Saturday morning, December 2, the last day of the Conference, Acting Dean Francis McIntyre, of the University of Hawaii, was stricken by an apparent heart attack, and died. In two short days, Dean McIntyre had won the friendship and respect of many of the participants, and we mourned his passing.

For valuable assistance in planning and executing the Conference and in editing this volume of proceedings, I have numerous debts to acknowledge. I am grateful to Irwin T. Sanders, of Education and World Affairs, and John Fayerweather, of New York University, for wise counsel in the early stages of planning the Conference program. To Eric W. Vetter, James T. Murphy, Hugh B. Carnes, Eugene T. Byrne, Jr., and James J. Linn, my Tulane colleagues who culled from the discussion sessions the principal points for inclusion in this volume, I express sincere appreciation for a task that was harder than I had imagined. Doris G. Campbell and Ann Hopkins, who expertly planned and executed all arrangements for the Conference, were indispensable associates. Ann Z. Bernos, Jeanette Warren, Janet McDaniel, and Ed Brinkley were more than equal to my incessant demands for the typing of correspondence, duplication of Conference materials, and retyping of papers for this volume.

Without the constant counsel and encouragement of Jack Grayson, dean of the Tulane Business School, the Conference would have been much less than it was. Indeed, it was he who originated the idea of holding the Conference. This is not the standard polite acknowledgment to one's boss, but an expression of deep appreciation and profound respect for a colleague who can move mountains.

STEPHEN A. ZEFF

New Orleans, Louisiana
January, 1968

CONTENTS

CONTENTS — Continued

CONTENTS – Continued

PROGRAM

Conference on Education for International Business

Tulane University

November 30, December 1, 2, 1967

THURSDAY, NOVEMBER 30, 1967,
MONTELEONE HOTEL, QUEEN ANNE ROOM

4:30 p. m. to 6:30 p. m.—Registration

6:00 p. m. to 9:15 p. m.—Reception and Dinner

Welcome and opening orientation paper by Dean C. Jackson Grayson, Jr., Graduate School of Business Administration, Tulane University (co-author of *EWA Report*), outlining major points in the *EWA Report* and setting forth objectives of the Conference.

Address by Dr. G. A. Costanzo, Senior Vice President in charge of the Overseas Division, First National City Bank, New York City, discussing recent developments in the conduct of business across international boundaries and their implications for the collegiate education of future business executives.

FRIDAY, DECEMBER 1, 1967,
UNIVERSITY CENTER, TULANE UNIVERSITY CAMPUS

CURRICULUM STRATEGY

KENDALL CRAM ROOM

9:00 a. m. to 10:00 a. m.

Chairman: Professor Stephen A. Zeff, Graduate School of Business Administration, Tulane University

"The Place of International Business in the Business School Curriculum: Major Issues and Controversies," Professor John Fayerweather, Graduate School of Business Administration, New York University.

Coffee break.

10:15 a. m. to 12:00 p. m.

Four concurrent discussion sessions, in which curriculum issues and controversies will be reviewed and discussed critically, an attempt being made to trace different approaches to the unique curriculum philosophies of different schools. (Size of each group, 30 to 40.) Each discussion session will have a discussion leader and a two-member panel. The task of each discussion leader will be to keep the dialogue on the central points, while attempting to bring out the contrasting curriculum philosophies of different schools and the apparent implications of these philosophies for decisions in international business. He should also attempt to bring out the experience that schools having different approaches have had to date. The panel is intended to stimulate discussion with pointed questions, critical observations, and statements about experience at their schools. Each session will begin with a short statement from each panel member about what has been learned from the experience at his school.

Concurrent Panel Sessions:

A. ANDERSON-HUNT ROOMS

Discussion leader: Dean Donald J. Hart, College of Business Administration, University of Florida
Panel: Professor Laurence P. Dowd, Director, Center for World Business, School of Business, San Francisco State College
Professor Endel Kolde, School of Business Administration, University of Washington

B. PRESIDENTS ROOMS

Discussion leader: Dean George E. Manners, School of Business Administration, Georgia State College.
Panel: Dr. Richard D. Robinson, Alfred P. Sloan School of Management, Massachusetts Institute of Technology
Professor Leo Spier, College of Business Administration, Pennsylvania State University

C. STUDENT SENATE ROOMS

Discussion leader: Dean Kermit O. Hanson, School of Business Administration, University of Washington
Panel: Professor Robert W. Adams, Graduate School of Business Administration, University of Michigan
Professor Lee C. Nehrt, Graduate School of Business, Indiana University

D. IMOGEN STONE ROOM

Discussion leader: Dean Clark E. Myers, School of Business Administration, University of Miami
Panel: Professor Dan T. Smith, Graduate School of Business Administration, Harvard University
Professor Michael Y. Yoshino, Graduate School of Business Administration, University of California (Los Angeles)

12:15 p. m. to 1:45 p. m., Rathskeller Luncheon

Chairman: Dean C. Jackson Grayson, Jr., Graduate School of Business Administration, Tulane University. Remarks by Professor Hans Picker, Director, Comité Latinoamericano de Decanos de Escuelas de Administración, and by Dean George P. Shultz (co-author of the *EWA Report*), Graduate School of Business, University of Chicago. Welcome by President Herbert E. Longenecker, Tulane University.

STRATEGY FOR OVERSEAS ACTIVITIES

KENDALL CRAM ROOM

2:00 p. m. to 3:15 p. m.

Chairman: Dean Alfred L. Seelye, Graduate School of Business Administration, Michigan State University

"Challenges in Assisting in the Development of a Business School or a Management Training Program Abroad." Three papers.

First paper, Dean William D. Carmichael, Graduate School of Business and Public Administration, Cornell University.

Second paper, Professor W. Warren Haynes, Chairman, International Teachers Program, Graduate School of Business Administration, Harvard University.

Third paper, Dean Reinaldo Scarpetta, División de Ciencias Sociales y Económicas, Universidad del Valle, Cali, Colombia.

Coffee break.

3:40 p. m. to 5:25 p. m.

Four concurrent discussion sessions, organized in the style described above.

Concurrent Panel Sessions:

A. ANDERSON-HUNT ROOMS

> *Discussion leader*: Dean Paul Garner, School of Commerce and Business Administration, University of Alabama
>
> *Panel*: Professor Claude Mc Millan, School of Business, University of Colorado
>
> > Dean Sterling D. Sessions, Escuela de Administración de Negocios para Graduados (ESAN), Lima, Peru

B. PRESIDENTS ROOMS

> *Discussion leader*: Dr. Sherman F. Dallas, Director, School of Industrial Management, Georgia Institute of Technology
>
> *Panel*: Dean Edgardo Reyes Salcido, Escuela de Graduados en Administración, Instituto Tecnológico y de Estudios Superiores de Monterrey, México
>
> > Professor George B. Simmons, School of Business Administration, University of Massachusetts

C. STUDENT SENATE ROOMS

> *Discussion leader*: Professor Ross M. Trump, School of Business and Public Administration, Washington University
>
> *Panel*: Professor Edward L. Elliott, College of Commerce and Business Administration, University of Illinois
>
> > Associate Dean Thomas A. Graves, Jr., Graduate School of Business Administration, Harvard University

D. IMOGEN STONE ROOM

Discussion leader: Dean James S. Schindler, School of Business Administration, State University of New York at Buffalo

Panel: Professor Thomas M. Hill, Alfred P. Sloan School of Management, Massachusetts Institute of Technology

Professor Roderick F. O'Connor, School of Industrial Management, Georgia Institute of Technology

INTERNATIONAL HOUSE, downtown New Orleans

6:45 p. m. to 9:30 p. m.

Cocktails and dinner. Brief remarks by Dr. Paul A. Fabry, Managing Director, International House, and Dr. Marshall A. Robinson, The Ford Foundation. Address, "Strategies for Education in International Business: The Business School in the University Constellation," Chancellor Herman B Wells, Indiana University.

SATURDAY, DECEMBER 2, 1967,
UNIVERSITY CENTER, TULANE UNIVERSITY CAMPUS

**OVERALL STRATEGY FOR EDUCATION
IN INTERNATIONAL BUSINESS**

KENDALL CRAM ROOM

9:20 a.m. to 9:50 a.m.

Chairman: Professor Stephen A. Zeff, Graduate School of Business Administration, Tulane University

"Critique of the *EWA Report*," Dean W. George Pinnell, Graduate School of Business, Indiana University.

Coffee break.

10:15 a. m. to 12:00 p. m.

Four concurrent discussion sessions on separate topics. Each session will begin with two 20-minute talks, followed by a discussion period organized in the style shown above.

Concurrent Panel Sessions:

A. ANDERSON-HUNT ROOMS

"Research in International Business."

Discussion leader: Professor Raymond Vernon, Graduate School of Business Administration, Harvard University

Panel: Professor Robert Z. Aliber, Graduate School of Business, University of Chicago

Professor Stefan H. Robock, Graduate School of Business, Columbia University

—4—

B. PRESIDENTS ROOMS

"Technical Assistance on the Campus: Visiting Students, Faculty, and Businessmen Studying in the United States; An Evaluation of Experience."

Discussion leader: Dean James M. Hund, School of Business Administration, Emory University

Panel: Associate Dean Thomas A. Graves, Jr., Graduate School of Business Administration, Harvard University

Acting Dean Vernon K. Zimmerman, Director, Center for International Education and Research in Accounting, College of Commerce and Business Administration, University of Illinois

C. STUDENT SENATE ROOMS

"Technical Assistance Abroad and the Curriculum and Research at Home: The Problem of Feedback."

Discussion leader: Associate Dean Hoke S. Simpson, Director of Executive Programs, Graduate School of Business, Columbia University.

Panel: Professor Alan B. Coleman, Graduate School of Business, Stanford University

Professor Leo G. Erickson, Graduate School of Business Administration, Michigan State University

D. IMOGEN STONE ROOM

"Prerequisites for Effective Management of International Business Today."

Discussion leader: Professor David J. Ashton, College of Business Administration, Boston University

Panel: Mr. Frank Pace, Jr., President, International Executive Service Corps, New York City

Mr. William S. Lindsay, International Division Vice President, Corn Products Company, New York City

12:30 p. m. to 2:30 p. m. Rathskeller Luncheon

Chairman: Dean C. Jackson Grayson, Jr., Graduate School of Business Administration, Tulane University.

"The Next Ten Years in Education for International Business," Dean Courtney C. Brown, Graduate School of Business, Columbia University.

List of Participants

CONFERENCE ON EDUCATION FOR INTERNATIONAL BUSINESS
November 30, December 1, 2, 1967
Tulane University, New Orleans, La.

A school's official representative is listed first

1. AACSB BUSINESS
   SCHOOLS

UNIVERSITY OF AKRON
Professor Stephen S. Castle

UNIVERSITY OF ALABAMA
Dean Paul Garner
(discussion leader)

UNIVERSITY OF ARIZONA
Professor Gary Munsinger

ARIZONA STATE UNIVERSITY
Dean Glenn D. Overman

UNIVERSITY OF ARKANSAS
Dean Merwyn G. Bridenstine

BOSTON COLLEGE
Professor Alfred E. Sutherland

BOSTON UNIVERSITY
Professor David J. Ashton
(discussion leader)

BOWLING GREEN STATE
UNIVERSITY
Dr. William Hoskins

BRIGHAM YOUNG UNIVERSITY
Dean Weldon J. Taylor

UNIVERSITY OF CALIFORNIA
(Los Angeles)
Professor Michael Y. Yoshino
(panelist)

CALIFORNIA STATE COLLEGE
AT LOS ANGELES
Dean Floyd R. Simpson

CARNEGIE-MELLON UNIVERSITY
Acting Dean Richard G.
Brandenburg

UNIVERSITY OF CHICAGO
Dean George P. Shultz
Professor Robert Z. Aliber
(panelist)

UNIVERSITY OF CINCINNATI
Dean Kenneth Wilson

THE CITY COLLEGE OF THE CITY
UNIVERSITY OF NEW YORK
Professor Samuel Ranhand

UNIVERSITY OF COLORADO
Associate Dean Philip R.
Cateora
Professor Claude Mc Millan
(panelist)

COLUMBIA UNIVERSITY
Dean Courtney C. Brown
(speaker)
Associate Dean Hoke S. Simpson
(discussion leader)
Professor Stefan H. Robock
(panelist)

UNIVERSITY OF CONNECTICUT
Dean Robert O. Harvey

CORNELL UNIVERSITY
Dean William D. Carmichael
(speaker)

DARTMOUTH COLLEGE
Associate Dean John W.
Hennessey

UNIVERSITY OF DELAWARE
Dean Ruben V. Austin

DREXEL INSTITUTE OF
TECHNOLOGY
Dr. Charles Welsh

DUQUESNE UNIVERSITY
Assistant Dean O. W. Nestor

EMORY UNIVERSITY
Dean James M. Hund
(discussion leader)

UNIVERSITY OF FLORIDA
Dean Donald J. Hart
(discussion leader)

FLORIDA STATE UNIVERSITY
Dean Charles A. Rovetta

FRESNO STATE COLLEGE
Dean McKee Fisk

UNIVERSITY OF GEORGIA
Professor L. Aubrey Drewry

GEORGIA STATE COLLEGE
Dean George E. Manners
(discussion leader)

HARVARD UNIVERSITY
Associate Dean George F. F.
Lombard
Associate Dean Thomas A.
Graves, Jr. (panelist)
Professor Dan T. Smith
(panelist)
Professor Raymond Vernon
(discussion leader)
Professor W. Warren Haynes
(speaker)

UNIVERSITY OF HAWAII
Acting Dean Francis McIntyre

UNIVERSITY OF HOUSTON
Professor Melvyn R. Copen

UNIVERSITY OF ILLINOIS
Professor E. Joe DeMaris
Acting Dean Vernon K.
Zimmerman (panelist)
Professor Edward L. Elliott
(panelist)

INDIANA UNIVERSITY
Dean W. George Pinnell
(speaker)
Chancellor Herman B Wells
(speaker)
Professor Lee C. Nehrt
(panelist)

UNIVERSITY OF IOWA
Dean B. L. Barnes

UNIVERSITY OF KANSAS
Acting Dean Wiley S. Mitchell

KENT STATE UNIVERSITY
Dean Bernard Hall

UNIVERSITY OF KENTUCKY
Associate Dean Joseph L. Massie

LEHIGH UNIVERSITY
Dean L. Reed Tripp

LOUISIANA STATE UNIVERSITY
(Baton Rouge)
Associate Dean Clarence L.
Dunn

LOYOLA UNIVERSITY (Chicago)
Dean F. Virgil Boyd

LOYOLA UNIVERSITY
(New Orleans)
Acting Dean G. Ralph Smith

MARQUETTE UNIVERSITY
Dean T. R. Martin

UNIVERSITY OF MASSACHUSETTS
Dean-elect Wendell R. Smith
Professor George B. Simmons
  (panelist)

MASSACHUSETTS INSTITUTE
  OF TECHNOLOGY
Professor Thomas M. Hill
  (panelist)
Dr. Richard D. Robinson
  (panelist)

UNIVERSITY OF MIAMI
Dean Clark E. Myers
  (discussion leader)

UNIVERSITY OF MICHIGAN
Professor Robert W. Adams
  (panelist)

MICHIGAN STATE UNIVERSITY
Dean Alfred L. Seelye
  (chairman)
Professor Leo G. Erickson
  (panelist)

UNIVERSITY OF MINNESOTA
Professor George Seltzer

UNIVERSITY OF MISSISSIPPI
Professor James E. Parks

MISSISSIPPI STATE UNIVERSITY
Professor Lawrence A. Kratz

UNIVERSITY OF NEBRASKA
Dean Charles S. Miller

UNIVERSITY OF NEVADA
Dean Robert C. Weems, Jr.

STATE UNIVERSITY OF NEW YORK
  AT BUFFALO
Dean James S. Schindler
  (discussion leader)

NEW YORK UNIVERSITY
  (Graduate School of Business
  Administration)
Professor John Fayerweather
  (speaker)

NORTH TEXAS STATE UNIVERSITY
Dean O. J. Curry

NORTHEASTERN UNIVERSITY
Assistant Dean Carlo E.
  Gubellini

NORTHWESTERN UNIVERSITY
Dean Ralph Westfall

UNIVERSITY OF NOTRE DAME
Dean Thomas Timothy Murphy

OHIO STATE UNIVERSITY
Professor Reed Powell

OHIO UNIVERSITY
Dean Harry F. Evarts

OKLAHOMA STATE UNIVERSITY
Dean Richard W. Poole

MUNICIPAL UNIVERSITY OF
  OMAHA
Dean John W. Lucas

UNIVERSITY OF PENNSYLVANIA
Professor Franklin R. Root
  (panelist)

PENNSYLVANIA STATE UNIVERSITY
Dean Ossian MacKenzie
Professor Leo Spier (panelist)

UNIVERSITY OF PITTSBURGH
Associate Dean H. J. Zoffer

PURDUE UNIVERSITY
Professor Charles Lawrence

UNIVERSITY OF ROCHESTER
Professor William C. Wichman

ROOSEVELT UNIVERSITY
Dean Richard R. Weeks

RUTGERS—THE STATE UNIVERSITY
Professor William A. Dymsza

SAINT LOUIS UNIVERSITY
Dean Stephen W. Vasquez

SAN FRANCISCO STATE COLLEGE
Dean William Niven
Professor Laurence P. Dowd
(panelist)

SAN JOSE STATE COLLEGE
Dean Milburn D. Wright

UNIVERSITY OF SANTA CLARA
Professor D. Robert Papera

UNIVERSITY OF SOUTH CAROLINA
Professor Garnett F. Beazley, Jr.

UNIVERSITY OF SOUTHERN
CALIFORNIA
Associate Dean Paul R. Cone

SOUTHERN ILLINOIS UNIVERSITY
(Carbondale)
Professor Andrew F. Powell

SOUTHERN METHODIST
UNIVERSITY
Professor Sydney C. Reagan

STANFORD UNIVERSITY
Associate Dean Samuel A. Pond
Professor Alan B. Coleman
(panelist)

SYRACUSE UNIVERSITY
Professor Peter G. Franck

TEMPLE UNIVERSITY
Dean Seymour L. Wolfbein

UNIVERSITY OF TENNESSEE
Dean Arthur E. Warner

UNIVERSITY OF TEXAS
Professor Lee A. Tavis

TEXAS CHRISTIAN UNIVERSITY
Dean Ike H. Harrison

TEXAS SOUTHERN UNIVERSITY
Dean Milton Wilson

TEXAS TECHNOLOGICAL COLLEGE
Dean George G. Heather

TULANE UNIVERSITY
Dean C. Jackson Grayson, Jr.
(chairman and speaker)
Professor Stephen A. Zeff
(chairman)
Professor Eric W. Vetter
(reporter)
Professor Hugh B. Carnes
(reporter)
Associate Dean Eugene T.
Byrne, Jr. (reporter)
Professor James T. Murphy
(reporter)
Professor James J. Linn
(reporter)

UNIVERSITY OF TULSA
Dean M. M. Hargrove

UNIVERSITY OF VIRGINIA
Dean Frank S. Kaulback, Jr.

VIRGINIA POLYTECHNIC INSTITUTE
Dean H. H. Mitchell

UNIVERSITY OF WASHINGTON
Dean Kermit O. Hanson
(discussion leader)
Professor Endel J. Kolde
(panelist)

WASHINGTON UNIVERSITY
Professor Ross M. Trump
(discussion leader)

WEST VIRGINIA UNIVERSITY
Professor Thomas S. Isaack

UNIVERSITY OF WISCONSIN
(Madison)
Associate Dean Edward J.
Blakely, Jr.

2. NON-AACSB U. S.
   BUSINESS SCHOOLS

GEORGIA INSTITUTE OF
TECHNOLOGY
Dr. Sherman F. Dallas
(discussion leader), Director
Professor Roderick F. O'Connor
(panelist)

KANSAS STATE UNIVERSITY
Acting Dean Blair J. Kolasa

LOUISIANA STATE UNIVERSITY
IN NEW ORLEANS
Dean John E. Altazan

UNIVERSITY OF SOUTHWESTERN
LOUISIANA
Dean Herbert A. Hamilton

3. LATIN AMERICAN BUSINESS SCHOOLS

BRAZIL

ESCOLA DE ADMINISTRACAO DE
EMPRESAS DE SAO PAULO
Dr. Gustavo de Sá e Silva,
Director

COLOMBIA

UNIVERSIDAD DE LOS ANDES;
Bogotá
Dean Eduardo Wiesner D.,
Facultad de Economía

UNIVERSIDAD DEL VALLE; Cali
Dean Reinaldo Scarpetta
(speaker), División de Ciencias
Sociales y Económicas
Professor Hans Picker, Director,
Comité Latinoamericano de
Decanos de Escuelas de Ad-
ministración

CHILE

UNIVERSIDAD DE CHILE; Santiago
Professor Abraham Toledo, Director, Instituto de Administración (INSORA), Facultad
de Ciencias Económicas

UNIVERSIDAD CATOLICA DE CHILE;
Santiago
Professor Rolf Lüders, Director
del Centro de Investigaciones,
Facultad de Ciencias Econó-
micas y Sociales

MEXICO

INSTITUTO POLITECNICO NA-
CIONAL; Mexico City
Dr. Octavio Gómez Haro

INSTITUTO TECNOLOGICO Y DE
ESTUDIOS SUPERIORES DE
MONTERREY
Dean Edgardo Reyes Salcido
(panelist), Escuela de Grad-
uados en Administración

UNIVERSITY OF THE AMERICAS;
Mexico City
Dr. Melvin E. McMichael,
Director, International Busi-
ness Center

NICARAGUA

INSTITUTO CENTROAMERICANO DE
ADMINISTRACION DE EMPRESAS
(INCAE); Managua
Sr. Ernesto Cruz

PERU

ESCUELA DE ADMINISTRACION DE
NEGOCIOS PARA GRADUADOS
(ESAN); Lima
Dean Sterling D. Sessions
(panelist)

VENEZUELA

INSTITUTO DE ESTUDIOS SUPERI-
ORES DE ADMINISTRACION
(IESA); Caracas
Dr. Santiago E. Vera I., Presi-
dent

4. OTHERS

DRS. D. J. PRINS, Head of Secre-
tariat and Documentation
Centre
International University Contact for Management Education; Rotterdam

MR. ROBERT L. GULICK, JR.,
Dean of Admissions and
Registrar
American Institute for Foreign
Trade; Phoenix

DR. MARSHALL A. ROBINSON
The Ford Foundation, New
York City

MR. BRUCE C. COTTON, Vice
President, Transylvania College

DR. G. A. COSTANZO (speaker),
Senior Vice President in
charge of Overseas Division
First National City Bank;
New York City

DR. HERBERT E. LONGENECKER,
President
Tulane University

MR. WILLIAM S. LINDSAY
(panelist), International
Division Vice President
Corn Products Company; New
York City

MR. HERMAN F. SMITH,
Project Director
Educational Testing Service;
Princeton, New Jersey

DR. PAUL A. FABRY,
Managing Director
International House; New
Orleans

MR. FRANK PACE, JR. (panelist),
President
International Executive Service
Corps; New York City

C. JACKSON GRAYSON, JR.
Tulane University

Background and Objectives of the Conference

A conference is a conference is just another conference . . . unless. Unless the people have a direct and immediate interest in the topic, unless they participate in the dialogue, unless there is both information-giving and receiving by those with interest, experience, and curiosity, a conference becomes just another conference. We all have had enough of those.

This Conference on Education for International Business has been designed to avoid becoming just another group of assembled friends. We have the ingredients for a successful conference. International Business is a topic of direct and immediate concern to all deans of Schools of Business Administration, most of you assembled here have either prepared papers or will take part in panel discussions, and the program is designed to encourage inquiry and controversy. Now I would like to take a few minutes to give you some background as to why we are here.

This Conference arises because of a direct interest of Education and World Affairs (EWA) in international affairs. EWA was founded as a nonprofit, educational organization in 1962 to assist in strengthening United States colleges and universities in their international teaching, research, and service activities. In 1965, EWA launched a

C. JACKSON GRAYSON, JR., is Dean and Professor of Business Administration, Graduate School of Business Administration, Tulane University. He has an MBA from the University of Pennsylvania and a DBA from Harvard University. He first joined the Tulane faculty in 1959 after holding several teaching and administrative positions at Harvard. He became Dean in 1963, and was on the IMEDE faculty, in Lausanne in 1963-64. He has been a newspaper reporter and FBI agent, and is a Certified Public Accountant. He has published *Decisions Under Uncertainty: Drilling Decisions by Oil and Gas Operators* (Harvard Business School, 1960). Among his research interests is the application of computers to farm management.

study entitled "The Professional School and World Affairs" to examine the reciprocal impact between professional schools and international affairs. Professional schools had been going through a period of growth, ferment, and re-examination. Little national assessment existed of the current trends or the future prospects regarding the professional schools in their international dimensions.

Such a study could easily have been one of sight and sound, signifying only the obvious. Almost every professional school already recognizes that the international dimension is important and that there should be opportunities for overseas work for United States professional people. Rather, this study was designed to close the gap between the evolving *practices* and the *self-awareness* and *articulation* of purpose and meaning. Typically, professional schools have been so busy getting tasks accomplished that they have not searched out the significance and implications of what is obviously a high level of professional school activity in international affairs.

Therefore, a study was initiated.

The overall responsibility for the study was vested in a general study committee composed of Task Forces which were to do the primary work. There were four such Task Forces: Agriculture and Engineering, Law and Education, Medicine and Public Health, and Business Administration and Public Administration. It is the work of the latter Task Force with which we are concerned.

Serving on the Task Force on Business Administration and Public Administration were nine persons representing the two professional fields, with the following ones from the area of business administration:

> Robert D. Calkins, President, The Brookings Institution
> George P. Shultz, Dean, Graduate School of Business, University of Chicago
> C. Jackson Grayson, Jr., Dean, Graduate School of Business Administration, Tulane University.

Working in this same Task Force were professionals in the area of public administration who provided valuable suggestions as the Task Force proceeded with its work.

The first meeting of the overall study committee was convened in 1965, and the final reports of the Task Forces were presented in late 1966 and early 1967. Information for the reports of the Task Forces was gathered by questionnaires, personal visits, published materials, and telephone calls. The work of our Task Force covered about a year and a half, and in the middle of this work our efforts were greatly assisted by the addition of a staff member—a Professor of Accounting at Tulane University—Stephen A. Zeff. Professor Zeff was an invaluable member in helping to gather together the materials and in drafting the report. Additionally, he was one of those largely instrumental for the organization and design of this Conference.

Let me give you the general setting for the work of the Task Force in three dimensions: the international environment, the business schools, and business itself. In the international environment, we have:

1. An unprecedented speed of international communications and transportation (Jumbo Jets, satellites, SST's)
2. A world population explosion
3. Continuing and rising intranational and international political tensions
4. An increasingly pragmatic, technological, and experimental approach to decision-making—as contrasted to solely idealogical formulae
5. An increasingly global population.

In the business schools, we have:

1. Expanding graduate work in master's and doctoral programs
2. Increasing quality of faculty and students
3. Increasing numbers of students in graduate programs whose undergraduate work has been in engineering, mathematics, or social sciences
4. Emergence of a firmer, conceptual base, as schools begin stressing scientific knowledge underlying all business instead of instruction in past and current practices of business
5. Increasing interrelationships among government agencies and their policies
6. Increasing importance of continuing education.

In U. S. business itself, we have:

1. Unparalleled expansion of investment in countries outside the United States
2. Creation of subsidiaries and affiliates by acquisition, direct investment, and joint venture
3. New forms of organization structures and novel operational problems in logistics, financial planning, nationalistic forces, profit retrieval problems, etc.

Now, with these settings as the scenario, we of the Task Force decided to address ourselves to the following two broad questions:

1. What have been the experiences of schools which entered the international field, and what may be learned from them?

2. What possible strategies may be employed by business schools seeking to expand into this field at various levels of commitment?

At the survey level, we grouped the activities under five main headings:

1. Curriculum
2. Student exchange
3. Research
4. Technical assistance
5. Continuing education.

We found quite a wide variety of programs, plans, and conceptual bases on which the schools were proceeding, and we presented these in our report. We attempted to explain this diversity, in part, by the different objectives and conditions at each school, but mainly by an unresolved controversy that permeates faculty discussions of international business curricula.

This controversy is now at two levels: conceptual and pragmatic. At the conceptual level, there are those who believe that international business represents an extension of the existing business curriculum. There are also those who contend that international business constitutes a separate and distinct field of study, while drawing occasionally on existing curricula for support. On a pragmatic level, there is recognition by some that faculty members cannot, or will not, meet the challenge of acquiring competence in the international dimension. Thus, they say, it is necessary to support the existing curriculum with special courses in international business.

The authors of the report took the position that there is not now a sufficient formal body of knowledge to justify a host of courses with "international" used mainly as an adjective. Rather, we believe that broad and steady research should be undertaken to determine the proper form and substance of the field, and we urge that comparative studies be continued and expanded in all fields.

We also looked at the possible strategies that schools might employ in their approach to international business, and we posed three questions that each school faces:

1. How best to mount a broad attack on international business problems?
2. How to design a curriculum?
3. How to relate the entire program to the existing educational efforts of the school?

Each school must naturally work out its own strategy. Nonetheless, we suggested in the report the main determinants that should influence the strategy selection, and we listed thirty-four kinds of activities ranging from:

1. A minimum commitment of resources, such as accepting qualified students from abroad, to
2. A major commitment, such as accepting technical assistance contracts and performing most of the work abroad.

We then stratified these activities into four general classes:

1. Threshold strategies
2. Lower-intermediate strategies
3. Upper-intermediate strategies
4. Grand strategies.

The report was submitted to the overall study committee, and all of us breathed a sigh. Shortly thereafter, on a bus from Washington to Friendship Airport with Steve Zeff, I first had the idea of a follow-up conference to this report. Subsequently, I approached EWA with a request for financial assistance to stage such a conference with two principal objectives in mind:

1. First, although there have been several conferences on education for international business, we felt that there had not been a conference to examine the entire range—the total package—of activities constituting education for international business. By this we meant to include curriculum, student exchange, technical assistance, research, and continuing education.
2. Second, we wanted to polarize the issues that have been silently, but powerfully, shaping the diverse programs found in business schools today. We wanted to bring out the contrasting philosophies, define the underlying beliefs, and examine the explicit and implicit assumptions. Our strong belief was that while discussions of practices or approaches are helpful, the delineation of conceptual issues underlying such practices is more beneficial to the long-run development of this kind of education.

In short, we wanted an active dialogue and not just another conference. We set out, therefore, to gather several groups. We wanted to have the recognized professors and deans who were active in this field. They would be the speakers, panelists, and chairmen of discussion sessions. We also wanted those responsible for the general leadership of their schools—the deans. We recognized that there could be a lot of dialogue in each individual school, but the deans themselves must be a party to this dialogue for significant action to take place.

Such an interaction clearly could not take place in a mammoth conference. Therefore, we decided to hold the size of the Conference to a level where the necessary exchange of ideas and experience could take place. We decided to invite, primarily, the deans of accredited schools of business in the United States and selected deans of business schools in other countries. Later, we expanded the invitation list slightly to include some other schools and institutions which had expressed a strong interest in the Conference.

The grant from EWA permitted us to hold the Conference here at Tulane and to pay the travel expenses of the speakers and panelists, plus the cost of the dinners and luncheons during the Conference. Unfortunately, the grant was not large enough to cover the travel costs of others in attendance.

Though we had suspected that there would be a strong interest in such a conference, we were overwhelmed with the response. Of the 126 accredited business schools in the United States, there are 94 represented at this meeting, the deans themselves constituting the majority of the representation.

We have as speakers and panelists practically all of the recognized professors and deans who are active in writings and actions in the international field.

We have ten deans from schools of business in Latin America and one representative from Europe.

And we have several leaders from business who are representative of the level of involvement of American industry abroad.

We have an issue of direct and immediate concern to those assembled here. We have those who have information to pass on to others. We have those who are seeking information in order to map out strategies for their own schools. We have representatives from schools which have given help and from those which have received help. We have a program that invites discussion and controversy.

In short, I think we have the ingredients of a successful conference. Let the dialogue begin.

G. A. COSTANZO
First National City Bank

International Business and the Cordon Bleu

In talking to you this evening about the educational requirements for international business and banking, I promise to protect you from the experience of the retiring business school professor.

At the farewell dinner honoring him, he was asked whether he had any final advice for the staff. He replied, "Yes, in the future, accept only one-armed students." When he was asked to explain, he said: "You will avoid students who write 'on the one hand this, and on the other hand that.'"

We have that problem too. Indeed there is little difference between us: we only sit on different sides of the aisle. You are trying to educate the youngsters we need so desperately. We in business can't operate without your help, and you can't very well perform your function without our cooperation, especially in the sphere of international business and banking.

THE PRESENT AND FUTURE OF INTERNATIONAL BUSINESS

The problem for both business and education, I want to suggest this evening, is to understand that the international arena moves the game to a new environment; it does not alter the fundamentals of the

G. A. COSTANZO is Senior Vice President of the First National City Bank in charge of the Overseas Division. He has a PhD in economics from the University of Virginia. He was formerly Deputy Director of the Western Hemisphere Department of the International Monetary Fund, where he negotiated many of IMF's stabilization programs with various Latin American countries. Before joining IMF, he was the American member of the Greek Currency Committee, and was architect of the Greek currency stabilization program of 1953. He has also served in various international policy positions with the U. S. Departments of State and Treasury. He was Assistant Professor of Economics at the University of Maryland before World War II and was a part-time lecturer at Georgetown University in the immediate post-War period. He served during the War with the U. S. Navy as a Japanese Language Officer.

game. You can see this, first, in the scope of international business and banking; and second, in the nature of the demands which that activity places upon its participants.

To begin with, international business has become big business. U. S. direct investments abroad now total about $60 billion, compared with only $8 billion at the end of World War II, and are growing at a rate of 10 per cent per annum in spite of governmental restraints.

Another, and perhaps more significant, measure of the dimension of U. S. international business is a recent estimate by Dr. Judd Polk, of the U. S. International Chamber of Commerce, on the value of the output of U. S.-owned production facilities abroad. His estimate is in excess of $120 billion, the third largest in the world after the U. S. and the USSR. Obviously, an activity of this dimension can no longer merely be a peripheral concern of U. S. businessmen; it has become a matter of central importance now. For there is every indication that businessmen will continue to increase their direct investment abroad.

But size does not tell us much, unless we understand the challenges it will bring. One of these will be to adapt to the accelerating pace of technological change. We are on the threshold of still another era of dynamic technological progress. It is certain to alter the face of international business as we know it today. In the 1970's a network of communications satellites and coaxial cables will encircle the globe, making possible the instantaneous transmission of business data from almost any place in the world to any other. This development, plus the multiple-access computer, must produce an information explosion that will become a driving force in business as well as an incredible asset for management control.

Moreover, technological progress is rapidly beginning to eliminate some of the obstacles to the development of a truly international corporation, as it provides more sophisticated ways to coordinate and plan operations. The development of corporate planning techniques has occurred in recent years in response to the needs of the giant domestic corporation. These techniques are already being applied by corporations with far-flung international operations to integrate the international side of their business into their overall strategy. As a result, there will be much more freedom to allocate responsibility to those in the best position to exercise it than has been the case in the past.

The success of international businessmen in organizing their operations for maximum efficiency and flexibility will largely determine their ability to meet a second challenge in the years ahead—namely, increased competition in world markets.

As more and more companies in the United States and elsewhere begin to recognize the opportunities to be found in world markets and to expand across their own national boundaries, there will be a substantial increase in competition. Indeed, trade in manufactured goods among the industrial nations in the postwar period has been growing even faster than industrial output. Historically, this is unprecedented.

It is clear that as U. S. companies become more dependent on external markets, their potential vulnerability to foreign competition will increase. As a result of lower labor costs, Western European and particularly Japanese companies are posing serious problems of price competition. But U. S. companies are generally credited with an edge on technological development. This is a matter of particular concern to our competitors. The struggle for markets will turn increasingly on research and development programs and will result in an accelerated growth of science-based products and industries.

The existence of a technological gap has already begun to arouse some anxiety among Europeans, who envision themselves in a position of economic subservience if the gap continues to widen. Consequently, the international businessman finds himself faced with the challenge of nationalism.

Nationalistic resentment of foreign investment is a phenomenon that poses a real threat to the future. The potential conflict between nationalism and international business arises from the fact that investment by a foreign corporation is double-edged. For example, on the plus side, foreign investment brings a capital inflow to the country, together with new technology. It also means more jobs for the local labor force. In addition, it may reduce imports and/or generate exports.

But the entry of the modern international firm into a country generates revolutionary forces which permeate the whole economy. Traditional business practices suddenly become obsolete. The local family-run industrial empires, after literally a century of profitable operations, are faced with the urgent necessity for revolutionary changes for survival. And, of these changes, the most difficult is adaptation to modern business management. Obviously, this creates resentment and fans the fires of nationalism. This does not mean, however, that nationalism and international business are incompatible.

Indeed, international business must make a real effort to understand the problems of the host countries and the roots of nationalism. I am confident that through understanding, forms of cooperation and accommodation will emerge which will ease the transition to the new and inevitable era of international business. The joint venture is one form of adaptation. I see great opportunities in joint ventures and other forms of cooperation between international business and the traditional family-run enterprises abroad. Another form of adaptation is for the American to assume a local character, to become less obviously and distinctly American. One possible approach is to employ local nationals wherever possible and to reduce American personnel to a minimum. By placing local nationals in top jobs, the company will be represented by men who will be unlikely to evoke resentment on nationalistic grounds.

But whatever approach is finally adopted, the burden rests squarely on the international business community to conduct its operations so as to avoid resentment in the countries in which it operates. A failure to recognize and react to the threat posed by nationalism would prejudice the future of international business.

ATTRIBUTES OF THE SUCCESSFUL INTERNATIONAL BUSINESSMAN

Overall, then, you can expect that the scale, complexity, and importance of international business spurred by technological change will increase immeasurably. Moreover, differences in economic growth, ingrained nationalistic habits, and the differing nature of competition itself all tend to change the ground rules. As a result, the man who has been an effective executive in domestic operations is not always equally effective if he is placed in an international context. Experience suggests that international businessmen must possess certain qualities that are not essential for success in business at home, yet make the difference between success and failure in overseas operations.

Simultaneously, however, the fundamental nature of international business will not change. The world market will continue to be a patchwork of national markets with wide variations in living standards. I believe this point has a most important bearing on our discussion, for the men who succeed in the business world of the 1970's and 80's must possess the same basic qualities that they do today.

In short, the question before us is how do you train a man to keep pace with technology, meet competition, and avert what might be called nationalistic backlash? What kind of man can meet the challenges in the international business world of the future? Here are some tentative suggestions.

First and probably foremost is the matter of a man's attitudes and how they have been formed. He must want to live and work in any part of the world for an indefinite period of time. He must understand what this commitment entails, and he must be capable of fulfilling it.

It is not an easy matter for business recruiters to identify such a man. It may interest you to know that at First National City Bank (FNCB) we have never been able to develop a pre-employment test that correlates reliably with success on the job. There is probably no group of businessmen in the United States today with more diverse backgrounds than those in international business. I know English majors as well as MBAs who are heading up international divisions of leading U. S. corporations. Still, we have developed some expertise over the years in identifying the men most likely to succeed in international careers. It's necessary to look at the whole man, his intelligence, background, personality, education, and skills. For international business is not the place for narrow-minded individuals of limited scope. Men who have traveled widely or lived abroad or whose outlooks have been broadened by association with professors at our liberal arts colleges have the background for a career in international business.

In addition, there are certain characteristics common to the men who succeed in international business. As a group, they tend to be extremely flexible when confronted with new situations. They can adapt to foreign cultures and operate effectively within them. Conversely, they are not easily frustrated when they discover that the old answers no longer seem to apply to the new problems that confront them.

What's more, they have probing, analytical minds. They can reach decisions even when they must work with limited information, as is still frequently the case in international business. They are empathetic in their approach to new people and new situations. They take time to listen to an opposing point of view and proceed into new areas with an open mind. They employ a diplomatic approach in their dealings at all levels. They frequently possess a genuine interest in closer ties among nations and feel a sense of involvement in the task of economic development and an improvement in living standards throughout the world. It is this strain of altruism that is often what attracts them into international business to begin with.

These, then, are the personal characteristics that distinguish the subtle differences between the international businessman and his domestic counterpart. If an individual does not possess these characteristics, then he is most probably ill-suited for a career in international business.

Secondly, if we can locate an individual who has the background and personal characteristics that I have mentioned, he is going to need a kit of tools for his job overseas.

The first and most obvious of these, but also the most important, is language. It is impossible to over-emphasize the need for fluency in the language of a host country. Men who try to do business without a firm footing in the language are placed at an inordinate disadvantage. It is unrealistic to rely on others knowing English. What is worse is that our foreign competitors often make a mockery of us by handling several languages fluently. Americans have tended to delude themselves about languages, paying lip service to their importance, but rarely learning to speak them.

Moreover, the need for more sophisticated business tools is increasing as the conduct of international business itself becomes more sophisticated. In light of the developments in technology and business techniques, knowledge of the principles of corporate planning and budgeting will be helpful. So will a basic understanding of the computer.

To be sure, this is an area that can be filled in during the course of an individual's career. In a corporate environment which has recognized the importance of continuing education, the business schools have begun to work closely with corporations to provide tools as well as special skills so as to speed an individual's progress.

What I have been suggesting, essentially, is that the international company is looking not for readers of cook books, but for cordon bleu chefs, not for potential candidates who simply go by the business texts, but for those who can be creative in a foreign environment of change as well. And so beyond sensitivity and adaptability and the modern business tools, we find an imperative need for —

> **The ability to analyze.** His training should have been such that he takes an analytical approach to whatever problem he encounters.
>
> **A knowledge of languages.** If he does not have that knowledge, he should at least understand that he must

acquire a fluency.

A broad-based familiarity with what is going on in the world. This would include at least survey history courses and contemporary events.

A grounding in international economics. The British experience of the past few weeks is proof enough of the need to understand the fundamentals of the international monetary system and the inter-relationships among monetary and fiscal policies, prices, the international balance of payments, and exchange rates.

This background is by no means icing on the cake. Rather, the items I have just enumerated are what make the difference between the domestic and the international business recruit. This, I realize fully, is a tall order; nevertheless, it is an order that must be filled. And I am happy today that we are filling it to a degree.

An increasing number of young men hired for international executive development programs have graduate degrees. At FNCB, 77 per cent of the men in our training program have graduate degrees of one sort or another; 35 per cent of the graduate degrees are MBAs.

Of course, corporate recruiters rarely encounter the ideal candidate. They usually wind up by hiring a person with a good international orientation who has expressed an interest in business, or a fellow who is a crackerjack business type who has expressed an interest in working overseas. The company then provides a training program designed to fill in the gaps.

We are also discovering that we can satisfy some of our requirements and at the same time slow down what has been called the "brain drain." We can do this in two ways. One is to hire the foreign national who has come here for a graduate education. The other way is to hire nationals abroad and bring an American education to them.

Within the context of his own country, the local national who has had a U. S. university education or its equivalent is preferable to an American. He is at home in the country, meaning that he will be dealing in his native language, with a people and a culture he has known from birth. Nor does the local national have to be moved onto location, nor does he have to be paid a premium for living outside his own country. And with an increasing number of foreign students being educated in the United States, a pool of talent is being created which international business is beginning to draw upon.

And we find recruiting on the spot even more advantageous for us and for our host countries. We have begun to introduce the executive development program overseas where local conditions warrant such a move. We have been successful enough in this experiment to amend our manpower plans for American personnel. In the next five years, we plan to hold recruiting of Americans for our international staff at present levels, although we anticipate a doubling of overall manpower needs as we continue to expand rapidly abroad.

Altogether, then, the whole subject of education for international business and banking is extremely fluid. We can say that, fundamentally, domestic management and international management differ not in the basic rules and techniques, but only in the nuances created by different environments. We can say also that education for overseas assignments demands an added emphasis on a knowledge of language, economics, and international affairs.

But when we have said this in whatever detail, we must add finally that what determine a man's ultimate suitability for international business are his attitudes.

To be sure, this leaves the educator at a disadvantage. He can provide all of the knowledge required, and he can stimulate the development of the crucial attitudes in receptive persons, but he cannot implant them in unreceptive minds.

This is also the case for the businessman. We can give a man the opportunity to demonstrate his capabilities, but we cannot assure that he will take complete advantage of them.

And so, as I suggested before, short order cooks won't do. Give us the cordon bleu chefs, if you can.

JOHN FAYERWEATHER
New York University

The Place of International Business in the Business School Curriculum:

MAJOR ISSUES AND CONTROVERSIES

It is a great pleasure to be here today and to be part of a conference which symbolizes an important milestone in the evolution of international business education in this country. We have come a very long way since I started work in teaching an international course almost 20 years ago. The change from being a marginal, relatively insignificant subject area to status as a major concern of an assemblage of people of your caliber is tremendous. Education and World Affairs has done us a notable service by giving this process a vigorous shove ahead, and Tulane is to be commended for adding to that shove by bringing us all together. I would also like to add a personal note of respect for Steve Zeff who did a major portion of the writing of the *EWA Report* and has done the lion's share of putting together this Conference, a task which we all know requires no small amount of energy, ingenuity, and persistence.

JOHN FAYERWEATHER is Professor of International Business, Graduate School of Business Administration, New York University. He has MBA and DCS degrees from Harvard. Prior to joining the NYU faculty in 1961, he was on the Harvard and Columbia business faculties, having directed Columbia's first Management Program in International Operations, a 6-week executive program. He is founder and managing editor of *The International Executive*, and has been executive secretary since 1965 of the Association for Education in International Business. He was president of AEIB in 1961-62. He has published *The Executive Overseas* (Syracuse University Press, 1959), *Management of International Operations* (McGraw-Hill, 1960), *International Marketing* (Prentice-Hall, 1964), and *International Business Education: Curriculum Planning* (NYU Graduate School of Business Administration, 1966), among other works. He was chairman in 1962-63 of the AIESEC-US Board of Advisors, and was consultant to the Department of Health, Education and Welfare on the recent International Education Act. Since 1965, he has been engaged in research on nationalism and the multinational corporation.

My objective this morning is to lay before you the major questions which I believe must be resolved one way or another if a business school is to discharge its responsibilities in preparing men and women for modern business careers. I do not intend to belabor the importance of the international component in those careers. The evidence is so overwhelming that I don't think it requires lengthy exposition before as sophisticated an audience as this. A very large portion of U. S. industrial and financial firms have an important direct stake in international business, either as investors and sellers or as importers. Virtually every other enterprise has a significant indirect concern with international business either because of its competitive impact or because international elements are important variables in their operations; for example, the effects of the U. S. balance of payments problem on money markets, with implications for banks of all types throughout the country. It seems to me readily apparent, therefore, that business schools must think of themselves as preparing students to function in a world society, not simply in a domestically-oriented society. Your presence here today, I think, attests to the fact that the business schools of this country have accepted this proposition, and we have gone on to the more complex questions of what we do to fulfill these responsibilities.

My role in this Conference is to identify critical issues and to indicate to you certain ways of thinking about them which I believe to be useful. Let me emphasize at the outset that I have no delusions about my views on any subject being the last word. My positions on a number of questions have changed substantially over time, and I fully expect that they will continue to change. I trust, however, that this statement of my current views will serve its intended function of stimulating what I am sure is going to be an extremely fruitful discussion over the next couple of days.

IDENTITY OF "INTERNATIONAL BUSINESS"

Any discussion of curriculum planning must start from assumptions as to the nature of the subject matter at hand and its educational implications. What is international business? Some people claim that it is a distinctive new field, even a discipline unto itself. I cannot agree with that position. I have tried very hard in my own teaching and writing to isolate things which I could identify as international business distinct from other fields and disciplines. So far, I have failed. The best that I can do is to put together certain concepts which are particularly useful in dealing with the problems encountered by business in international operations. But all of these concepts are essentially derived from existing functional business fields or basic disciplines like economics and political science, for example, the determination of export strategy which is largely a blend of marketing principles and international trade theory or strategy in the ownership pattern of a multinational organization and which combines consideration of business policy and political science.

But this does not mean that international business does not have an identity in the spectrum of business subject matter. It can be identified as a phase of study when considered in conjunction with — or better, as an extension of — traditional fields of study. It adds a new dimension to them, typically a broader and more complex dimension. International business is, therefore, in the first instance identified as a part of traditional fields, for example, international marketing, international economics, international business policy, and so forth.

As a second phase in the identification process, one can, I think, discern a unifying theme which runs through these separate international phases of the traditional fields. That unifying theme is essentially the substantial difference in the environmental variables to which the concepts of each field must be related. These environmental variables recur in fundamentally similar form with respect to each field, and there are elements of the process of relating to them which also recur from field to field. These elements of commonality do provide something which may be called "international business," even though I am not prepared to classify them as a field or a discipline in the same sense as other aspects of business or basic disciplines.

IMPLICATIONS FOR THE CURRICULUM

The foregoing, I believe, leads logically to the conclusion that there are two essential components of preparation for international business responsibility. First, functional capabilities appropriate to the international environment, and, second, skill in perception and adaptation to the environmental variables with respect either to different foreign countries or to the global economic-political context. The implications of these two need to be spelled out further.

The contrast in speaking of functional abilities appropriate to the international environment is with those whose suitability is limited to a more parochial environment, for example, just to the United States or just to industrially advanced countries. Some forms of depreciation accounting, for example, are suitable only to the degree of inflation encountered in the United States and not to extreme inflation such as one finds in Brazil. To perform effectively in international business the manager must clearly acquire skills in his chosen field which are suitable for whatever conditions he may encounter. So far as our business education is concerned, there are two possibilities here which depend upon the level of abstraction which each functional field or piece of a field has achieved. First, there are situations in which a level of abstraction has been achieved in which the content of instruction has universal applicability. To cite a simple example, the ratio of profit to capital employed is a broadly useful concept for measuring the effectiveness with which the capital is being utilized. To the extent that instruction is pursued at such a universally applicable high level of abstraction, specialized instruction for international business is theoretically not necessary. As a practical matter, however, it often turns out in such situations that the incorporation of international content proves useful as a means for demonstrating and reinforcing the universal applicability of the concepts. And this inclusion of international material has a secondary benefit in broadening the outlook of the student.

Second, we have those situations in which the concepts considered in general non-international courses are strictly applicable only to the United States and nations reasonably similar to it. In advertising, for example, a number of our approaches are pertinent to a market dominated by a large, affluent middle class, and are not particularly meaningful in a country with a mass of impoverished people and only small middle and upper classes. Where the instruction in general courses is of this nature, the development of functional skills appropriate specifically to other environments becomes a separate educational task. This is the primary logic for separate courses on the international aspects of specific functions — international accounting, international business policy, international marketing, and so forth. In an international marketing course, for example, the student may grapple specifically with the problems of advertising in less-developed countries and modify the concepts which he has previously acquired in general courses to fit these different circumstances.

Some years ago, a very large portion of instruction in business schools fitted the second of these categories. By now, however, I think we have generally moved a long way towards the first. That is, much of our instruction used to be concerned with specific features of U. S. business like the supermarket or our particular type of commercial bank, but our courses have increasingly moved towards a level of abstraction well beyond this limited parochial view. The extent to which the concepts we are purveying have full universal applicability, however, varies greatly from field to field and within individual fields from one subject to another. And of course, there is substantial variation among schools in this regard. The determination as to whether functional competence appropriate for international business is developed adequately in general courses or requires separate treatment in individual functional courses must therefore be made on a case-by-case basis, depending upon the level of abstraction achieved in individual schools and courses.

The second aspect of international business competence, skill at perception and adaptation to environmental variables, is quite a different order of pedagogical problem. To indicate its dimensions, we need only contemplate its domestic counterpart. Businessmen are effective in applying functional skills in their home society because they have been conditioned to perceiving and relating themselves to that society since they were babies. Relating one's actions to an environment is a total process with physical, emotional, and intellectual elements. The proposition before us is the complex and difficult one of achieving a modest portion of this skill with respect to new environments in a fairly short educational period. Clearly our expectations should be modest. In particular, it seems unlikely that we can make any significant progress at the emotional level.

At the intellectual level, we may hope for some achievement. Probably we could hope to do quite a bit if our assignment were limited to preparing an individual to work in only one other specific country. Except in rare cases, however, this degree of specialization is a poor service for the American student whose international contacts are most likely to be with a variety of countries and with the world environment as a whole. A more realistic and useful objective, therefore, is to develop in the student certain generalized skills which are appropriate to the process of perception and adaptation in any new environment.

These, in essence, are the types of skills which are rooted in basic disciplines like economics and anthropology. Regrettably, except in the case of international economics, the basic disciplines themselves have not cast their concepts in a form which appears to be particularly suitable for the business student. Perhaps they will in due course, for certainly major progress has been made in constructing behavioral science courses useful for the general business student.

In the meantime, however, we find that this aspect of education for international business is most effectively achieved in varying forms of applied environmenal study — in area courses like Latin American Business; in comparative courses either of full business systems or in the functional areas, like comparative management; and in the international functional courses. The area courses tend to be most useful for this purpose primarily because the environment itself is given greater direct attention. However, the latter two types of courses may often be equally effective, because the requirements of perception and adaptation are given particular urgency by relating them directly to functional objectives. That is, if the student is told to develop a distribution plan for tractors in Turkey, he will be strongly motivated to get a good picture of the nature of the agricultural communities in that country and the requirements which the situation presses upon his distribution system.

I don't much like to assign priorities as between these two aspects of international business, the functional and environmental skills, because I think that both are extremely important. However, I recognize that in the design of curricula, priorities are often required. To the extent that they are, I think there is no question that the functional skill takes precedence over the acquisition of skill in environmental perception and adaptation. In part, I think this conclusion stems from the lower level of effectiveness of our educational approaches in the latter category. The fact is that we are still not very skillful in developing the capacities of people for environmental adaptation, and until our skills progress farther it is unsound to devote too much of our time in that direction. And in part, my conclusion stems from the experience of the business community. By and large, they have found that the functional competence of individuals is more critical to their successful performance in international business than their environmental skills, at least where the latter are at a certain minimum effective level. The typical observation by an international executive is, "I am a lot more interested in how much the man knows about finance than what he knows about foreign countries. The more of the latter he knows the better, but first make sure that he has a solid training in financial management (— or marketing, or management, or whatever the field may be)."

TYPES OF COURSES

The development of functional skills appropriate to international environments and the development of skill in perception and adaptation to these environments provide the goals for international business curricula. Now to consider the way in which specific types of courses may contribute to these goals.

First, how much can be accomplished in the general run of non-international courses — the core courses and the non-international courses in each functional field? The possibility of introducing international studies into these courses is particularly appealing because it offers a convenient channel for reaching the broad mass of students as distinguished from those with specialized international interests. I personally am very anxious to push as far as I can in this direction for precisely that reason. However, there are significant limitations to how much we can and should try to do along these lines. The critical question is the extent to which inclusion of international material in a general course will contribute to or detract from the basic mission of that course, which is to develop a fundamental functional competence of the student. Two weeks ago I participated in a conference sponsored by Indiana University which focused on the international content of four types of courses: accounting, business policy, finance, and marketing—a very interesting study which I think is about six or seven months from publication, and I think it will be very helpful to all of us. One point which emerged force-fully from the discussions was that the feasibility of including inter-national material varied tremendously. In some fields, where func-tional concepts are at an early stage of development (business policy is one example), the instructors feel that the inclusion of international material distracts from the study of the concepts themselves and therefore decreases the effectiveness of the course in the achieve-ment of its basic mission. On the other hand, there are instances in which the inclusion of international material was cited as enriching and strengthening the impact of the basic functional content of the course. I believe that these differences can, in large measure, be traced to the question of level of abstraction, which was discussed previously. On the whole, it appears that where the concepts in a course are well established at a high level of abstraction, the inter-national material can be incorporated readily, and that it enriches the content of the course. On the other hand, where the instruction is concerned with concepts essentially applicable only to the United States, international material becomes a confusing sideshow which takes time away from the all-too-crowded effort to develop the main functional skills.

Quite aside from the question of the nature of the subject mat-ter in these courses, we must also consider the nature of the faculty members involved. Unless a professor is reasonably conversant with the international aspects of his subject, he will usually not be equipped to discuss them well. Indeed, it is quite likely that he will not want to have them in his course for this very reason. Certainly our objectives will not be furthered by forcing international content on unwilling instructors. Thus, in a number of cases the inclusion of international content in general courses is further limited by the abilities and receptivity of the faculty members involved.

While as a general proposition the inclusion of international content in general courses is certainly desirable, we must also recognize its limitations in terms of the objectives already set forth. If, as I assume, international content will be appropriate only in courses teaching concepts at a high level of universal applicability, then the international content does not provide an essential element in the development of the functional skills. Its contribution lies in the reinforcement and illustration of the universality of the concepts. Towards the second objective, development of environmental skill, this sort of content, I think, makes only a very small contribution. Where an international illustration or case is introduced in a general course, there is rarely time to make the thorough analysis of the environmental situation necessary to develop this sort of skill. I think, therefore, that the best we can expect from the general courses is to develop in the minds of the students a sense that business is something which is conducted in the world, not just in the United States, and that the skills they are acquiring have meaning in this broader environmental context.

While I emphasize that this is a limited achievement, I do not intend thereby to underrate its importance. If every student came out of our schools with this point of view, I think we would have made major progress, and I think it is progress which is quite practical of achievement. In my own school, I know several professors who, simply because they personally have strong international interests, have brought substantial international content into general courses without any sacrifice in their basic mission, and making, I think, a substantial contribution to their students. And, as I am sure many of you know, two schools in Europe, INSEAD at Fontainebleau and IMEDE at Lausanne, conduct all of their instruction in this manner, with cases drawn from a variety of countries in every course. I doubt that anybody has attempted to determine whether they would develop greater functional competence in their students if they did not have this multi-country approach, but the general consensus seems to be that they are doing a good job, and this encourages us to believe that international content may be included in general courses effectively.

The second approach lay in the establishment of specialized international courses within the various functional fields. There are two types which may be considered: operational decision-making and comparative courses. Each has a quite different role.

The primary role of the operational decision-making type of course has already been suggested in the early discussions of levels of abstraction. Where the general functional courses do not present skills fully appropriate to international management in their particular field, a gap exists which is appropriately filled by a specialized course. For example, it is effectively argued that the general marketing courses in many schools do not adequately prepare a student for export and overseas marketing management responsibility. The merits of this argument have to be examined critically in each case, but where it is true there exists a logic for establishing a separate international marketing management course to provide, for those students who seek it, functional skills appropriate to the international environment. Such a course will, in addition, contribute towards the development of environmental skills. The other courses I will discuss next are more appropriate for this purpose, but to a degree an international decision-making type of course contributes towards this end by repeatedly forcing the student to examine thoroughly the environment to which his decisions must be related.

Comparative courses have quite a different rationale in international business curricula. The systematic study of the differences and similarities in the business systems of various countries does, of course, contribute to the development of functional skills appropriate to these differing environments. But it is my contention that the benefit to functional competence gained in the process goes well beyond that useful specifically for international operations. In other educational fields, comparative studies have an established place in basic learning. Comparative religion and comparative political systems are, for example, well accepted in the fundamental study of those fields. Why should not comparative business studies make the same contribution in our schools? I think there is a good argument to be made that a comparative marketing course, for example, broadens and deepens the fundamental understanding of marketing processes and that it is, therefore, a useful contribution to the study of any marketing student.

The comparative courses also make a significant contribution in developing environmental adaptation skills. Day after day in a comparative course, the student is required to analyze the differences in the business systems of various countries in terms of the environmental variables of each country. Thus, a constant awareness of environmental difference and skill in assessing its significance is one of the main pedagogical gains from experience in a comparative course.

In a third category of courses, environmental study becomes the central objective. I include in this category area studies and the basic disciplines—international economics, sociology, anthropology, and political science. Each of these in one way or another contributes to the ability of the student to understand the nature of the environmental variables encountered in international business. Each, however, presents somewhat different possibilities and problems for the international curriculum. International economics is such a well-established subject and so clearly useful to international business study that its role requires no defense. The nature of the course content does call for comment, however. We find in international business programs in some places a gentleman's version of international economics in which the theoretical content is watered down for easy consumption. After touching lightly on the theoretical concepts, the course hops on to a similar treatment of various aspects of commercial policies and international institutions. Unquestionably, such material is better than no international economics. But I submit that it is wiser to concentrate on a solid presentation of the basic concepts and, if time is limited, to not even deal with such matters as tariffs, the World Bank, and the like. There is a fair chance that the student may study the latter after he is out of school, but the odds are a thousand to one against his taking time to grapple seriously with the basic theoretical concepts of international economics.

Potentially, anthropology, sociology, and political science have roles equal in importance to economics in the understanding of environments abroad, but it is unlikely that we will find it practical to package them into separate form for international business curricula in the near future. Ideally, we would like to have students study them in college before they enter business school. If not, many of them will gain some useful competence through the general behavioral science courses which are now beginning to appear in core curricula. In most cases, however, their insights will, I think, be gained as a practical matter through application in comparative and area-study courses. For this reason, I think there is a strong argument for utilizing professors with behavioral science competence to teach this type of course.

Area-study courses are theoretically the ideal vehicle for the acquisition of environmental adaptation competence. That is to say, in a Latin American business course the primary focus should be on acquiring a thorough understanding of the aspects of the Latin American environment which bear on the operation of business and the way in which they affect business. Unfortunately, area courses have much difficulty in actually achieving their full potentials. Many of them are overly concerned with descriptive, factual content of fairly limited breadth, for example, a course in Latin American markets in which the emphasis is on statistics and assorted other detailed market characteristics. A more sophisticated problem lies in the nature of the teachers. Ideally an instructor in an area course should be strong in economics, anthropology, political science, and sociology. In fact, few of us are. For example, my own teaching of a Latin American business course suffers from my mediocre competence in economics. More commonly, such courses are placed in the hands of economists who do a good job in that respect but who are not particularly effective in, for example, the sociological and anthropological aspects. And a further problem lies in the fact that too few teachers approach such courses with the understanding that they are essentially teaching area study *per se,* and that the particular area being examined is essentially a case or exercise in application of this broader skill. In many cases, in the minds of both the teacher and the students, the fundamental objective is to learn as much as possible about the specific area. In fact, I am sure that certain generalized environmental skills result from the process, but it would be better if these generalized skills were given explicit attention.

Except in the case of international economics, therefore, the environmental study courses are still at an early stage of evolution. This does not mean that they are not useful in international business curricula, but it does mean that their adoption should be based upon an understanding that they are experimental and their character should be under constant review.

I have left to the end a fourth type of course—the international business survey course—because I feel it has the least to offer towards the objectives of an international business program. The content of such courses varies tremendously. Characteristically, they include a brief statement of international economics, some discussion of other environmental variables like cultural differences, and some coverage of the differences in the main functional fields as encountered in international operations. I should emphasize that my comments here are not addressed to certain courses which may appear to have a survey objective because they bear a general label like "International Business" but which are in fact international business policy courses properly considered as part of the functional groups already discussed. Course titles are often deceptive, and one must look behind them at actual content. The chief problem with the survey courses is that they try to do several things and in the process end by doing none of them very well. Many of them attempt to develop international functional competence in several fields—accounting, marketing, etc. But two or three classes devoted to international marketing, for example, is not enough to have real impact on the student. They are probably more effective in developing environmental competence, for their content is focused on environmental variables throughout. Yet even this type of course typically jumps from subject to subject and from geographic area to geographic area so rapidly that the impact is limited. The coverage of international economics, for example, may be completed in but two to three weeks and then the discussion will move about rapidly amongst functions and country situations. A redeeming grace in a number of these courses is the assignment of a term report to study a particular business problem in one country, and here at least the student does have a quite intensive experience in environmental adaptation. On the whole, however, the main impact is the conveying to the student of a sense of the variability and complexity of the international environment. This is a useful contribution and in some cases where only one competent international faculty member is available, only one course is possible, or some other conditions make it peculiarly appropriate, the survey course may be worthwhile. On balance, however, I think that the objectives of the international business curriculum can be better achieved through the alternatives already discussed.

The superficial character of the content of the typical international business survey course underscores a serious problem of which we must be aware in our international curricula, namely, the risks of lack of rigor both in intellectual content and in pedagogical approach. At the present early stage of development of teaching in this field, it has been all too easy for a relatively mediocre teacher to put together some interesting and exciting but not particularly rigorous course material and attract an assortment of students many of whom were anticipating an easy, interesting experience rather than a challenging acquisition to their management competence. This image of international business studies exists in some schools, and the potentials for its emergence in others are a real risk against which we must guard. They are greatest in the international business survey courses because of their breadth of content and because they are organized outside the rigorous standards of established functional fields. The risks are substantially less where the content of a course is already well established as in the case of international economics or where the potentials for development of a rigorous sequence of intellectual concepts is available as, for example, in the comparative approach to a functional subject.

Perhaps a good way to summarize this discussion of various courses is to suggest an ideal structure which we might reach 10 or 15 years from now. It would have these components. First, the general run of functional courses in business schools would all be taught at a high level of abstraction. The universal applicability of the functional skills they were developing would be demonstrated by assorted cases and other references to international business situations.

Second, comparative courses would have become a standard part of the basic theoretical conceptual education of students in each functional area. They would no longer be thought of as part of the international studies, and would quite likely intermix comparisons of a sectoral as well as a spatial nature. That is, for example, a comparison of accounting in public vs. private organizations as well as between countries.

Third, environmental studies in the form of courses in international economics and area study would be firmly established. The latter would have developed a rigorous systematic content incorporating various behavioral sciences and some development economics.

Fourth, I suspect that the international management decision-making types of courses may have largely disappeared, their functions being performed quite adequately by the general courses taught at a high level of abstraction and by the comparative courses.

A "COMBINED MAJOR"

This discussion of types of courses still leaves us with the question of how we put them together in packages for student consumption. In considering international business programs as a whole, I find it helpful to think of two categories of students. First, those who already have a strong interest in international business, and second, the general run of students whose interest varies from moderate to zero.

Designing programs for the students already anxious to pursue international studies is easier than handling the second category, because there is no problem of attracting them into courses with international content. Indeed, the problem is often to be sure that they do not take an excessive amount of international study at the expense of developing the basic business skills. Probably the most controversial issue here is the question of whether or not a school should establish an international business major. While I know that a number of able people disagree with me on this point, I persist in stoutly opposing the idea of such a major. There are, I recognize, certain values in the major in channeling the strong interests and energies of students anxious for international careers into the studies which will maximize the gains of high intellectual motivation. I am also aware that there are cases in which a vigorous program of international business studies would have been extremely hard to start without a segregated international business program because of resistance, lack of instructor competence, or apathy in other sectors of the business school.

However, on balance, I think the arguments against a separate major for international business are very persuasive. The essential purpose of a major, to my view, is to provide the student with a rigorous and penetrating intellectual experience with a solid, cohesive body of conceptual knowledge. This is not possible in international business. There is no solid body of concepts which we can separately identify as international business. The material which one finds grouped in an international business major can be interesting, valid, and challenging, but it lacks the cohesion and penetration which a major should provide. Rather, it is a combination of economics, behavioral sciences, and various functional fields, which for lack of time are not examined with the rigor and penetration which should be expected in a major.

The decision on establishing an international business major should be made essentially on these intellectual, conceptual grounds. However, the negative viewpoint can be further reinforced by the attitude of business. I have a strong impression both from businessmen themselves and from business school placement offices that there is no great demand for students presenting a major in international business, that companies are primarily interested in people with strong functional competence. I do know that some schools with international business majors can point to a fine placement record for their students, but this, I suggest, is due more to the fact that they have attracted some very good students than that the companies have valued the international business major itself. I think we are all aware that companies in their recruiting are much more interested in acquiring good people without regard to the functional label they may wear—Dr. Costanzo made essentially that point yesterday when he said they want people with a good analytical mind. But to the extent that the label makes some difference, I am quite convinced that the international business major is little contribution and often a negative factor in company decisions for hiring.

Rather than an international business major, I lean heavily towards some blend of majoring in a traditional, functional field and acquiring a strong supplementary competence in international studies. At my own school we have formalized this concept in what we call a "Combined Major." I don't happen to know of any other school which has adopted this formal label, but I think the essential concept is appearing in many places. Indeed, I have the clear impression that at a number of schools which have an international business major, very much the same philosophy is applied. That is, a man majoring in international business is strongly encouraged to take several courses in one of the basic functional fields as electives so that he may at least satisfy the company recruiters as to having functional competence. The essence of the combined major approach is that the established requirements for a major in the functional field be met, including the pursuit of international operational and comparative courses in those fields where they are available. Beyond this, international supplementary studies are provided typically in the form of international economics and area study.

The combined major idea fits readily into the established pattern of business school studies. Beyond it lie possibilities for substantial innovations which we have scarcely begun to explore. Their essential characteristic would lie in quite different approaches to developing the environmental skills required for international business. We already have a few probings in this direction in the form of Columbia Business School's three-year program in collaboration with its School of International Affairs, and the two-year MBA-International Studies concept developed by Johns Hopkins' School of Advanced International Studies. A very interesting scheme along these lines is in the making at Transylvania College, which proposes a Latin American MBA program with a heavy environmental study content in the second year. It is quite possible that a few years hence we may find quite imaginative approaches to utilizing the elective component of the second year MBA program for international environmental studies. But I doubt if useful innovations will appear at the expense of rigorous study in the conceptual content of the basic functional fields.

The design of programs suitable for the great majority of students with little or no present international leaning is more difficult. Yet it is an extremely important matter. A very substantial portion of these students will find themselves in one way or another carrying responsibility for international operations either abroad or in parent organizations, and international business will impinge to some degree on the responsibilities of virtually all of the balance. Thus, I am convinced that we have a responsibility to prepare all students to think about business in world rather than strictly domestic terms.

Progress in this direction comes slowly and with difficulty. It would appear that our main hope lies in the infusion of international content into general courses. As I have already suggested, I think that to a degree this is both feasible and desirable. However, there are limitations which restrain the pace at which we can move in this direction and the accomplishment which we may expect. In some cases, the addition of international material would, as I have already indicated, be at the expense of the optimum level of accomplishment of the basic functional mission of the courses; in other cases, the lack of international teacher competence or interest would make the process ineffective. Furthermore, we must recognize that in the time available in the general courses it is not possible to give sufficient attention to the environmental variables to develop any significant environmental skill. So far as it is practical and useful, therefore, we should certainly seek to include international material in general courses, but this is not going to do the whole job for the general students.

Over the long term, I am more optimistic for the potential contributions of the comparative type of course. As I have already indicated, I think that these courses can make a valuable contribution to the basic functional competence of the general student by broadening his understanding and perception of the nature of his field. Thus I look to the day when they can defend their status as part of the required program of a departmental major without reference to their international character. But in the process of performing this function, they will, as a by-product, contribute substantially to the development of environmental skill. I might note that we already have some evidence of the potentials in this direction. I recently made a study of the number of students in my own school who took one or more international course. The range ran from 49 percent in finance to 16 percent in accounting, with an average of 36 percent for all fields. Since no more than 10 to 15 percent are combined majors in international business, this indicates that a fair portion of non-international specialists are taking the international courses, of which several have the comparative approach. However, the 64 percent taking no international course underscores our major problem for the future.

Beyond the explicit conveying of international content to the general student through infusion of material in general courses, and the expansion of comparative courses, we may hope to progress by internationalizing the basic school environment. This in a way is outside the immediate scope of the topic assigned to me, but I do want to reflect on it for a moment. It is clearly what the wide range of subjects discussed in the *EWA Report* add up to, and it is, I am sure, an important contribution to the pedagogical objective of reaching the general student. In this connection I find very helpful a term which Harlan Cleveland drew out of the research which he and his associates undertook at Syracuse University a few years ago on all aspects of Americans in overseas assignments. He found that the people who did well abroad often came from what he called "*National Geographic* homes." The point was that people who grew up with a constant awareness of the differences in environments around the world and of the way in which we were related to them, were the ones who were most effective in international affairs. In business schools we start later, and the job of internationalizing the individual is therefore more difficult. But we can, to a degree, do the same thing. If throughout his stay with us, the student is exposed to a "*National Geographic* business school," it cannot help having a significant impact on his point of view. Therefore, all of these things discussed in the *EWA Report*—foreign assignments for teachers, participation in AIESEC, international executives on the campus, and so forth—collectively do, I am sure, have an important pedagogical impact.

RECOMMENDATIONS

I think a good way to summarize my comments this morning is to make some very concrete recommendations. From time to time, people who are starting or revising international programs ask me what courses I would recommend. Subject to modifications to fit the particular circumstances of each school, I generally come out with something along these lines.

If only a limited commitment is possible, I suggest international economics and a comparative business systems course. The economics provides an essential base for comprehending the logics of international business. The comparative business systems course is the best available vehicle for developing environmental skills. While it is not likely to be as rigorous as I would like, still it draws directly upon well-established concepts in the functional field and basic disciplines, and, if well taught, it can be a solid educational experience.

As a next step, I encourage people to move as rapidly as possible to establish international courses in each of the functional fields. My preference here is for the comparative approach, but, as a practical matter, an operational approach or a combination of comparative and operational seems to be most likely to get off the ground, and my chief interest is to get each of the functional fields moving on the international plane as quickly as possible. Once an international specialist is established in a functional field, he then becomes a center for stimulus and development of instructional material and ideas which will contribute to the infusion of international content into other courses.

The addition of area studies is, I think, the final stage in the growth of an international business curriculum. From what I have already said, it will be clear why I have not included an international business survey course in these recommendations. Only where some peculiar set of circumstances in a school makes this the only apparent way to get international studies started do I think that it is a sound step.

All of this leads by degrees toward a blend of strong functional education with parallel development of international functional and environmental competence. The international component is strong and useful, but the primary emphasis remains on the basic business skills.

Now I have had my say, and the next step is to open up these and doubtless other questions to what I am sure is going to be a most stimulating discussion process among the working groups.

LAURENCE P. DOWD
San Francisco State College

Curriculum Experience with World Business at San Francisco State College

I. INTRODUCTION

    A. General place in School of Business curriculum

        1. The Center for World Business was established at the request of the San Francisco international business community over 15 years ago; interest continues, as evidenced by our active Advisory Council and Board of Associates and the number of graduate students coming from business organizations.

        2. As the *EWA Report* points out (p. 40), San Francisco State College (SFSC) is one of few schools with a fully developed concentration.

        3. A graduate Principles of World Business course is now required for all MBA candidates, and consideration is being given to making a similar course a part of the

LAURENCE P. DOWD is Director of the Center for World Business and Professor of World Business, School of Business, San Francisco State College. He has an MA in Oriental studies from the University of Hawaii and a PhD in economics from the University of Michigan. Prior to going to San Francisco State in 1960, he was on the Michigan faculty, where he supervised a study of the practical potential of the St. Lawrence Seaway for Midwest business. A second study was related to the implications for Michigan business of the EEC. From 1955 to 1957, he was a Fulbright lecturer on foreign trade management at Kobe University, Japan. He is author of *Principles of World Business* (Allyn and Bacon, 1965) and a number of articles in professional journals. During 1966-67, he was on leave in Europe to study the philosophies and problems of medium-size European enterprises. He spent considerable time interviewing senior executives of European subsidiaries of U. S. companies on their views regarding the education that men and women should have prior to assuming the management of international business operations.

undergraduate core requirements.

4. Both undergraduate and graduate concentrations require completion of the respective cores for all business administration majors.

B. General Approach

1. Basically we have a dual approach:

   a. Environmental — knowledge of cultural, economic, legal, political, and institutional environments influencing the conduct of business in other nations.

   b. Management principles — functional approach emphasizing perception and adaptation competence in applying the various management functions to business in other nations, including some aspects for which there is no similarity in the United States.

2. Both approaches utilize comparative analysis where it is pertinent or applicable.

II. ASSUMPTIONS

A. Internal (within the School)

1. Business today is a "world" concept rather than being merely "international"; i. e., companies operate *within* foreign environments or nations, in addition to crossing environments or national boundaries. ("International" means *"between* nations"—substantial business is carried on between nations; but constantly more is being carried on *within* other nations. We concentrate on business wherever it may be carried on in the world.)

2. All students should have a strong functional emphasis— accounting, finance, marketing, personnel, operations, etc. This knowledge is gained basically in the usual functional courses offered in business schools. In addition, students concentrating in world business should have a world functional orientation. This is achieved in such courses as World Finance or World Marketing Management.

3. All business administration majors should have exposure to basic world business principles pertinent to the management of any business as it is (or may be) influenced by international factors.

4. Not all students, however, should be world business specialists. That is, as business administration majors are expected to acquire knowledge of principles of account-

ing, finance, marketing, etc., and learn to integrate them into other areas of business administration, so also should they acquire knowledge of world business principles and be able to apply them where desirable or necessary, but without being specialists.

B. External (outside the School)

1. Not all business schools should have intensive international or world business programs, because:

    a. Only a small portion of business school graduates will go directly into world business activities. Although some will become involved later in their careers, many will never be involved directly.

    b. Actually, relatively few students will reach "senior management" levels where integrated, world-wide decisions are made. Most will remain in a functional area for their entire working life. Of these, only a portion will be involved in the functions on a world-wide basis.

    c. Relatively few business or world business students will be assigned to overseas positions. The majority of overseas management personnel, and a constantly increasing portion, will be nationals of foreign countries. (Although there is some evidence of modification, most foreign nationals will be with firms engaged in business in their country.)

    d. Although the total of U. S. businessmen overseas will enlarge as more and more firms become world-oriented and will have some small part of their management stationed overseas, few of those students assigned overseas will know, while engaged in their undergraduate or graduate preparation, the specific area to which they will be assigned.

    Furthermore, many will be transferred to responsibilities in different areas as they advance in management positions. That is, firms seem to be moving in the direction of assigning the best qualified functional man *rather than* the area specialist to the position open in a foreign area.

    e. Only a relatively few firms, mainly the largest, can become "multinational." Because of limited financial and managerial resources, most firms interested in foreign involvement will not be able to move into more than one or two countries at most. Education must be provided for all firms, including small and medium size, rather than merely for large firms.

III. OBJECTIVES OF SFSC CENTER FOR WORLD BUSINESS
CURRICULUM

A. General

1. The Center for World Business provides specialized education at both the undergraduate and graduate levels for those seeking careers in world commerce, finance, operations, or international development.

2. As part of this program of study, all students must complete the general education requirements of the College as well as the business core required by the School of Business. The total educational pattern complies with that established by the American Association of Collegiate Schools of Business (AACSB).

3. Beyond this, we have already adopted Strategies (1), (3), (5), and (6) of those listed on Page 36 of the *EWA Report*, and we are working actively toward Strategies (2) and (4).

B. Specific

Our specific objectives in both the undergraduate and graduate programs include:

1. Knowledge of basic principles, including pertinent economic concepts;

2. Knowledge of differences in foreign cultural, economic, legal, political, and institutional environments;

3. Knowledge of basic management methods where different from domestic;

4. Perception and adaptation of functional knowledge necessary for efficient management of small- and medium-size, as well as large, firms in foreign areas as a consequence of environmental differences or traditional or customary methods; and

5. Ability to manage functions anywhere in the world — rather than the international orientation, emphasizing merely the transaction *between* nations.

IV. SOME PRACTICAL LIMITATIONS

A. Integration with other business courses

1. Our faculty would agree that *ideally* world business principles, including environment and methodology, should be integrated into usual business-school courses. How-

ever, this cannot be done *practically* in the foreseeable future because:

    a. The volume of material to be covered in most courses, functional or otherwise, precludes the addition of a world approach. Most faculty complain they cannot cover all desired, or needed, material in their existing courses, without adding on world materials.

    b. Few faculty members have world knowledge.

        (i) Most are fully involved in maintaining domestic competence in an ever more dynamic domestic business environment, and

        (ii) Many are simply uninterested in acquiring world competence in their functional area.

2. Consequently, acquisition of world environmental or functional knowledge must be left to the specialist.

    a. This is similar, however, to the entire area of business administration. We have accounting, finance, marketing, statistics, etc. specialists who concentrate on their field rather than acquiring advanced knowledge of other fields. For example, few accounting professors have much specialized knowledge of marketing, yet marketing is used in accounting every day. Similarly, few finance professors have knowledge of personnel management, or statistics professors a knowledge of operations management.

B. Research

1. Far more world business research is necessary; however, we are limited by budgetary restraints which require that SFSC be primarily a teaching institution. This is not all bad, because all our courses are staffed by experienced faculty rather than "teaching assistants," as is true at some schools. There is a danger that too much research involvement will be at the expense of high quality teaching.

2. Business generally has not yet accepted the desirability of world business research. Securing financial assistance from business organizations, even those involved intensively in world business, has proved extremely difficult.

3. At present, most research is being carried on by advanced undergraduate and graduate students as part of seminar requirements.

C. Overseas Involvement

1. In general this can make a professor more qualified to teach world business. There is a tendency, however, to become an "area specialist," with a further tendency to characterize the whole world as similar to that in which the professor has had his specialization. There should be foreign involvement, but not exclusively in one area.

V. CONCLUSIONS

A. The SFSC Center for World Business follows a curriculum pattern which provides:

1. A broad general education, including courses in the social sciences, humanities, and natural sciences, mostly at the lower division level. (By AACSB regulations, at least 40 percent of the student's program must consist of non-business courses.)

2. A business core, including knowledge of the basic principles in the usually accepted functional areas.

3. Advanced functional knowledge in one of the usually accepted areas.

4. A world business specialization involving:

   a. Knowledge of differing foreign environmental influences on business.

   b. Knowledge of differing, and sometimes unusual, applications of principles and methodology of the functional areas.

B. The following teaching approaches are used in the curriculum:

1. The usual lecture-discussion approach, utilizing standard textbooks as well as special materials emanating from such organizations as Business International, the National Industrial Conference Board, etc.

2. Case analyses. Some business cases are included in most of the business core and world business courses.

3. Management simulations. The INTOP management simulation[1] is now an integral part of at least six world busi-

_____
[1][For references to materials discussing the INTOP game, see the **EWA Report,** pp. 43 and 66 (ftn. 11).—Ed.]

ness courses. In an unusual experiment at SFSC, we are simultaneously playing INTOP in some eight different classes. Some problems have been generated as a result of the impossibility of all students, not only world business but also others, to meet at one time; but we have worked out techniques to overcome this problem. And we believe the experiment is working very successfully. It is providing a wonderful opportunity to integrate all management functional principles, domestic and world-wide.

ENDEL J. KOLDE
University of Washington

Curriculum Strategy:

THE UNIVERSITY OF WASHINGTON PROGRAM

The International Business Program at the University of Washington has a history that extends back over 50 years. It may be relevant as a historic fact that in 1919 when Pan Xenia, a national foreign trade honorary, was established, the University of Washington was selected as its home, and the chapter at Washington became its Alpha Chapter. It seems fair, therefore, to assume that the School had already at that early date gained recognition in its international work. For the last 50 years, the Washington business school has offered a sufficiently wide assortment of international courses to enable students to major in this field.

For the first 40 years the international program was of the traditional type—a *Foreign Trade* program consisting primarily of import-export trade, international finance, and a modest amount of economics. For the last ten years the School has had a program in International Business rather than Foreign Trade.

ENDEL J. KOLDE is Professor of International Business, Graduate School of Business Administration, University of Washington. He has a DHS degree from Stockholm and MA and DBA degrees from the University of Washington. He has served as an executive in the export-import business, as senior international economist in the petroleum industry, and as consultant to multinational companies in aircraft, chemical, food, natural gas, power, and maritime industries. He has also served as advisor to governments in Europe, the Middle East, and the Orient, and to such organizations as the OEEC, European Productivity Agency, the European Common Market, EFTA, and the UN. He joined the Washington faculty in 1951, and since 1956 has developed the present multi-course programs in International Business at the graduate and undergraduate levels. He has authored numerous publications, including "Business Enterprise in the Global Context" (*California Management Review*, Summer, 1966), which won the McKinsey Foundation for Management Research award as an outstanding contribution to the management literature.

The major break with the traditional foreign-trade approach came in 1957 when the program was reviewed and revised. Certain changes in courses and requirements have continued to this day. In its basic attributes, however, the new approach has· undergone but one significant change during the last ten years; namely, it has crystalized, become established, and proven its philosophical and pedagogical values for the contemporary educational needs of the business school.

1. INTEGRATIVE, INTERDISCIPLINARY APPROACH

What is this new approach?

First, it is an interdisciplinary approach, at least if one looks from the pre-international business perspective. It rejects the functional frame of reference which was characteristic of foreign trade and finance, and substituted a much broader and more flexible frame of reference which attempts to integrate other business administration subfields and which draws heavily upon a number of nonbusiness subjects (or which at least in 1957 were so considered), especially political science, cultural anthropology, international economics, organization theory, and area studies (including regional science).

This new approach required, of course, quite different staff capabilities, imposing some real burdens on the faculty. And let me say that it was not painless. If some of you are now trying to make the same kind of transition and encounter a great deal of faculty resistance, don't despair; we, too, had this problem and still haven't solved it completely, though we have learned to live with it.

2. PRIMARY OBJECTIVE

The basic rationale of our new approach was the realization that:

(1) the main differences between domestic or uninational and international or multinational business administration derived from the environmental complex, the greater diversity, and the external plurality that an enterprise faced in the international realm than in the domestic context and in the managerial responses that flow from this plurality, and

(2) that the typical business student had, at best, only rudimentary notions about the world outside the United States.

Having accepted these two premises, it did not take great genius to discover that the environmental plurality of multinational business embraced a great many factors that were nonbusiness and non-economic in terms of our traditional notions and that, in the light of the students' needs and time constraints, our international business program had to expose the student to the entire environmental complex before trying to teach him specific managerial applications or expecting him to be able to provide realistic solutions to international business problems.

With these premises in mind, a new course, entitled "'International Business Environment," was established in 1957. To our knowledge it was the first course of its kind. It marked the end of the Foreign Trade era and the beginning of the International Business Program at Washington.

In this course the focus was deliberately diverted from the specific, from the operational, and perhaps most importantly from business *per se*. In their stead an effort was made to unravel the broad international panorama in its entirety, that is, to study its relevant characteristics regardless of their traditional academic domain, to try to deal with whatever is important from an overall perspective, be it cultural, social, economic, physiographic, or political.

No room was left in this course for a narrow functional perspective. This was done deliberately to provide some counterbalance to the strong functional biases by which both the faculty and the students were indoctrinated.

3. EMPHASIS ON SUBSTANCE

Since the typical business student is ill-informed, if not illiterate, in international affairs, and since, as noted above, the study of international business environment must include certain aspects of many nonbusiness disciplines, the primary educational need here was (and continues to be) to provide the student with substantive knowledge. This does not mean statistical data, as in traditional economic surveys, but facts, concepts, and relationships that make up the environmental complex.

As we have gained in proficiency in dealing with this matter, we have tried to focus more and more on the factors and relationships which generate changes in the international environment—the prime movers of international dynamics, so to speak. In this effort we find it increasingly useful to integrate into our courses certain working tools and basic truths of political science, sociology, cultural anthropology, economics, and regional science.

Thus, we are here unconcerned with any unified theory as such, or model building as such, though many theories and models are studied. The real objective is to make the students more knowledge-able individuals in world affairs, and to bring their international hori-zons somewhat closer to the level where their understanding of the domestic environment lies; that is, to equip them with an under-standing of the forces which circumscribe business behavior in foreign societies which more nearly equal their grasp of the interplay between society and business in the United States.

4. FOREIGN AREA ANALYSIS

A second benchmark course in this new program was "Foreign Area Analysis." This was a follow-up course to the International Busi-ness Environment and was designed to provide the student with systematic means of conducting research on foreign areas. It should not be confused with export market research or the kind of review courses of regional economies, such as Latin American Business Prob-lems, or Far East Trade Problems. Indeed, this one new course replaced three or four such area survey courses which we had had before.

The main concern in this course is not statistical manipulation or the accumulation of information. Instead, it is concerned with acquiring knowledge of sources of information, international and supranational agencies, research programs, and most of all, the methods that lend themselves to effective analysis of foreign areas.

5. INTERNATIONAL GENERALIST

The phrase "international generalist" would be a succinct sum-mary of the primary objective of the I. B. program at Washington. Our students should expect to gain from the program:

—a new frame of reference (perhaps a composite of frames),
—a considerable body of substantive knowledge of world af-fairs, and
—basic analytical methods for researching foreign areas, es-pecially in their dynamic aspects.

Needless to say, the degrees of sophistication that are expected and actually attained are quite different on the undergraduate and graduate levels. However, the objective remains the same.

In this generalist package are currently such components as:

—basic international economics and economic policies
—major international political issues
—international integration
—economic development and social modernization of under-developed areas

—inter-nation linkages, including trade institutions and multi-national companies and their evolution
—interactions between national and corporate interests (especially their conflicts) in the international realm
—social and political responsibilities of multinational business, including basic issues of ethics and morality.

The order in which the subjects are listed does not indicate their importance or emphasis in the program but gives some idea of the order in which the component areas are studied. Actually the listing is illustrative only; except for the one on economics, the items are not singled out as chapters or segments of the program.

6. SECONDARY OBJECTIVE

On this generalist foundation we try to erect a superstructure of additional offerings which focus on specific managerial problems encountered in international business. We are much less certain how to proceed on this secondary level than we were on the primary level. Our problems and experiences here are echoed in the *EWA Report* and seem to be shared by many other schools.

We have tried to work here with two different approaches simultaneously; that is, to teach certain managerial courses under the label of International Business and have others housed in the functional departments. The experience to date on this is quite contradictory and thus inconclusive. International aspects of business policy, organization, labor relations, personnel, and marketing are taught primarily in I. B. courses. However, I must hasten to add that this in no way restricts the respective functional specialists to treat international subject matter in their courses. To the contrary, the introduction of international aspects into functional courses is encouraged, and many professors have been expanding their functional coverage. Despite an apparent overlap, we have had no real problem in coordination, for the functional people have been happy to leave to I. B. staff the basics and especially the common denominators, and to reserve for themselves certain areas connected with their own research of overseas experience, or other more specialized aspects.

In accounting and finance, we have separate international courses. Their objectives and coverage are set by the respective functional departments, and they are not integrated with the I. B. program as such.

The accounting area has been our strongest functional area in terms of research and contributions to international business knowledge. It has also lent most valuable strength to our I. B. program, both in adding possibilities for technical competency and in increasing student interest on the graduate, especially doctoral, level.

There is a great deal of complementarity between I. B. and international accounting courses. The experience with the courses in international finance has been less satisfactory. Here the functional faculty has strongly resisted all attempts to align their offerings with the I. B. program, and have elected to limit their approach to the perspective which is characteristic to traditional courses in international finance. Because of the isolation of international finance from other international offerings, it has been necessary to build a two-course sequence in international finance so that the internationally uninitiated students can get at least a minimal sophistication in the field. Much of this is repetitious of the basic I. B. courses. At the same time, the I. B. courses have had to beef up their own treatment of finance.

As a consequence, a disproportionate share of the School's resources which are devoted to international offerings is absorbed by the finance courses, which add very little to the I. B. program as such.

I cite this experience as a concrete illustration of the kind of difficulty that may arise and block the path toward a cohesive and efficient program in I. B. The functional specialist does tend to rebel against the idea that a person from outside his functional specialty is permitted to teach in that area—this to him is often an invasion of what he considers his exclusive "competence region." To be sure, he is confusing technical with environmental, and *Americana* with universal knowledge, but he does not know it, and often does not care.

The solution of this problem must remain for future experience or wiser people to uncover. My subjective speculation is that if the deans are wise they will insist on a coordinated and closely integrated program of international offerings in business, and will resist, at least in the early stages, this proliferation of functional international offerings. After the base program has jelled and a competent core of I. B. faculty has been developed, the danger of dis-integrated functional proliferation is likely to disappear.

RICHARD D. ROBINSON
Massachusetts Institute of Technology

The International Business Field
– – What Makes It Different?

To those concerned with management education, but who feel that international business is not a distinct field, that it has no place in the curriculum of a self-respecting school of management, let me say this. One could agree with them IF—and this is a large if—IF the more traditional functional management courses were expanded so as to deal with environmental variables without regard for nationality and to deal also with the nature of the international business system.

Take an example. If, in a marketing course, rather than holding the political-economic-social variables to values within the range of domestic experience, the full range of possible values for these variables was dealt with, then the marketing course becomes multinational in the comparative sense. If it deals with the problems of relating two national marketing systems, it becomes international. To be more specific, *if* the marketing course deals with market problems inherent in a centrally-controlled economic system as well as the more market-oriented; *if* it deals with problems characteristic of the non-literate society as well as the literate; *if* it deals with marketing problems created by greater speed of structural changes than that characteristic of the domestic market; *if* the marketing course includes such considerations as these so that the marketing system

---

RICHARD D. ROBINSON is Senior Lecturer in the Sloan School at Massachusetts Institute of Technology. He has an MBA from Harvard University and a PhD from MIT. Prior to joining the MIT faculty in 1962, he held a variety of positions, with emphasis on the Middle East. From 1953 to 1956, he was Turkish Area Specialist for the American Universities Field Staff. He has written numerous books and articles, including *International Business Policy* (Holt, Rinehart and Winston, 1962), *The First Turkish Republic: A Case Study in National Development* (Harvard University Press, 1963), "Measuring the Impact of a Business on a Developing Society" (in Ettinger, *International Management Handbook*), *International Management* (Holt, Rinehart and Winston, 1967), and *Highlevel Manpower Development, The Turkish Case* (Harvard Center for Middle Eastern Studies, 1967).

and analytical techniques have been *generalized multinationally* and the domestic case—that of a market-oriented, literate, more slowly evolving society—is seen as but a special case; *if* these things be true, then my plea to include such comparative material within a differentiated, international business field has no force. If the marketing course also examines the relationships, in marketing terms, between different national marketing systems, then nothing remains for international business. If one develops all of the functional courses in this manner, including business policy, a differentiated international business course would be redundant. But, by the very nature of things, few schools can generalize either their research or courses to the comparative and international levels in this fashion, for the bulk of the students intend to—and probably will—be concerned almost entirely with the domestic market. It comes down to a matter of time and interest priorities. But that is true of every subject under the sun. Otherwise, we would have one field and one course—that dealing with human society. Consequently, I feel that we have a meaningful distinction here—comparative on the one hand, international on the other.

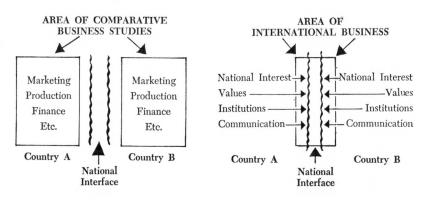

I see the contemporary specialists in international business as pushing their functionally-oriented colleagues in finance, marketing, production, organization, personnel, operations research, industrial relations, policy, etcetera, to broaden their respective horizons, to concern themselves with the much wider range of relevant variables present when one moves geographically, and to adapt analytical techniques accordingly. Ultimately, what is probably left to one teaching in the field of international business are those problems arising out of the conflict among national or regional business systems—that is, conflicts in national interest as manifest in the market place, conflicts in values and priorities (not the least of which is that relating to time horizons), conflicts in institutions (such as law, finance, and taxation), and conflicts arising out of intercultural communication. On the other side of the coin, of course, are those devices, techniques, attitudes, and skills useful to the international manager in resolving or minimizing the cost of such conflicts on the national interface. I suggest that this is the proper area of something called international business.

To deny that this is a valid field for academic effort is to suggest by analogy that such subjects as international politics, international economics, and international law are equally not academically respectable. It is true that international business borrows very heavily from all three, as they borrow from each other, but the core problem in international business is quite different. International economics seeks to find the optimum allocation of goods and services among nations, given very different factor endowments and economic systems. International politics seeks to find the optimum allocation of political power among nations, given very different power endowments and political systems. International law seeks to find the optimum resolution of conflict of national law, given very different legal concepts and legal systems. International business, on the other hand, seeks to find the optimum relationship between business interests in two or more countries, given very different priorities of objectives and business institutions. It is pointless to go into more definitional problems here, but I think you see my point. At the moment, the international business specialist is concerning himself with many problems which one day may find their way into the functional areas as the relevant courses become comparative. He will then be left with what is truly his area—the problems arising out of the international relationship of business interests, whether represented by buyers, sellers, manufacturers, assemblers, financiers, distributors, managers, or workers.

Part of the difficulty in understanding what international business is arises, I think, because those researching and teaching in the area are compelled—through default—to concern themselves with problems which are not, strictly speaking, international business. If the marketing specialists were adequately researching and teaching marketing in its global context, those identifying themselves with international business would not have to concern themselves directly. An analogy would be the plight of the international economist if economic theory concerned itself solely with the economics of perfect competition in a market economy. He would then be compelled to study the economics of imperfect competition, up to and including the centrally-directed economy. But in fact, economists have concerned themselves with research and teaching the entire array of possible economic systems. Therefore, the international economist can concern himself more with international economics, that is, with the optimum allocation of goods and services among nations, given very different factor endowments and economic systems. He himself does not have to ascertain what these factor endowments and economic systems are.

Educationally, the general failure of the functional areas in management to encompass the business systems of all countries forces the teacher and researcher in international business to concern himself with understanding these business systems—that is, with the comparative approach. He has a very small body of globally relevant theory and research to draw upon, and is thus very much poorer than the international economist. This means that, given the present state of the arts, much of this material must be included within the international business courses. In so doing, three strategies are possible:

- First is the comparative approach, which may take the form of examining a sample of the more important operating problems characteristic of the various national business systems and which are quite different from their purely domestic counterparts.

- Second is the international approach, that is, concentration on the true field of international business, which is the search for optimum relationships between business entities embedded in different national systems, different in terms of priorities of objectives and business institutions.

- Third, one can combine the comparative and international approaches.

In considering educational strategies, one can cut along a different dimension. One can opt for (1) a core course either combining both the comparative and international approaches or not; or (2) one can organize the comparative and/or international material into separate functional courses; or (3) push it into the traditional functional courses which nonetheless may remain heavily weighted toward the domestic environment. One can best visualize these strategies in a nine-box matrix, thus:

	Comparative Approach	International Approach	Combination
International Core Course			
Special International Functional Courses			
Expansion of Traditional Functional Courses			

The optimum choice of strategy in a particular school of management depends in large measure on the size, interest, and academic level of its student body on the one hand, and on the competence, interest, and relative size of its faculty on the other. Characteristically, one starts with the international core course concept in which both the comparative and international material is treated. As student interest and faculty competence expands, some special international functional courses appear — characteristically comparative management, comparative industrial relations, international marketing, international finance, and international commercial law. To a degree ascending in the order listed, such courses are likely to use the international approach as well as the comparative. Eventually, as globally valid theory and research techniques appear in the functional areas, the traditional functional courses may be expanded to be of global reach, *if* time and interest permit. At that point, the international business course shrinks back to the confines of international business proper, that is, to the problems arising out of international business relations, the problem on the international interface.

LEO SPIER
Pennsylvania State University

The Role of University Education In International Business

Increasing commitments in international business reflect the need for professional personnel who can synthesize
social sciences information with business techniques in the
most complex environmental conditions. This requires an international business curriculum capable of training graduate
students in analytical techniques for top-level decision making. Courses covering (1) Environment (interdisciplinary
analysis), (2) Macro Theory and Policy, (3) Micro Theory
and Policy, and (4) a Research Seminar in International
Business comprise a basic program. In support of these
courses, there should be a solid PhD program, extensive
interdisciplinary research programs, keynote speaker and faculty and student exchange programs.

The significance of American private and public involvement in
international activities is overshadowed only by the complex problems that it raises. Foreign private investment is valued at more
than 60 billion dollars; military and political commitments stretch
from Vietnam to Israel and NATO; foreign aid flows to every corner
of the world; and the dollar has become the principal basis of exchange in world trade. All these developments illustrate emphatical-
ly the international ramifications for the United States. They place

LEO SPIER is Associate Professor of International Business in the College of Business Administration, Pennsylvania State University. He has MBA and DBA degrees from the University of Washington. From 1962 to 1967, he was on the
University of California (Berkeley) business school faculty, where he was
responsible for establishing and developing a comprehensive research and course
program in international business. His duties at Penn State are similar. He has
been particularly interested in the European Economic Community, and has published in several journals. His current research interest is in (1) studying the
implications of differing national economic policies upon international liquidity,
and (2) developing a model from the behavioral sciences to study the environmental impacts in international business.

exceptional diplomatic burdens on America's businessmen and government representatives, and consequently impose great responsibilities upon the educational organs of our society to produce men who can meet these international challenges. For instance, means of competition differ among nations; philosophies on the use of capital or employment compensation also vary; methods of control no longer fit "optimal" patterns; indeed, the entire meaning of what *is* optimal now assumes differing but nonetheless relevant proportions. While there is little disagreement regarding the significance and impact of these issues on the life of every American, there reigns considerable confusion on what the problems are and how they should be resolved. Consequently there is much disagreement among university educators regarding the nature, the scope, and the *modus operandi* of an international business program.

To understand the purpose and objectives of international business and its ramifications as a field of study, we need to focus on the underlying role that such a field must assume in university education. The study of international business involves, in large part, problems of human behavior generated by a variety of environmental norms and values. As such, it must incorporate interacting economic, social, and political forces, and must deal with their dynamic properties over time and space, as well as with their non-quantifiable aspects that make measurement an art, not a science. When we deal with different societies, we can no longer afford to rely on intuition or to generalize from assumptions based on the economically oriented values of our more familiar domestic environment. Instead, we must find a more systematic and comprehensive approach from which the complex international variations in behavior can be examined analytically.

Man functions as an entity, not as a scientifically segmented part, and man's decision-making norms and values reflect the unique mix of the particular environmental properties to which he is exposed. It is because of this that many economic policy measures of U. S. government and business acquire political and social implications abroad. Foreign societies react in ways dictated by the norms and values of their indigenous environments, which may be alien to ours.[1] It is the responsibility of the academic world to study these problems and to prepare the international executive appropriately.

1Ernest Dichter, "The Strategy of Human Motivation," **Public Relations Journal,** October 1967, p. 59.

THE PLACE OF INTERNATIONAL BUSINESS

International business envelops three basic areas of learning: the functional study of management practices; the scientific study of social phenomena and other applied disciplines; and the study that relates scientific phenomena to management practices under complex and differing environmental conditions.[2] The business scholar is in a unique position that allows him to bring to managerial decision-making a detachment from specialization and an ability to synthesize different sciences. He lacks only the expertise of the specialist, and he can overcome this lack by using the already established findings of each social science, rather than by searching for new ones. Thus the business scholar can provide the student with the combined advantages of a specialist and a generalist by integrating findings from diverse social science disciplines into a total system with a purpose of its own. As an example, a law school is founded on its ability to draw from the disciplines of political science, economics, and sociology, and to integrate the tools from these bodies of knowledge for the purpose of regulating present and future societal needs. Law is an expression of organized conduct based on social, political, and economic premises; law schools synthesize them into a meaningful entity.

The international business program must provide means for carrying out the ever-increasing private and public commitments of the United States to international affairs. The purpose of international business as a profession is to provide continued leadership in anticipating the changing needs of world business, and to resolve the potential problems arising from the complexities of these needs. Since these needs evolve from the comparative and global dimensions of international business, the modern executive must deal with the multiple variations of environmental forces in societies different from his own, and must formulate strategies that will optimize the firm's total operations. In essence, the decision-making tasks of world business require a "man for all seasons," having a capacity to generate opportunities within relatively unknown and complex environmental conditions.

NEW STRATEGIES FOR CHANGING NEEDS IN INTERNATIONAL BUSINESS

Recent developments in international activities require not only new structural designs of business operations, but a different man-

2Herbert A. Simon, "The Business School: A Problem in Organizational Design," **The Journal of Management Studies**, Vol. 4, No. 1, February 1967, p. 1.

agement philosophy. For example, the creation of newly independent nations has regenerated strong nationalistic biases toward international business ventures.[3] Second, the aim of developing countries to create their own industries and the drive by the Common Market nations toward industrial consolidation and political reformation, continuously shift the economic trade advantages between countries. Third, export barriers increase to bolster one economy's industry, or to create a new industry in another economy, or to develop political power in another. Fourth, direct foreign investment is welcomed with greater reluctance in order to avoid domination in some countries or to maintain the "national identity" in others. Finally, the reserve currency position of the United States and the advanced technological and management status of its economy imply a major shift in its comparative advantage toward capital and technology. These situations can no longer be resolved by traditional means; they require a fresh approach in order to assure effective world business operations.[4]

The international decision-making burden now shifts from a function of overseas lower- and middle-level clerical and staff personnel to a full-time responsibility of home-based executive management personnel and high policy-level staff specialists. Routine export-import transactions take a back seat to strategies of investment, marketing design, or management control.

The business school can make a unique contribution by equipping the executive for his enlarged role in world affairs.[5] It must provide him with (1) a fundamental grasp of the basic tools of economics, social psychology, political science, and the humanities, and (2) the basic knowledge of the functional fields in business. The main purpose of this undergraduate curriculum is to provide the student with as wide a perspective as possible of the complex and diverse environmental influences that confront the managerial decision-maker. Undergraduate studies in a business school should

---

3"Ownership Policies at Work Abroad—Responses to Nationalism and Needs for Capital and Friends," **Business International,** management monograph.

4Some changes are already evidenced in the increased use of joint ventures, multi-national holding companies, and diverse forms of minority equity control, which are not only physically feasible, but helpful in overcoming foreign environmental obstacles. Kaiser Industries and the Hilton Hotel Corporation are cases in point, where capital and management know-how have allowed little or no direct equity control.

5In essence, a business school is a professional school "which must participate **effectively in** the social and information systems of business, on the one hand, and in the social and information systems of sciences, on the other." Herbert A. Simon, **op. cit., p. 1.**

aim primarily for professional preparation of the graduate student, and should leave any specific advanced training to the graduate school and to the business firms.

AN INTERNATIONAL BUSINESS PROGRAM

With this undergraduate foundation, the international business curriculum can be directed toward synthesizing the diverse social sciences and developing more meaningful equipment to handle complex managerial issues in the international environment that may arise in the future. The program need no longer look as formidable as many present university curricula appear to be.

It does more harm than good to the advancement of a solid program to proliferate courses by functional specialization and by geographic areas.[6] First of all, functional exposure is the domain of the undergraduate curriculum. The student should already be familiar with the basic concept of foreign-trade multipliers, with adjustment for structural disequilibrium of the balance of payments, with fundamentals of organization theory, marketing systems, or the use of factor analysis in sociology. Second, teaching by detailed geographic area constitutes primarily a rehearsal of situational experiences. For one thing, there are too many alternative strategies for the students to commit to memory. For another, this approach encourages the students to make generalizations from specific situations without a proper analytical framework. Area studies have their place—in advanced research seminars where PhD students and qualified MBA students submit methods to the acid test. In other words, research findings should build the foundation for the establishment and development of courses.[7] Fewer courses, but ones with solid research foundations, will produce better potential scholars and international business executives than will a large number of courses having topic ideas but no research findings to back them. Only research seminars should be used for exploratory purposes.

An international business program at the graduate level can be covered by three basic courses and one recurrent elective seminar. This relatively small core group allows for a sufficient number of elective courses in other fields to enhance the student's knowledge in areas of special interest surrounding international business, e. g., investment finance, economics of underdeveloped areas, etc. More-

6See, for instance: J. Fayerweather, J. Boddewyn, and H. Engberg, **International Business Education: Curriculum Planning** (New York: New York University, 1966), pp. 14, 58-63.

7EWA Report, pp. 44, 53

over, it would give graduate students without a business background an opportunity to acquire the basic requisites for international business.

There are three integral components to a dynamic international business program. Neglect of any one of the three, or attempts to separate one from the others, will defeat the purpose of the whole. The components are (1) a solid graduate course program at both the master's and PhD levels, (2) a comprehensive research program with an Institute for Comparative and International Studies as its nerve center, and (3) programs for keynote speakers and international faculty and student exchanges.

COURSE PROGRAM

The four courses that are suggested below are neither conclusive nor absolute. The "determinants of strategy" in selecting a proper program depend upon location of the school, availability of academic research, teaching, and monetary resources — and more importantly, philosophy of the direction of education and of an international program.

(1) *The International Environment: An Interdisciplinary Approach for Comparative Analysis of Decision-Making Behavior*

In this course, a multidisciplinary model of environment is developed to aid the student in the analysis of managerial decision-making behavior among diverse societies. The basic assumptions are that within the environmental make-up of society are existing structural relationships of material and human resources that produce crucial behavioral qualities. These qualities, in turn, underlie specific norms and values of the socio-political and economic institutions by which man allocates power and wealth. Man's decision-making behavior is the characteristic product of the environmental properties to which he is exposed. A study of the behavioral dimensions of socio-political and economic norms and values provides the student with a comprehensive set of tools for systematic analysis. It helps explain not only specific reasons for dissimilar behavior, but permits more accurate prediction of behavior to given issues.

(2) *Macro Theory and Policy in International Business*

This course concerns the application of international economic trade and monetary tools to current national policy issues. Problems surrounding the Trade Expansion Act, the Voluntary Program, Common Market agricultural measures and antitrust policies, foreign aid, the Revenue Act, etc., are analyzed against a background of terms of trade, multiplier effects, capital structures, liquidity, economic market concepts, etc. Their ramifications for international business activities are then examined in terms of both domestic and foreign perspectives. The purpose of this course is to provide the student with a "clinical" basis for testing theory on current policy issues and to develop an ability to cope with domestic and foreign policies as they affect the international activities of the firm.

(3) *Micro Theory and Policy in International Business*

This course pertains to the analysis of international issues surrounding the internal operations of a company. Significant variations from domestic operations are examined; an analysis of the changing patterns of international operations is made for its potential implications. For instance, alternative strategies of operations for the multinational firm will be developed to test allocation of the firm's resources, to examine issues of transfer pricing or capital budgeting, to design marketing and information systems that may allow optimization for different subsidiaries in several countries, and to study diverse formats for efficient control under minority equity holdings and joint ventures.

(4) *Seminar in International Business*

This course is designed primarily for PhD candidates and qualified MBA students. Seminar techniques will be applied to such research topics as international cartel arrangements and commodity agreements (stabilization and factor movement effects, market structures); capital budgeting and investment functions; comparative studies of regionalized world markets; characteristics of multinational industrial organizations; the state of development of economic and political institutions, and their effects on international business.

These topics must be closely correlated with current research issues of the international business community in order mutually to expose the points of view of students, professors, and business executives. This also provides a basis for anticipating changes in international business that require attention. Moreover, these topics also build the foundation for an extensive and continuous research program to assure constant re-examination of issues and analyses and to allow for the needed modifications in a dynamic environment. These seminars will coordinate the information systems of the social sciences with those of management practices and will devise strategies for total information systems through integration of the dynamic forces in the international business environment. Specific area studies will serve as test bases. Alternative seminar methods may be substituted in which a broader topic is parceled out for specific but differing research assignments.

(5) *PhD Program in International Business*

The doctoral program constitutes an important link in a successful international business curriculum. First, it provides a criterion for measuring the performance of the program relative to other academic institutions. Second, it produces a more dynamic program where constant research efforts reinforce and continue to develop the curriculum. Third, unlike the master's program, it must concentrate on building up areas of specialization for the candidate and for the field of international business.

The following requisites should be covered in a doctoral program:[8]

(A) There must be a solid course foundation;

(B) Areas of competence must be selected to support the major in specialization;

(C) A comprehensive research program must be maintained —preferably under the auspices of an "Institute for Comparative and International Studies." This center would have the responsibilities for (1) providing the doctoral candidate with the means for developing his research skills, and (2) initiating and developing diverse aspects of research in international business and in related areas;

(D) A keynote speaker program and a faculty and student exchange program, to provide continuous exposure to pertinent subject matter in international business and world affairs; and

(E) An introductory course in international business on the upper-division undergraduate level should be provided for joint teaching efforts of doctoral candidates under close faculty supervision.

These requisites may be amplified as follows:

(A) *Course Foundation.* The course program should essentially cover the same salient features as that of the master's candidate. Flexibility, however, is always advisable to allow the doctoral candi-

---

8The doctoral program must, of course, be correlated with the specific requirements of the University. This may mean that the doctoral candidate has anywhere from one to three minor fields of competence in addition to his major. We will assume here the maximum range in order to give fullest possible coverage for such a program.

date to substitute courses for those in which he already can prove competence.

(B) *Areas of Competence.* In consultation with his adviser, the PhD candidate must select a specialization within international business and build the minor fields of competence around that specialization. The reasons for this specialized direction are (1) the general exposure already received from the course foundation above, and (2) the need as a scholar to show competence in one or two aspects of the complex field of international business for teaching and research purposes. If, for instance, a candidate desires to build up a specialization in international financial management, he might concentrate his efforts in a seminar project on international financing methods between subsidiaries. He might further research such topics as means of foreign private investment, minority equity controls, etc. Finally, he should present his findings to an introductory undergraduate course for practical exposure. These fields should be supported by courses in finance, quantitative techniques, money and banking, and political science programs relating to fiscal and monetary administration. If a candidate wants to gain competence in international management controls in developing nations, he should study alternatives in decision-making processes and constraints from developing economies. He might concentrate his research efforts on the international management environment to compare organizational structures or strategies or risk minimization in developing countries. Again he must support this effort through courses in organization theory, operations research analysis, comparative economic systems, social ecology, and social change.

(C) *Institute for Comparative and International Studies.* An Institute for Comparative and International Studies must support the international curriculum. Primarily it should concern itself with generating new ideas and preparing students for scholarly research. Consequently, research is and should be the life-line for a dynamic international program that is capable of revising itself continuously and adjusting to changes in the world. Moreover, the Institute can serve as an information and nerve center for business and government contacts with the academic world. Such research must not be restricted to any one social science discipline, but should encourage intercourse of ideas among all faculties through regular meetings and joint research efforts. Finally, it may provide in special cases for joint research with foreign scholars to provide alternative viewpoints on a specific issue such as allocation of decision-making responsibility concerning a subsidiary.

(D) *Keynote Speaker Program and Faculty-Student Exchange Program.* For continued and diversified exposure to current issues, noted experts from business, government, and the academic worlds should be invited to speak to joint faculty-student colloquia on their areas of specialization. For instance, a member of the U. S. trade negotiation team to GATT might shed valuable light on the position of government; in turn, a member of the textile industry may produce varying, but nonetheless significant, themes on the same issue. Such a speaker program would assist in maintaining vital contacts needed for research and training.

Along similar lines of thought, it would appear useful to organize a faculty-student foreign exchange program to provide a broader mutual exposure. Some of the more successful programs contract with foreign host universities to send (and receive) a faculty proctor and a selected group of graduates. The host university arranges for lecture programs and part-time employment of the guest students; the faculty guest lectures to host students; and periodic faculty-student seminars between host and guest provide for continued interchange of ideas. Furthermore, the faculty member would be invited to participate in specific projects at the Institute.

One major point that may require some careful re-evaluation on the part of many American universities is their present over-emphasis of relations with non-European institutions. It seems that we overlook the pressing needs for solutions arising from issues in the European Community, from England's struggle to modernize, from Eastern Europe's desire to gain closer relations with the West, from the still-unexplored possibilities for making business administration a respectable and acceptable part of the European societies, and from the lion's share of international activities that take place between Europe and the United States. This is not to say that other world areas do not have their place in research and exchange programs, but it does propose to channel some of these efforts into the somewhat neglected European issues which require as much if not more attention, as recent political and economic developments illustrate.

(E) *Introductory Undergraduate Course.* Many universities deem it desirable to familiarize the undergraduate students with the complexities of international business. Such a course should remain sufficiently broad to provide a maximum exposure to the diverse issues, on the one hand, yet sufficiently specific to show the importance of intense study, on the other. As part of such a course, doctoral students could present their diverse research problems and findings in liaison with one another and under close supervision of a faculty member. The benefits are manifold. First, the undergraduate gets diverse points of view and broad coverage of specific issues. Second, the doctoral candidate learns the results of research exposure and is introduced to the ramifications of teaching. Moreover, the faculty member can evaluate the doctoral candidate in a more objective light.

CONCLUSION

It suffices to point out again that the program presented here is not to be taken as a rigid plan, but as a set of guidelines designed around a set of ideas regarding the role of international business in university education. International business plays a vital role in the economies of the world. Its complexity—cutting across the total dimensions of human behavior—makes separate study of international business imperative. Most importantly, international business education must provide the kind of leadership which anticipates changes in world affairs and supplies the future business executive with the means for dealing with differing environmental behavior. This requires resolving national differences for effective and optimal operation of the global enterprise.

The place of education, therefore, is to create new opportunities that will advance the purpose and objectives of world business; it must not be satisfied with supplying manpower for business issues that are already obsolete. This requires a comprehensive program of teaching, research, and interrelation among business, government, and the university. Moreover, it presumes synthesis of diverse social sciences and applied analysis to complex business and government problems. Therefore a solid international business program should be taught at the graduate level, with a thorough preparation in the functional and social science fields at the undergraduate level. The program must be supported by clearly defined and correlated research efforts and a doctoral program, and impetus must be maintained through contact with the business community and government. Only then will an international business program remain dynamic, continue to anticipate changes, and prepare its students to cope with the complex and viable managerial problems that face the world of tomorrow. Perhaps the first step is to re-orient our philosophy toward the idea of world business instead of international business.

ROBERT W. ADAMS
University of Michigan

International Business
at the University of Michigan

At the University of Michigan, substantial revisions have been made in both the MBA and PhD programs which will become fully effective next year. In the committee and faculty discussions that preceded these revisions, many problem areas were considered. One of these was the role that international business should play in education for a career in business administration. In my remarks, I shall describe briefly the changes that were made in the MBA program and in the role of international business in that program. A description of these changes, the reasons for them, and what we hope to accomplish should furnish some insights into our curriculum strategy and philosophy.

Considering first the MBA program as a whole, its broad strategic objective is certainly to train students for a career in business; that is, to become an executive in the corporation as it will be in the next 40 years. The specific objectives used as a guide in the review of the curriculum were as follows:

to insure a knowledge of basic business functions and provide the opportunity for intensive study in major fields;

to develop ability in identifying problems, obtaining relevant information, devising and evaluating alternative approaches, and choosing and implementing decisions;

to increase the capacity for quick, flexible adjustment to the rapidly changing conditions of the business world;

ROBERT W. ADAMS is Professor of International Business in the Graduate School of Business Administration, University of Michigan. He has a PhD in industrial economics from Massachusetts Institute of Technology. From 1946 to 1965, he was economist and manager of the General Economics Department of Standard Oil Company of New Jersey. He joined the Michigan faculty in 1965 and is Director of the Institute for International Commerce at the university.

to enlarge understanding of the political, social, and economic order and of the businessman's responsibilities to society; and

to provide the foundation for continuing self-education and development.

Clearly these broad objectives have important implications for international business. It seems logical to expect that the corporate world in the next 40 years will become increasingly international. Not only will there be a greater number of international companies, probably dominating the scene, but they will also be involved in more countries around the world. Executive personnel will become practically "stateless." The normal business firm will be the international corporation, with major commitments abroad, and with the entire world enterprise getting management's attention.

To train future executives for such a situation is the objective of the international business component of the business administration curriculum.

Given these various objectives, what changes have been made in the curriculum to achieve them?

By way of introduction, let me mention that there has been no change in the formal length of the MBA program. It has been maintained at 4 semesters of full-time work. The time is divided approximately half and half between required core and elective courses. Requirements for advanced standing have been tightened.

The first important change that I shall mention is that the structure of the core curriculum was changed quite markedly. In the old program, the core consisted entirely of the traditional tool and functional courses. In the new, the number and extent of tool and functional courses have been reduced, although still more than meeting the requirements of the American Association of Collegiate Schools of Business. This has permitted the inclusion of integrative and cross-functional courses in the core curriculum.

The new core curriculum is integrated into a single unified program. The individual courses build on each other and must be taken in the prescribed sequence. They start with a liberal sprinkling of foundation courses, progress through a series of decision-oriented courses, and wind up with an integrated Business Policy course.

The result is a breaking down of the traditional boundaries between functional areas, a broader total program, and a stress on the interrelationships among the functional and tool areas.

With respect to international business, it was felt that as a minimum, the business executive of the future who is being trained now needs to have at least an awareness of some of the environmental differences in doing business in other countries, and some conception of how these differences complicate business problems.

This is provided for by including an international component where appropriate in the core curriculum courses. Each student gets some international marketing problems in the course in Marketing Management in the second term. In the third-term course, Business, the Economy, and Public Policy, some aspects of the international environment will be included as well as policies concerning them. Finally, in the capstone Business Policy course in the fourth term, a substantial proportion of the case problems pertains to international corporations. Thus every student will meet international implications of business administration principles as a normal part of his core, integrated program.

The second change in the MBA program that has relevance to international business is the new provision for a concentration requirement. Each MBA student is now required to concentrate in at least one area. This normally involves an introductory course, an advanced course, and a seminar with a substantial amount of independent study and research. This concentration requirement assures at least a minimum amount of work at an advanced level, without requiring an undue degree of specialization.

This provision for an area of concentration can affect the student in two ways. For one, it permits the student concentrating in some functional area, as for example, marketing, to add an international dimension to his field of specialization. We are now offering international courses in the functional areas of marketing, labor relations, and finance. Doubtless others will be added to this list in due course. These give the student the option of getting additional training in the international aspects of his area of concentration.

The second possibility is for the student to concentrate in the area of international business. The philosophical question of whether international business is really a separate discipline seems to me to be largely irrelevant, at least for the present. As it evolves, the international corporation finds it useful to have executives trained in peculiarly international problems in order to acquire some skill in solving these more complex problems. There clearly are some concepts relating to international and foreign aspects of business that the executive of the future will find useful. Until such time as the other functional courses make no distinction between domestic and international business, we shall offer the student the opportunity to get this specialization.

What makes up a concentration in International Business? What are the concepts to be included?

The introductory course, The World Economy, is a new one replacing the former course, International Economic Relations. This changed course is designed to acquaint the student with the environmental differences that distinguish international business. In the past, the International Economic Relations course was mainly concerned with the relationships among countries in terms of trade theory, the balance of payments, and public policy issues. There was no explicit attempt to bring in the cultural, social, and economic differences within different nations as they bear upon business decisions. These were only brought in as needed in the decision-oriented courses. We found that the American student had little conception of the differences among nations, and that insufficient time and effort was being devoted to giving him any real understanding. Therefore, we have increased the number of hours in the introductory course from three to four and will devote about half the time to a comparative study of the environmental differences in other nations and about half to the economic relationships among nations.

The second course in the concentration sequence in International Business will be one of the decision-oriented courses, building on the environmental material in the introductory course: Management of International Operations, International Finance, International Marketing, or Comparative Labor Relations.

The final course in the sequence is a seminar. In this we attempt to do two things: one is to include some international business policy cases to integrate the material in the international area with material in other functional areas. The other is to have the student do independent study and research on a project in international business.

Within the strategy for international business education as we have defined it, I do not think that there is any room for, nor any need for, considerable expansion of the program beyond its present scope, except for one or two more international courses in functional areas.

To be specific, I do not see that a series of area study courses would help this program meet its objectives. The corporation of the future will be concerned with all areas of the world, and the future manager can ill afford to take the time to become an expert in any one area. The student should acquire a sensitivity to different environments, some conception of their scope, the origin of the behavioral and attitudinal differences, and how to deal with them—that is, either adapt his own behavior or try to modify them. For the occasional student who, for some reason, wishes to specialize in some particular area of the world, there are area study centers elsewhere in the University where he can take courses; and he is in fact encouraged to do so.

In summary, then, we have not really taken sides in the controversy as to whether international business is a separate discipline. As a minimum, we feel that the businessman who is being trained today should be aware: (1) that some things are different outside the United States—and not necessarily worse for being different—and (2) that the business principles which he is learning have worldwide applicability. This we are trying to do in the new core curriculum. At the other extreme, the problems of international business sufficiently complicate the traditional functional areas that there is ample justification for making provisions for a separate area of specialization. Within these extreme positions, the student may exercise freedom of choice.

We think this arrangement fits our conception of purpose. But the problem is not yet solved, and there will continue to be further discussion, evaluation, and evolution.

LEE C. NEHRT
Indiana University

The Imperative of International Business for the Business School Student

I would first of all like to respond to what seemed to me to be the most important question raised in the *EWA Report,* following which I shall describe the direction which our International Business program has taken at Indiana University and how far we have gone.

The question to which I refer is, "Is there some minimum exposure to the international dimension of business operations that should be acquired by all business students?"

Let me back off a bit from the question to a relevant side issue in education. Several years ago, Kingman Brewster, Jr., President of Yale University, gave a talk in which he advocated a significant change in the undergraduate curriculum, designed to prepare college graduates for today's world. His remarks were echoed by a number of other educators. The gist of their thinking was that a very high percentage of U. S. college students graduate without ever having studied anything foreign or international, except perhaps a

LEE C. NEHRT is Associate Professor of International Business in the Graduate School of Business, Indiana University. He has MBA and PhD degrees in international business from Columbia University. Prior to joining the Indiana faculty in 1962, he was with the Atomics International Division of North American Aviation. In the summer of 1963, he was in Yugoslavia to negotiate the establishment of an MBA program through an exchange relationship between Indiana University and the University of Ljubijana. From 1965 to 1967, he was in Tunisia as advisor to the Minister of Planning and Economics, concerned primarily with foreign investment, foreign trade, and productivity. His published writings include *Foreign Marketing of Nuclear Power Plants* (Indiana University Press, 1966) and *International Finance for Multinational Business* (International Textbook, 1967). He co-edited the proceedings of the December, 1963 International Business Administration Conference, held at Indiana University.

comparative literature course. They have had no exposure to U. S. foreign policy, to international politics, to the history of Western Europe or some other area, to any of the other cultures in the world, to the aspirations and problems of the people in the underdeveloped world, to the various meanings of communism, socialism, and capitalism, to the 3 billion people outside the United States, etc. Then, these "educated" people venture into life, not as citizens of a second-rate power, such as the United States prior to World War I, not as citizens of an isolationist country, such as the United States prior to World War II, but as citizens of the world's most powerful country, with interests of many kinds in every part of the globe. In their lifetime, whether these students become biologists or geologists, doctors or teachers, politicians or businessmen, they will be expected to vote intelligently on international issues, and they may be called upon to go overseas for the government, for international organizations, for private organizations, or for business. Why should so many students start from point zero in appreciation of the realities of the problems they will face? What is needed is a mechanism by which every college undergraduate, regardless of his major, would take a number of courses which will give him some appreciation of the politics, economics, or general culture of peoples outside the United States. This would not require the addition of new courses — a multiplicity of appropriate courses already exist at nearly all universities and colleges. It needs only the addition of some specialized requirements within the existing requirements for social science studies.

This happens to be a very keen side-interest of mine, and I apologize for burdening you with it, but I couldn't resist preaching to such a select audience.

The analogy between this problem of the internationalization of the university's undergraduate students and the question of international exposure for business students, is close, but has some differences. The role of a business school is not to prepare students for life. It cannot serve as a substitute for programs in general studies. It is a professional school and should prepare students for the kinds of problems they will encounter during their careers. The question, then, is, "What is the probability that today's business student will, at some time in his career, be working for a company which has some international operations, and have a responsibility for some aspect of those operations?" In a report prepared for the Department of Health, Education and Welfare, John Fayerweather raised this question and noted the need for research in this direction. Without talking to the companies which interview graduate business students, and in the absence of data on the rate of increase in the number of U. S. companies which are "going international," I would suspect that very few of today's students will be able to avoid responsibility for some aspect of international business at some time in their careers. The remainder should understand the extent to which international business can affect the operations of a firm which is purely domestic in its own operations, for the manager who is ill-prepared may find himself handicapped.

But this brings us to the concomitant question: "If business students should have some minimum exposure to international business, how can this limited objective be accomplished?"

The various approaches have been discussed in the *EWA Report,* and you are familiar with them. I wish to comment, however, on one of them. It appears that most people are in agreement that the most desirable method is through an internationalization of existing courses. The problem seems to be in the implementation of such a scheme.

Many of you are aware of a study which is now nearing completion, at Indiana, under the direction of Professor Schuyler Otteson, concerning the extent to which internationalization of the curriculum has taken place in schools of business. They have fairly complete data from about 80 schools. The study is not complete and I am not in a position to discuss it, but I understand that one of the findings is that only a very few institutions have achieved some degree of integration of the international dimension into a few of the regular courses. There are many reasons for this, which I will not mention at this time, but I should like to draw another analogy.

The goal of Marxist communism is the gradual withering away of the State. The various entities of the society should gradually become self-motivated and self-operating, carrying out those functions which were initially the responsibility of the State. The problem is that most communist governments now consider this a utopia which *may* be achieved in the next generation or the one after that. You are familiar enough with Yugoslavia's political economy, however, to realize that with sufficient faith, effort, and suffering, it is possible to approach this goal.

I don't like this part of the analogy, but the State obviously represents the establishment of an international business department which offers specialized courses in I. B. The goal is the infusion of the international dimension into the standard business courses and a diminished responsibility on the part of the International Business Department. The probability that this will happen very quickly is very low. *I do feel, however, that an International Business department or area must be established initially and that it must then work diligently and continuously to diminish its role.* If a dean feels that he can achieve the internationalization of the various functional courses without establishing some central organism from which the spirit of internationalism emanates, I feel that he is either fooling himself or he has established for himself another full-time job.

The second portion of my remarks concerns the experience of Indiana in building up its International Business program. At its inception, in about 1960, the policy was to offer a number of International Business courses so that MBA and DBA students might major in International Business, but with the goal of internationalizing as many of the standard courses as possible. To avoid creating too strong a structure, a department was not established. The head of the program was not a department chairman but, rather, a Director of International Business Studies. To assure the cooperation of the various functional departments and to serve as an initial step in internationalizing the functional courses, the international marketing, international finance, and international management courses were made the responsibility of those respective departments and taught by professors from those areas. International Business Studies itself offered three courses of importance: Introduction to International Business; Comparative Business Systems; and a Seminar in Selected Issues in International Business. The last served also as a seminar for doctoral students for the preparation of dissertation proposals. In addition, area courses, such as Business and Economic Conditions in Latin America, were offered intermittently. An MBA student majoring in International Business was required to have a minimum of three courses in the field. Introduction to International Business and Comparative Business Systems were required; the third course would be either International Marketing, International Finance, or International Management. A DBA student majoring in International Business was required to have a minimum of five courses, including the three required for MBA students, plus International Economics (which is taught by the Economics Department). The above-mentioned organization, courses, and requirements remain in effect today, although the content of each of the courses has changed significantly with experience and as the availability of literature has changed.

If I were to refer to the "Determinants of Strategy," as presented in the *EWA Report*, it would appear that Indiana has a "major commitment" to International Business and is involved in most of the elements of the "grand strategy." We have been fortunate in receiving significant Ford Foundation grants in 1961 and again in 1966, the latter permitting the establishment of an International Business Research Institute. These funds have made it possible to provide grants to non-international business faculty members to engage in international business research, much of it performed abroad. In addition, Indiana now has technical assistance projects to help establish MBA programs in Pakistan, Thailand, and Yugoslavia. This has resulted in additional foreign experience for a number of faculty members.

Last year, with a total graduate enrollment of about 600 students in the Indiana Business School, international business courses had a total enrollment of about 270 students. This represented an increase of 53 percent over the preceding year. About 13 percent of the graduate students were international business majors, about 30 percent took the introductory course in international business, and about 45 percent took at least one other international business course. There are now 15 DBAs with international business majors, of whom 10 are in residence, the remainder doing field research. Finally, to end the statistics, we discovered only several days ago that the number of companies that come to Indiana and ask to interview international business majors has increased this fall by 120 percent over last fall.

All this appears to spell "success" in one direction, *but* to what extent is Indiana achieving its stated goal of internationalizing a significant number of its regular courses? The answer is "very little." The small extent to which it has been achieved can be traced to the efforts of only several professors in the functional areas.

Based on our experience, therefore, it appears that the only way to insure that all business school students receive some international business as part of their education is to have a course on the international environment and dimensions of business as a required part of the program. Such a requirement has not yet been instituted at Indiana.

DAN T. SMITH
Harvard University

On Integrating International Business into the Curriculum

The differences between those who argue for and against international business as an area of study do not appear to be so great as is suggested by the categorical statement of the issue. The choice, I believe, is not between a completely separate field or full absorption into traditional areas. The problem is rather how best to fit into a curriculum the additional facts and broader perspectives needed to deal with the more complex situations which usually exist when business activities extend beyond one country. Modifications in several respects are probably required.

The addition of some international material into some of the basic courses seems desirable and, indeed, necessary. Those who later take special courses with emphasis on international aspects of business will have had some introduction to the subject. More importantly, those who do not take advanced courses with an international flavor will at least be aware of the inadequacy of a purely national point of view.

There is, to be sure, the danger that a little knowledge and superficial understanding, acquired from international material in basic courses, will give a false sense of mastery and perspective. But half-

DAN T. SMITH is Professor of Finance at the Harvard Business School. He has a PhD from Harvard. He joined the Harvard faculty in 1930. From 1953 to 1959, he held a series of policy posts in the U. S. Department of Treasury. He was 1963 president of the Tax Institute of America, Inc., and is 1967 president of the National Tax Association. He has been consultant to various corporations, The Brookings Institution, National Bureau of Economic Research, and the Committee for Economic Development. Among his publications are *Taxable and Business Income* (co-authored, NBER, 1949) and *Effects of Taxation on Corporate Financial Policy* (Harvard Business School, 1952). He is chairman of the International Business Area and chairman of the Faculty Committee on International Activities, Harvard Business School.

baked ideas are a perpetual danger in any introductory course, as is apparent to anyone who has been involved in a condensed presentation of macro-economics, or to those who have received such presentations. The pedagogical challenge to make students understand the complications and uncertainties, while simplifying. a subject enough to make it comprehensible to beginners, will always be with us.

Some international material can be worked into the basic courses in both the traditional functional fields and those dealing with macro-economics and environmental factors. The balance of payments and changes in exchange rates are as important as purely domestic fiscal and monetary policies; the latter, as we now know too well, cannot be set without regard to the former. A generation ago, the controversy in some faculties was whether to require any general work in economics as part of a program in business administration. It should be less of an issue now to broaden the coverage, though not the total time allotted, to include international aspects.

In the functional fields, the suitability of international material varies with the subject. Marketing and finance have conspicuous differences as one moves beyond a single country, as do many aspects on production. The more theoretical aspects of quantitative analysis or decision theory, by contrast, can probably be taught equally well with material from a single country. A specific danger is that the introduction of a single foreign setting into a functional course may give the impression that all foreign environments conform to one pattern, and the domestic to another.

Beyond the introductory courses, advanced work in most of the functional fields, with emphasis on international material, seems appropriate. International finance is probably the most obvious and most frequent to be offered. Marketing is equally suitable, and comparative organizational behavior seems to be of increasing interest to specialists.

In the advanced courses, one should distinguish, I believe, between the material useful for international business on the one hand and a purely comparative approach, or even a course dealing with problems of doing business in one or more foreign countries, on the other. The latter especially seems inappropriate. Let educators in each country develop their own programs of education for doing business in their respective countries. Our concern here should be to include some understanding and facility in dealing with the more complex problems arising when business operations go beyond a single country.

A straight comparative analysis may be useful for this purpose, but it leaves to the students the problems of determining the ways in which a business operating across boundaries or in more than one national jurisdiction differs from those operating alone and quite separately in one country as compared to another. The words "international," "multinational," and "transnational" may give, each in its own way, the distinction between a comparative approach and that which seems more appropriate in study programs here.

Along with the functional courses with an international emphasis, in a large curriculum there is need and should be room for an advanced course in international economics pointed to prospective administrators who have a taste for theory. Unless there is a fair amount of international material in the basic economics course, a term of international economics may be a prerequisite or co-requisite for the functional courses with international emphasis. The design of courses is likely to become difficult at this point; familiarity with the balance of payments, trade agreements, and distinctive national planning procedures is equally important for parts of international finance and international marketing. It is a duplication to present the background in separate courses, but to require a course in international economics as a prerequisite may preclude many students concentrating in a functional field from getting the international aspects of their special area.

In addition to a course on international economics and environment and the functional courses with international emphasis, is there anything left that is purely international? A course dealing with distinctively international problems of top management seems called for, including such topics as problems of entry into another country, joint ventures and conflicts of interest, executive recruitment, transfer and compensation, government relations, the choice between international pooling of funds or quasi-autonomy of subsidiaries, and the all-important matter of the extent of delegation of authority to secure the best combination of initiative and flexibility on the one hand and coordination on the other.

In selecting subject matter for such a course, one has to guard against material that is merely significant and in an international setting. To merit inclusion it should be distinctive because it is international. Frequently one will decide, on reflection, that material which arose in an international situation might equally well have developed in a large company operating several subsidiaries within a single country. As such, it should have no place in a truly international course.

One may regard the course in general management problems as a special course in business policy or simply as a capstone course in international business. The latter seems useful to increase the probability of coordination among the international functional courses for those who want to use international business as a field of concentration.

Courses dealing with a geographic region are familiar and useful. My own feeling, and that of my colleagues on my own faculty, is that they may be dropped in preference to the functional course, with students interested in particular geographic areas encouraged to register in regional seminars in other faculties, thereby gaining the benefit of securing a mixture of disciplines along with cross-cultural material.

Should there be a major in international business? For those of us who think a student may be well advised to choose his courses for the particular challenge of the subject matter and the professor, an international major seems as appropriate as any other, even though most students, as has been pointed out so often, are likely to start their employment in a functional area in domestic activities, making their way up in it before going abroad. The international major should, however, be able to stand on its own merits in a reasonably broad curriculum.

What about faculty organization? Those giving functional courses with an international emphasis clearly have a place in their respective areas or departments. But additional membership in an international area or department seems desirable to secure collaboration in courses which have the common thread of international emphasis. The problem of faculty organization is perhaps similar to that of a firm which has each product line organized on a worldwide basis. There is still some need for special attention to the international aspects of the whole business, at times achieved through a grid type of organization. Faculties, too, may have a few international specialists working with functional specialists on matters of common concern.

As regards faculty, it should be apparent that familiarity with a foreign language or having a foreign origin is not sufficient qualification for teaching or research in international business. Interest and the ability to deal with particularly complex problems are more important. Hopefully, an increasing number of faculty members will develop these aptitudes from participating in foreign academic programs of one sort or another. Widespread participation in such activities is useful for providing a basis for effective teaching of international material in the basic courses. Just as foreign students have difficulty in dealing with complex domestic subject matter in this country, so do faculty members have problems in dealing adequately with foreign material if they have never been in a foreign environment. Fortunately, faculty experiences seem to be becoming international about as rapidly as are the activities of business. The wider perspectives of the faculty should qualify them to present the wider and more complicated problems which confront so many of the current generation of students.

MICHAEL Y. YOSHINO
University of California, Los Angeles

Curriculum Planning in International Business at UCLA*

During the last two decades there has been a tremendous acceleration in international business activities. An increasing number of large and small firms and virtually all the industrially advanced nations of the world are now engaged in international business. We are witnessing the evolution of a new corporate entity—the multinational corporation. Moreover, domestic and international economies are now so closely intertwined that even those firms whose business operations are confined to their national boundaries cannot escape the influences of the international economic and political environment. This phenomenon was dramatically demonstrated in the far-reaching impact of the recent devaluation of the British pound upon the national economy of virtually every nation in the world.

It stands to reason, therefore, that professional business schools seeking to train future executives and educate future scholars cannot ignore the extraordinary development and growth of international business in our time. However, beyond a general consensus that something innovative needs to be done, the whole issue is clouded in marked uncertainty, groping, and controversy. And, at the same time that a number of American corporations expanded overseas without well-thought-out strategies, some business schools hastened to add

MICHAEL Y. YOSHINO is Assistant Professor of Business Administration, Graduate School of Business Administration, University of California (Los Angeles). He has an MBA from Columbia University and a PhD from Stanford University. He has co-authored *Comparative Analysis for International Marketing: Organizing for Planning and Control* (Allyn and Bacon, 1967), and has written several articles on international marketing. At UCLA, he is chairman of the International Business and Comparative Management Program.

*Professor Yoshino replaced Professor Root, who was unable to attend the discussion session because of severe weather and a consequent flight cancellation. Professor Root's paper is included in this volume, immediately following Professor Yoshino's.

courses and programs in international business without first clearly defining their objectives. Many of these crash programs have produced disappointing results.

How can the business school best meet the challenge? What approach would prove most effective for a business school to use in developing an effective program of education in international business? What constitutes a sound international business curriculum at professional schools of business administration? Such are the basic and provocative questions that need to be answered.

This paper examines the approach used by the Graduate School of Business Administration at the University of California in Los Angeles (UCLA) in setting up its international business curriculum. Although it is confined to the analysis of the experience of one school, it is hoped that generalizations may be extracted from the discussion which will prove valuable to other schools.

Before describing our international business program, we shall sketch some pertinent facts regarding our business school. UCLA has for some time now offered only graduate programs in business administration. Specifically, we now offer programs leading to the MBA, Master of Science, and PhD degrees. The distinction between the MBA and MS programs is that the former is designed for training in general management and does not offer the opportunity for major-field concentration, whereas the MS is for students wishing to specialize in a certain functional area.

The School has two types of MBA programs. In addition to a regular program, it offers a different one to selected students who, at their undergraduate level, had followed a major other than business administration. This program is not shaped in the form of the traditional series of courses, but as a two-year curriculum of coordinated and integrated courses for management training. When planning our program in international business, we first set ourselves two key tasks: (1) to define the field of international business and (2) to determine for whom the program was intended.

After a careful consideration of the essential nature of international business, we arrived at a consensus that international business is inherently different from functional areas such as finance, marketing, or production. We also perceived that although there are some problems that are unique to international business, a crucial part of its operations calls for the application of basic business concepts, theories, and analytical tools in various functional areas to the international business scene. Thus, the major focus in formulating our international business program was to help the student develop an understanding of the diversity and complexity of the international environment in which basic functions of business administration are carried out. In fact, the following excerpt from the *EWA Report* succinctly summarizes our own basic point of view on the subject:

> In order to preserve the integrity of a school's present—though changing—MBA program, the rigor and content should not be watered down by an infusion of an excessive number of "international" courses at the expense of thorough education in the more basic disciplines and specialized courses in the functional fields. *It is felt, in other words, that training in international business should in large measure supplement, and not replace, good fundamental study in business.* [Emphasis added.] (p. 53)

Turning now to the second question, it is our view that the international business program is relevant to three types of students. The first group consists of those who plan to make international business their career. Although students in this category have an intense interest in this field, their number is very small. The second category consists of students who may be called upon to perform international assignments from time to time. In fact, with the growing importance of international business and the gradual removal of artificial barriers between domestic and international business, it is not unrealistic to anticipate that the responsibilities of many future executives and staff specialists will increasingly take on a multinational character. The third type of students are those whose activities are confined to national boundaries. Yet, whether they foresee or like it, their involvement in domestic business operations will be affected in varying degrees by the developments in the international economic scene.

Though it is true that a program in international business should vary both in kind and intensity according to each of the three classes of students, it is nevertheless our view that an effective educational program in international business must meet the needs of all three types of students.

When UCLA committed itself to developing a curriculum in international business in the early 1960's, the school, at the same time, sought to avoid a crash program. To begin with, it intensified its efforts to recruit faculty members with a strong international orientation in each key functional area. In some cases, international specialists in functional areas emerged within the school through their research activities. This "grass roots" approach has offered two important advantages. The program has evolved rather than being superimposed on the existing curriculum, thus facilitating the ready acceptance of the international program by the faculty at large, among whom the "grass roots" members were a small minority. It also allowed integration of international business into each key functional area.

Furthermore, development of a specific international business program was based on the recognition that an effective over-all program of this nature must satisfy the needs of all three categories of students indicated earlier, and that because the needs of each category are different, differentiation of curriculum was indicated.

For the student interested in an international business career or in research in the field, we established international business as an area of concentration leading to Master of Science and PhD degrees. For the second and third categories of students, we decided to selectively introduce international business content into the existing business administration program.

Reflecting our view of international business as a field of study, students majoring in this field are urged to develop a thorough background in a functional area, either prior to or simultaneously with taking international business courses. The emphasis of the major field at the Master of Science level is to develop skills and points of view to enable students to apply basic concepts and analytical tools of functional areas in international context, and, in addition, to learn concepts and theories that are specifically related to the management of international business. At the doctoral level, the emphasis is on the development of research competence in the field. Due to the very nature of international business plus its current state of development, a strong emphasis is placed on the acquisition of a thorough knowledge in the use of basic analytical research tools.

Building on the common core of requirements for all doctoral candidates, doctoral students majoring in international business are urged to develop (1) a thorough background in international economics, (2) a competence in a functional area, and (3) research competence in the field of international business. To achieve the third goal, candidates for the PhD usually find it necessary to acquire some competence in an allied discipline, such as political science, anthropology, area studies, or law.

We have already noted the importance of developing a minimum competence level in international business for the great majority of students who do not major in international business. We are pursuing this objective in several ways. In our regular MBA program, gradual efforts are being made to introduce international elements in selected courses, such as economics, business and government, and business policy. In addition, MBA candidates may choose to satisfy their second year elective course requirements by taking international business courses.

In the integrated MBA program, a special learning unit (equivalent to a 4-unit credit course) on international business has been introduced as part of the required second-year curriculum. The program is taught by a panel of faculty members. Master of Science candidates with a field of specialization other than international business are strongly urged to take international courses in their respective functional areas.

Turning now to the content of our curriculum, the School has avoided the proliferation of courses in international business. The existing courses may be divided (somewhat arbitrarily) into three categories: environmental, comparative, and operational. Environmental courses are designed to develop a sound theoretical and conceptual understanding of the environment in which international business is performed, providing a background for subsequent courses. An important portion of these courses is devoted to rigorous treatment of international economics. The environmental courses, however, go beyond the traditional ones in international economics by introducing the students to concepts and theories from allied disciplines that are relevant to international business. They include such topics as nationalism, political culture and development, and cultural change.

The second type—the comparative courses—are designed to undertake cross-cultural comparisons and analysis of business systems, ideologies, and functions. These courses go beyond the mere description of cross-cultural differences and similarities in various fields of business administration by seeking to identify variables that explain the differences and similarities.

The distinction between the comparative courses and the operational ones is not clear-cut, inasmuch as both aspects are frequently covered in a given course. Comparative analysis will serve as a valuable input to operationally oriented courses. However, the latter primarily emphasize strategic issues involved in the management of multinational corporations.

To coordinate its international business programs, the School has established a committee consisting of faculty members teaching international business subjects. The committee approach (in lieu of establishing a separate department) is consistent with our view of international business; at least in our limited experience, it offers two advantages over establishing a separate department. First, it helps integrate international business with the existing curriculum, minimizing the danger of the international business program being isolated from the other areas. Secondly, it allows a high degree of broad faculty participation in both the teaching and curriculum planning in the field.

The very nature of this field and its relative "immaturity" makes it essential to draw from other related disciplines for the development of theories and concepts. Recognizing the important contributions that can be made by the other disciplines, concentrated efforts are being made to tap resources available throughout the University. As is well recognized, effective interdisciplinary collaboration is by no means easy to achieve. Our limited background in these areas coupled with the "culture-bound" view frequently found in other disciplines have presented serious barriers to such efforts. Cumbersome administrative procedures at times make fruitful interdepartmental collaboration in research and teaching difficult. Despite these drawbacks, the prospect is encouraging. On the positive side are a number of successful interdisciplinary research projects in which our faculty members have participated in recent years. Such participation has made it possible to establish good personal rapport with faculty members in other disciplines. By this means, and others, it is becoming increasingly possible to tap the resources of other departments.

Because the major purpose of this paper is to discuss the development of curriculum strategies, little has been said about our research activities. Although a detailed description of this aspect is not feasible in this paper, it should at least be pointed out that our faculty is vigorously pursuing research. The great majority of the faculty teaching in this area have had some field research experience overseas. Thus, there is, fortunately, a continuous flow of new research findings into the contents of courses.

In conclusion, it is hoped that, although this paper is not much more than a case study, it has provided some useful insights and guidelines for other schools.

FRANKLIN R. ROOT
University of Pennsylvania

International Business
as a Field of Study*

To devise a meaningful curriculum for international business, one must first develop a clear understanding of its scope and thrust as a field of study. What should be the instructional and research focus of international business? Is there a concept of international business that distinguishes it from other academic fields and, at the same time, reveals its relationships to the latter? If so, what is that concept? Answers to these questions are of fundamental significance for curriculum design and for the shape of the international business program in general.

THE EWA CONCEPT OF INTERNATIONAL BUSINESS:
COMPARATIVE BUSINESS STUDIES

Unfortunately, there is much confusion and disagreement about the nature of international business as an academic field of study. This is to be expected for an area of interest so new to most professors and administrators. Those of us who view international business as a distinctive field of study may take some comfort in the realization

---

FRANKLIN R. ROOT is Associate Professor of Marketing and International Business in The Wharton School, University of Pennsylvania. In 1967-68, he is on leave to occupy the Chair of Economics at the Naval War College. He has an MBA in foreign commerce and PhD in economics, both from the University of Pennsylvania. He joined the Penn faculty in 1955 after five years in the economics department at the University of Maryland. He has spoken and written extensively on international trade and finance, with particular attention to Western Europe. Since 1965, he has lectured on international trade expansion for the U. S. Departments of Commerce and State. Among his publications are *International Trade and Finance—Theory, Policy, Practice* (South-Western, 1966), *Strategic Planning for Export Marketing* (International Textbook, 1966), and "Antitrust Policy in the European Common Market" (*Quarterly Review of Economics and Business,* Autumn, 1963). He recently completed research on the expropriation experience abroad of U. S. companies.

*See footnote at outset of Professor Yoshino's paper.

that it required many years (and much research) for the functional business fields to come into their own as disciplines separate and distinct from economics.

Taking note of this lack of a "clear understanding of what international business encompasses," the *EWA Report* proposes a "conceptual framework" to guide the business schools in designing a curriculum. This conceptual framework, in effect, identifies international business as comparative business.

> In time — perhaps over the next ten years — some structure may be developed in the field. *The extent to which some formal structure can be developed will depend in large part on the scope and perception of comparative research studies now under way and to be undertaken in the future.* [EWA emphasis.] . . .
> Until we have much more of this kind of knowledge, any program of education in international business necessarily must be exploratory and experimental. (p. 52)

I cannot agree with this conception of international business. The perspective of comparative studies, however useful, is *not* the proper perspective for international business studies. Furthermore, the confusion of international business with comparative studies can only delay the emergence of international business as a distinctive field of study. It is hardly surprising that this mistaken concept leads directly to the following statement in the *EWA Report*:

> We have concluded that there is not now a formal body of knowledge, outside of international economics, sufficient to justify a host of special courses with "international" used mainly as an adjective. . . .
> Following the principle of comparative advantage, we have decided that the important overlay of specialized institutional knowledge can best be provided by universities abroad, and that the U. S. business school could best prepare students in basic disciplines that would allow them to make most effective use of time spent abroad. (p. 53)

There are probably few, if any, business fields with a body of knowledge sufficient to justify a "host" of special courses. Certainly, I would not propose a host of international business courses. But I would argue that there is justification for a limited number of courses in this field, apart from any international courses in other business fields. In any event, the second paragraph is a *non sequitur;* it amounts to a denial of any intellectual content in international business studies. If we are to accept this paragraph seriously, it means that there is no need for an international business curriculum. Instead, our students should study what they have been studying all along (the functional business fields, economics, etc.) and then become "internationalized" by spending some time abroad.

I submit that this conclusion derives from an erroneous conception of international business, namely, its identification with comparative business. I further submit that a proper conception of international business reveals that it is a distinctive field of intellectual inquiry and that it is capable of development into a discipline at least as rigorous as the accepted business disciplines. Let me now indicate what I think this proper conception to be.

AN ALTERNATIVE CONCEPT OF INTERNATIONAL BUSINESS: A SYSTEMS APPROACH

As an academic field of study, international business is primarily directed towards the description, analysis, and explanation of the actual and normative behavior of the private business enterprise as it seeks to achieve its policy goals and objectives in a multinational environment. The fundamental and distinctive characteristic of international business as a field of study centers on the *cross-national interactions* that link the enterprise to its immediate and wider multinational environment in a dynamic and systematic fashion. This conception of international business may be clarified by the use of a model involving three international systems.

We start with a conception of the firm as an international enterprise system (IES). Major variables in this system include the parent company and its multinational subsidiaries and branches. Subject to a common management, the elements of the IES are inter-connected by a complex set of "flows" that cross national boundaries—information of all sorts; managerial and administrative processes; the interchange of materials, components, end products, and manpower; the movement of capital, and other financial assets; the transfer of ownership; and so on.

The international enterprise system is itself a sub-system of what may be called the international micro-system (IMS) that includes the IES and all the many business, household, and government units that the IES depends upon as sources of its inputs (raw materials, power, component parts, labor, capital, etc.) and the disposition of its outputs (channel and facilitating agencies, household consumers, business users, government users). The relationships (flows) among these elements are cross-national to one degree or another and this is what makes the IMS an international system.

The international micro-system, in turn, is a sub-system of the international political-economic system (IPES) whose elements are national governments and national economies. It is this system that creates the environment or setting of international business. Indeed, it is the IPES that calls forth the massive enterprise adaptation that we describe as international business. The IPES is a nation-state system. Each state is sovereign, possessing absolute juridical authority inside its frontiers and in the determination of its relations with other states. Each state is also a nation. That is to say, its people tend to share a common history, a common culture, and a common national identity and ideology. The nation-state system is also a system of national economies. The national government controls its own monetary system and pursues its own policies in all aspects of economic endeavor. Although the frontier of a nation-state is first and foremost a political division, it also represents in varying degrees a set of economic, social, and cultural divisions. Hence cross-national relationships have many facets.

I would argue that this three-systems model offers a conceptual framework for the field of international business that makes it a distinctive field of business study. Research and instruction in international business should be directed toward the cross-national interactive processes or flows that connect the three systems and elements within each system. The exogenous and endogenous interactions of this systems model may be studied at several different levels and from several different perspectives. For example, research and instruction may focus on interactions among the systems as whole systems or, alternatively, on any subset of interactions. The interactive processes themselves may be investigated toward the end of constructing an abstract interaction model (as I have tried to do in the area of expropriation). Of particular importance is the study of interactive processes from the perspective of management—one of the principal actors generating and responding to the many cross-national flows among systems and system elements. In brief, I believe this conception of international business will prove to be exceptionally heuristic in the further development of international business as a discipline.

At this point, it is perhaps redundant to note that the social sciences do not share the conceptual framework I have outlined. International relations (political science) and international economics study the relationships among national states and national economies. Both are vital to a comprehension of the international political-economic system, but neither discipline studies the inter-connections between that system and the international micro- and enterprise systems.

The relationship between the international business field and the functional business fields is somewhat different. Many of the flows (interactions) in our systems model may be designated as financial, marketing, administrative, and the like, and they may be studied from the vantage point of the appropriate functional discipline—international marketing, international business finance, etc. By its very nature, however, the functional approach offers only a partial understanding of international business. What is also needed—what makes up the intellectual core of international business—is study (from various perspectives) of all the cross-national flows that form the enterprise and micro-systems and that relate them to each other and to the international political-economic system.

In the light of these remarks, let me turn now to a brief description of the MBA program in international business at Wharton and the problems that have been encountered in its creation.

THE INTERNATIONAL BUSINESS CURRICULUM AT WHARTON

Wharton was one of the few schools of business in this country to have an MBA major in Foreign Commerce before World War II. The curriculum was a mix of international economic theory (comparative costs, foreign exchange, balance of payments), commercial policy, and export and import trade. The latter subjects constituted the "business" content of the major. In their study, major emphasis was laid on intermediaries (export-import houses, export agents, foreign distributors, etc.); little attention was paid to manufacturers. Foreign operations were identified chiefly as resource investment that provided a source of imports. The approach was descriptive and institutional rather than analytical or managerial.

The inadequacy of this curriculum became embarrassingly evident to some of us around the middle of the 1950's. But the full transformation of the Foreign Commerce curriculum into an International Business curriculum was a slow affair. Several problems were encountered that even today—a decade later—have not been finally resolved. The contemporary MBA program is the end-product of negotiation and compromise between the International Business faculty, on the one hand, and its colleagues in economics and business, on the other.

The International Business faculty at Wharton now offers five courses: International Marketing and Foreign Operations, International Business Management, Studies in International Markets, International Business and Government, and International Business Seminar. Despite its title, the first course is an introduction to the entire field of international business. It studies the organization, operations, and policies of companies functioning in a multinational environment. The dominant perspective in all these courses is managerial, particularly at the corporate level. Environmental factors are introduced as inputs of the decision process and as constraints on operations.

Students in the International Business program are required to take international economics (unless they have taken it elsewhere) as one course of the four-course major. Two courses—International Marketing and Foreign Operations and International Business Management — are mandatory, but the remaining fourth course may be chosen with the approval of the advisor from a wide selection of courses drawn from the social sciences and functional business areas. In practice, students almost always select their fourth course from the International Business curriculum. In addition to course work, the student also writes a thesis on some problem area of international business.

The International Business major attracts about 10 percent of all MBA students at Wharton. Since 1960, the absolute number of student majors has about doubled to reach over one hundred. Furthermore, many non-majors take one or more courses in International Business as electives.

Within the past few years the Wharton faculty in the traditional business fields has begun to establish comparative and international courses. Comparative marketing and comparative management courses are already in existence, and courses in Comparative Industrial Relations, International Corporate Finance, and Comparative Accounting are under consideration. The International Business faculty has welcomed these new courses because they offer an opportunity for its students to deepen their knowledge of particular business functions from international and comparative perspectives. The further spread of internationally-oriented courses across departments will probably induce some changes in the International Business curriculum, but the limitations of any sole reliance on the functional approach will continue to justify a separate major in international business.

FACULTY RESISTANCES TO THE DEVELOPMENT OF
AN INTERNATIONAL BUSINESS PROGRAM

In closing, let me turn to a topic that should be of particular interest to this audience.

My own experience indicates that the creation of an International Business major, concentration, or program will probably encounter faculty resistances of various sorts.

First, there is the resistance of professors who have taught the traditional courses in foreign trade for many years. These people may be emotionally and intellectually committed to a foreign trade concept of international business, and vigorously oppose a radical transformation of the curriculum. Unless these professors can be educated to a broader conception of international business that embraces all of the complex operations of today's multinational company, they must somehow be bypassed in curriculum development.

Second, there is the resistance of professors in the traditional business fields who regard an International Business major or program as a transgression on their own disciplines. These professors claim that only they can say anything about organization, about corporate finance, etc. They are hostile to international business because it appears to ignore the lines that separate the functional business disciplines.

Closely associated with this jurisdictional resistance is the denial by some professors that international business is a field of study. An extreme manifestation of this attitude is the allegation that international business is nothing more than applied international economics. A more restrained argument is that international business is simply a mix of the functional business disciplines with an international ingredient. An effective intellectual response to these attitudes and arguments must rest on a conceptual foundation of international business that demonstrates its uniqueness as a field of study. This is not any easy task for an area of study that is in its first stage of evolution as an academic discipline. Earlier, I outlined my own conception of international business.

Finally, note should be taken of simple inertia. There are always professors who distrust any proposal to institute a new program of study simply because it is new. These persons always favor a postponement of curriculum decisions, and they afford support to active opponents of an international business program.

When the administration plays a neutral game, these resistances must be overcome by the arguments and determination of those faculty members who are actively promoting an international business program. After a wearying round of committee sessions, the result is likely to be either a complete defeat for the proponents of international business or a compromise program that fully satisfies no one. Much of this painful process can be avoided if the administration takes the lead in setting forth the future direction of the school and the potential contribution of international business in this regard. It is then up to the faculty to design the kind of curriculum that will help the school move forward into an age where business strives to transcend national boundaries. A sense of commitment to international business at the very top is a necessary, if not sufficient, condition for the development of a first-rate program in this exciting new field of business and academic endeavor.

Discussion Comments

Curriculum Strategy

Panel A: Dowd-Kolde

REPORTER: Hugh B. Carnes

The basic controversial issue seemed to be over the primacy of the functional or of the environmental. With the usual digressions into semantics, it was pointed out that the difference between national and multinational enterprise is ceasing to be relevant. It seemed to be generally conceded that the major constraint upon development of international business training is lack of broadly competent faculty.

A business representative questioned the impression of an absolute decrease in the number of Americans working abroad, and even indicated doubts regarding a percentage increase. He strongly endorsed Costanzo's "cordon bleu" plea, asked for adequate language training, and lamented the lack of international orientation in functional courses.

Kolde strongly attacked the applicability of traditional international economic theory to current problems. It is, he pointed out, anchored on trans-boundary transactions which presently play a minor, and decreasing, role in world business. He maintained that we have no discipline to deal effectively with problems of multinational business, and that the main job of management is the management of change. This idea led to a suggestion from the floor that "country" problems should be left to business.

There was general agreement that student ability outweighed, as a job-earning asset, any specialization. The feasibility of teaching environmental adaptability was, as always, questioned.

It was suggested that strategic areas or aspects of environment be determined and concentrated on; i. e., outside the United States, the student will probably confront a traditional society with a managerial elite based on family. Teach what is meant by a traditional society, by a family-oriented managerial elite. Another similar illustration was drawn from Roman vs. common law.

Panel B: Robinson-Spier

REPORTER: James T. Murphy

The roundtable discussion at this meeting tended to center on three topics: (1) knowledge accumulation by students and professors about the foreign environment; (2) problems of proliferation and specialization, including the relationship of international business courses to current curricula; and (3) selection of inputs.

(1) Work experience in foreign environments is obviously an excellent way, perhaps the best, for the synthesizer of tomorrow to gain an understanding of and appreciation for diverse values, as well as the appropriate responses to the values. But it is difficult to implement this approach for students, either professional or doctoral. Moreover the experience may be *too* specific; that is, by involving students in only one area, they may develop misleading generalizations. An additional disadvantage of teaching or studying in a particular locale—pointed out by Scarpetta (Colombia)—is that business systems may be changing so rapidly that the "rules of the game" shift about; "at distance" material, e. g., internationally-oriented cases studied in the United States, may facilitate the educational process. On the other hand—as pointed out by Robinson—students and teachers must recognize a fundamental learning problem in this area: namely, that of linking slowly changing with more rapidly changing business systems.

A second-best approach is through courses which stress concepts about working and living abroad; thus vicarious experience may satisfice in this regard. The specific content of such courses is itself a research matter; tools should be borrowed from any discipline which seems relevant for developing the necessary conceptual framework. If inter-disciplinary studies lack feasibility, an acceptable alternative would be a descriptive course; the quick acceptance and creation of this type of course seems obvious.

Taking a set of courses in a foreign environment is not a good alternative and must be ranked last. The goals of such courses need not necessarily, perhaps rarely, coincide with the goals of an international business emphasis or program in the curriculum of an American institution.

(2) On the matter of working an international emphasis into functional courses, using other vehicles such as information systems or organization theory or creating new courses, there was substantial agreement that specialization has dominated business school curricula and that international business programs should neither fall into that trap nor be a case in point. The existence of vested interests will tend to maintain an image of specialization and will force a slow adaptation of international business programs to a systems or interdisciplinary approach. Robinson thinks that we will have to accept a variety of pedagogical approaches for some time, but he does favor a systems approach by which international business courses would stress the linkages between various types of business systems. In his view, the introduction of international business into functional areas would lead to more specialization, but the expansion will be only temporary. As long as courses are carefully planned and are adaptable to other curriculum developments, the real nature of international business—i. e., a systems orientation—will assert itself.

Spier argued that involvement by seemingly uninterested parties in international business research projects would change attitudes gradually, and relevant topics would be introduced into *existing* functional courses without need for additional special courses.

In order to ensure competence, however, there do appear to be some areas for which real specialization is needed; that is, it would not be reasonable to expect the absorption of all aspects of international business into existing functional courses or into systems courses. Both finance and law were accepted as such special areas, and the participants were hard-pressed to justify others. There may be others, but not many.

Two questions and an example will summarize much of the foregoing discussion: What is the trade-off between an international businessman interested in a functional area *vis-à-vis* a functionally oriented man interested in international business? What is the degree of specialization in international business for a decision-making role within a firm? Using the area of finance and the topic of devaluation as an example, there seemed to be agreement that all students, professors, and decision-makers should be able to discuss the general characteristics of a devaluation as well as its implications for other countries. In a curriculum, however, an international finance specialist would be a predictor of such events and would be able to give more penetrating analyses of its impact. Within a firm, decision-makers would be sensitive to the growing pressures for devaluation in a particular foreign environment and would know enough to ask the right questions of specialists. Reinforcing his argument for limited specialization, Spier asserted that a systems or synthesis orientation for international business courses would increase the probability of asking the right questions of those few specialists who will exist in the international business area.

A more general summarization was given by Lombard (Harvard): " . . . business curricula are changing rapidly, and one input to that change must be the special needs and problems of international business. Eventually we will have a different and better blend of specialization and systems; international business topics will be a part of both."

(3) There was some discussion on the selection of good inputs to the international business program in order to increase the probability of turning out good synthesizers. Opinions ranged from "taking anybody you can get and do what you can" to "it's a puzzlement and really not different from selection problems in general." The belief was expressed, however, that students with interdisciplinary background would have a distinct edge in comprehending the real nature of an international business program.

REMARKS BY DEAN GEORGE P. SHULTZ AT LUNCHEON SESSION

In the main, this was a plea for the non-proliferation of courses. As Robinson wants linkages among business systems to be the proper base for course work, and Spier seeks a "synthesizing man," Shultz wants such course work to emphasize "true internationalism" — not differences or dissimilarities in a variety of topics. Existing and interesting courses can be developed for the latter, but they will be descriptive, institutional, and basically non-intellectual. Concepts should be emphasized together with the foundations of international trade and economics. More than anything else, we need high-quality research on the nature of international business, with a view toward developing a conceptual base or theory. An international business curriculum should follow and adapt to this research.

Panel C: Adams-Nehrt

REPORTER: Eric W. Vetter

The dominant theme in this discussion centered on the content of International Business programs. The points raised were not necessarily agreed upon by all present because of the limited time for debate.

The specifics a major in international business should acquire in his studies constituted the lead topic of discussion. Adams stressed the need for developing competence in understanding and interpreting environmental influences on business decisions and the reciprocal influence of the decision on the environment. This involves more than just an awareness of the environment. It frequently means that the concepts from the basic disciplines must be applied differently because of the environmental factors. Nehrt built on this by stressing the different risks associated with overseas business which tend to produce a different step-function of economic involvement abroad than might be experienced in the States. These considerations mean that international business decision-making involves different variables. The fact that the American company is a significant agent of change in the host country is particularly important.

Although the environmental factors may be the key to differentiating international business studies from general business administration, the best approach to gaining this understanding is unclear. A high risk factor may be associated with allowing students to pursue depth area studies and/or language skills, because the graduate may not be assigned by the employing company to the area he studied. Receiving attention at some schools is course work in foreign area analysis. Here students are required to engage in research involving the analysis of a country or an area of the world. The objective is to equip the student with concepts and skills that are transferable in making a study of other areas of the world. Thus, the methodology is stressed and not the specifics of a particular area or country. This type of approach is perhaps a partial answer to concern over the level of abstraction that exists in basic international business courses so that the material has real relevance. It was also suggested that the incorporation of a little international business material in basic business courses is becoming less necessary because of the increased attention by students and faculty to specialized international business courses.

The development of real expertise in international business is important for business schools. More than an understanding of international business factors is needed by the schools. More vital is the development of concepts in international business so that abstraction can be used to solve problems. A hopefulness was expressed that this would occur as the field of study matures.

Remarks on how to qualify academic instructors for the field bear on the possibility of the developing concepts. Upgrading the faculty through assignments abroad is a method found useful by several schools. Yet it is easy to over-emphasize the usefulness of this approach. Unless the professor engages in research while abroad, he likely will not gain a depth-understanding of his host country. In preparing the next generation of teachers, the view was expressed that perhaps all doctoral candidates in business administration should be required to gain a minimum awareness and understanding of the international business aspects of their major discipline. In this regard, the University of Washington reported that thirty to thirty-five percent of their doctoral candidates take international business as one of their fields of study. At Indiana University, ten percent of the doctoral candidates take international business as their major field of study, and over fifty percent enroll in one or more international business courses.

Panel D: Smith-Yoshino

REPORTER: Eugene T. Byrne, Jr.

One feature of the session on curriculum strategy was the lack of agreement on many major issues. This was especially so where the issues were discussed on pragmatic rather than ideal grounds. It should also be noted that participants' attitudes toward International Business programs often reflected the schism that is found in discussions of general business education. To this extent, much of the disagreement does not rest on questions relating solely to International Business.

It was asked whether international business should or could be taught as an option or whether it should be taught through internationalizing the current curriculum.

Neglecting the "good man is a good man" hypothesis, there appeared to be general agreement that international business education has a formal role in business school curricula. Generally, it seemed that the ideal would be to internationalize current curricula. All students and faculty are somewhat, and need to be, internationally acute. Such acuteness is more generally assured through an internationalizing of curricula than establishment of an International Business option. Despite the desirability of the ideal approach, a number of considerations render it impractical. Among these are: a definite lack of interested faculty, both within and without schools of business; a similar lack of interest among students; and an improbable change of attitudes in the near future.

Pragmatically, then, it appears that the short-run approach must be through development of International Business options. To prevent submergence of the long-range goal of internationalization, there should not be a separate department of international business but rather a faculty committee on international business. The goal of this committee should be to plan for the realization of the long-range objective.

Accepting the option as a short-run necessity does not alleviate the requirement to consider how the interdisciplinary nature of the subject should be reflected in specific programs. The basic question is whether to have students take appropriate course work in the discipline area itself or to seek to develop the necessary courses in the business school. Here again is a question that is not unique to international business, nor were the responses much different than one would expect. Many participants suggested that the crucial factor is whether the pedagogy of particular disciplines is consistent with the objectives of a business program. Experience indicates that consistency cannot be assumed and usually is not found.

Irrespective of how a given faculty decides the preceding questions, it must face the question of whether International Business programs should emphasize the multinational or the national. Participants' opinions were sharply divided among those who generally defined international business as the problem of operating in many countries and those who defined it as operating in different national environments. Certain responses reflected the current and future manpower needs of international firms for persons who know the peculiarities of operating in a national environment. Other responses suggest that national or comparative emphasis is not only unnecessary but intractable. Participants supporting the latter view added that many important dimensions relating to the operation of multinational firms are overlooked in a purely comparative study. The most common rejoinder was that most students and faculty are sensitive to those dimensions but require greater depth in their study of national milieux.

Should International Business programs carry a decision-making orientation or a conceptual-theoretic orientation? It is safe to note that this question is continually debated and that attention to international business does not bring about a consensus. Generally, those who support a decision-oriented approach are inclined to favor case-type research activities by faculty and students. Those who favor the conceptual-theoretic approach strongly support an intellectually-based form of research. Such research would produce a corpus of knowledge pertinent to the study of international business. Although causality is difficult to determine, it appeared that the supporters of a conceptual-theoretic approach also supported the position that course work in the discipline areas is desirable. An additional impression gained is that the "decisionists" are less opposed to so-called survey courses.

In addition to the research activities just mentioned, what other activities can strengthen international business studies? Generally, any activity that increases an individual's awareness of the international dimensions of business should be promoted. Among the prominently mentioned activities are international student recruitment programs; support of AIESEC activities as part of a general suggestion to include summer work-study programs abroad; and a plea to schools to recognize the (not too obvious) benefits of supporting faculty participation in any activity whose major concern is international business.

One might suspect, *a priori,* that international student recruiting should be followed by a program to effectively utilize the heterogeneity. However, the experience of a few participants in attempts to formalize student relationships was largely inconsequential. Most agreed that the natural interchange of ideas in and outside of the classroom is at least as good as any alternative method of promoting interchange.

HERBERT E. LONGENECKER
Tulane University

Remarks

I welcome the privilege of saying thanks, first of all, to Education and World Affairs, an organization formed a few years ago to bring together in a new kind of organization some of the thoughts, opportunities, and, perhaps, the provocative questions that could be formulated in realistic terms *by* members of the educational community and *for* members of the educational community. Certainly in its few years of existence, Education and World Affairs has demonstrated fully and convincingly the importance of a role of this kind of organization in providing the needed leverage in international education.

Secondly, I want to thank those in the Ford Foundation who had a part in making this Conference possible.

The hard work of some intelligent and persuasive people made it possible to bring this Conference together. We are privileged indeed to have the opportunity of sharing it with you.

May I go on to make one further observation. If our engagement in a discussion of this sort is really to be brought into meaningful terms in our own individual institutions, we must do something more than just shape up programs, exchange ideas, and perhaps do a little tinkering with curriculum here and there. Those of us who have been thinking about the urgency of deeper involvement of our institutions in international affairs are concerned that we lack the re-

HERBERT E. LONGENECKER is President of Tulane University. He holds **MS** and PhD degrees from Pennsylvania State University. For 17 years, he was a member of the biochemistry faculty at the University of Pittsburgh, serving as Dean of Research in the Natural Sciences from 1944 to 1955 and Dean of the Graduate School from 1946 to 1955. He was Vice President in charge of the Chicago Professional Colleges at the University of Illinois from 1955 to 1960, following which he became President at Tulane. He has been a member or chairman of numerous boards, commissions, and committees of many educational, scientific, and civic organizations. Since 1963 he has been chairman of the Advisory Committee of College and University Presidents to the Institute of International Education.

sources, not so much in the ideas as the funds. As you bring your ideas together in this session you will certainly find many useful things that can be done within the framework of existing resources. But at this particular moment in the development of our educational institutions, many of us are confronted with the same problem. Certainly the private institutions are deeply concerned with questions related to the possible source of the resources. And I believe that the public institutions likewise are being confronted more and more with some of the same questions. The problem of financing the kind of ideas you should develop and should be encouraged to develop is one that will have to be met. A number of people from all our institutions have been laboring arduously for the past several years to develop some conviction about the dimensions of international education that should have support. They have been working in Washington, and specifically in Congress. Most of you know that a very vital bill, the International Education Act, was passed last year. But you all know that authorization is one thing and appropriation another. Today the prospect of funding the Act is bleak. I suggest that with the new enthusiasm your Conference will have developed, you join in seeking a prompt activation of programs for which clear purpose and need are already established. As a result, I suggest that your work here will be made meaningful.

HANS PICKER
Universidad del Valle, Colombia

Committee of Deans of Latin American Schools of Business Administration

Brief Statement of Purposes and Operations

It is a great honor for me to be here and, in the name of the Committee, I would like to thank Tulane University and Education and World Affairs for inviting me. I appreciate the opportunity of discussing, if briefly, the work of the Committee of Deans of Latin American Schools of Business Administration.

The Committee is formed by twelve institutions. First we have the graduate schools of management which are presently operating in Latin America. From North to South, these schools are the Escuela de Graduados en Administración del Instituto Tecnológico y de Estudios Superiores de Monterrey, México; the Instituto Centroamericano de Administración de Empresas (INCAE), Managua, Nicaragua; the División de Ciencias Sociales y Económicas de la Universidad del Valle, Cali, Colombia; the Facultad de Economía de la Universidad de Los Andes, Bogotá, Colombia; the Escuela de Administración de Negocios para Graduados (ESAN), Lima, Perú; the Escola de Administracão de Emprêsas de São Paulo, Brazil; the Facultad de Ciencias Económicas de la Universidad de Chile, and the Facultad de Ciencias Económicas y Sociales de la Universidad Católica de Chile, both in Santiago. In addition, we have as observers three institutions that will shortly have graduate programs in management. These are the Facultad de Comercio y Administración de la Universidad Nacional Autónoma de México, Mexico City; the Instituto de

HANS PICKER is Professor of Finance in the División de Ciencias Sociales y Económicas, Universidad del Valle, Cali, Colombia. He is also Director of the Comité Latinoamericano de Decanos de Escuelas de Administración (Committee of Deans of Latin American Schools of Business Administration), which is headquartered in Cali. He holds an MBA from Northwestern University.

Estudios Superiores de Administración (IESA), Caracas, Venezuela; and the Instituto para el Desarrollo de Ejecutivos en la Argentina (IDEA), Buenos Aires. Finally we have another observer, PACCIOS, an institution which belongs to CIOS (Conseil International pour l'Organisation Scientifique, represented in the United States by the Council for International Progress in Management [CIPM]). PACCIOS is a federation of all the management institutes in the Americas.

The institutions that form the Committee have several common features, which are, first, a full-time faculty, or mostly a full-time faculty, with master's degrees and PhDs. Second, they accept students from other degree areas. Third, they have programs at the graduate level or the equivalent, and finally, they grant academic degrees.

The purposes of the Committee are, first, to promote the international dimension of the business curriculum in the business education of Latin America, which is especially important to us in the light of Latin American integration and the creation of the Common Market. The second purpose is to achieve an efficient operation by pooling some academic resources among these schools.

To accomplish these general purposes we have designed a program composed of eight projects:

The first project, perhaps one of the most important, is to create work groups of Latin American professors belonging to these graduate schools. It is at the level of our faculties, we believe, that an effective international academic collaboration can occur among our schools. A different work group will be created for each field of study. These work groups will meet at least once a year in a specific city and will be sponsored by one of our member institutions, where, during one week, our professors will (1) discuss academic matters such as academic interchange of experiences, (2) analyze the similarities and differences of teaching undergraduates, graduates, and executives, the similarities and differences of teaching their own fields in the various Latin American countries, (3) recommend major research projects among our schools, and (4) analyze the future trends in their fields in Latin America.

In some cases, participating professors will conduct seminars for a group of local executives. In these cases the work group will provide not only an exchange of information among the professors, but also teaching methods will be given "on the spot" trial. Such seminars should broaden the views of both lecturers and businessmen. In addition, fees from the local executives will help finance the work-group gathering.

We have already had two meetings, one at ESAN in Perú in marketing and another at the Instituto de Administración (INSORA) in the Universidad de Chile on industrial relations and human resources in general. Very important conclusions were reached in these two meetings, such as the undertaking of joint comparative studies and research projects in topics highly relevant for academicians and for the business community, and the editing and issuing of books of readings. In March, 1968, we are going to have a meeting in Monterrey on quantitative methods and production management, and another meeting on accounting and financial management in July, 1968, in Chile. Coinciding with these two meetings, the participating professors will conduct a seminar for the local business community as explained before. A meeting of coordinators of the graduate programs will take place in May, 1968, in Colombia, and during the following months we will have additional work-group meetings in the fields of business policy, applied economics and sociology, and again in marketing and human resources.

The second project is related to an interchange of professors among our institutions, which we believe is essential in internationalizing our faculty, and, therefore, in internationalizing our students. This will also assure a better use of the human resources of the Committee and stimulate a certain specialization of the schools in the long run.

Third, we wish to design a special program for our faculty development that contemplates the specific needs of Latin America, thereby improving our academic standards and research capabilities.

Fourth, we are establishing an academic clearinghouse to which all the institutions will send cases, articles, translations of books, etc., which in turn will be distributed and redistributed among our institutions.

Fifth, we are building a fund to support the exchange of students among our institutions in order to have, let's say, Colombians go to Chile, Chileans go to Mexico, etc., again with the main purpose of internationalizing our students and stimulating a certain degree of specialization in the schools. As part of the program, the student will decide in which specific field and at which graduate school of management he would prefer to study.

Sixth, we are trying to standardize the admission tests of our schools. Having scarce resources, we need to select applicants with the highest professional and academic potential. Furthermore if we want to exchange our students, our product has to be homogeneous, and one way to accomplish this, we believe, is to standardize admissions. Finally, we would like to have a common test for selecting our students who go to study in North American universities or in other parts of the world.

Seventh, we are organizing major seminars for executives. Next year, we are going to conduct six seminars in six Latin American countries, sponsored by the Organization of American States (OAS), in the field of international marketing. They will be four-week seminars, full-time, and each seminar will be given by two of the faculty members of the Universidad del Valle. We expect to extend this arrangement to other schools of the Committee.

Eighth, there's a yearly dean's conference. We have already called two conferences, the first in February, 1966 at the Universidad del Valle, Cali, and the second in March, 1967 at ESAN, in Lima. The third will be held in March, 1968 at the Escuela de Graduados en Administración, in Monterrey. For this occasion, and following the meeting, we will have a round-table discussion in New York with some 15 top North American executives whose companies operate in Latin America, some 15 top executives from Latin America, and four scholars presenting papers on future changes in the sociological, political, economic, and technological aspects of Latin America. They will be asked to predict how these changes will affect future business in the medium term and, in turn, how these future changes should or will change business education in Latin America. The round-table is being organized jointly with Business International, Inc.

These are the eight projects we have under way, and briefly, these are the purposes and the plan of action of our Committee. Our institution is financed with contributions from its members. That is, no outside funds have been raised, except for the financing of specific joint projects. We expect to maintain very close relationships with all of you and perhaps specifically with the American Association of Collegiate Schools of Business.

WILLIAM D. CARMICHAEL
Cornell University

Challenges in Assisting in the Development of Management Education Abroad

The topic which this panel has been asked to consider is formidable. The challenges associated with assisting in institution-building overseas are substantially more numerous and complex than the three of us can hope to cover. Ours is a topic under which questions come more easily than answers, and generalizations are hazardous. Of necessity, we must be concerned with institution-building assistance in widely varying situations and stages of development, and we must recognize that what is an effective analysis or prescription in one instance may be entirely inappropriate in another. Moreover, we are handicapped by the fact that there has been very little systematic evaluation, to date, of the growing body of experience in assisting in the development of management education abroad.

In approaching this complex problem, let me confess at the outset that my relevant experience is limited and that my perception may be correspondingly distorted. For six years Cornell has been involved,

WILLIAM D. CARMICHAEL is Professor of Economic Policy and Dean of the Graduate School of Business and Public Administration at Cornell University. He has an MPA (public and international affairs) and MA in economics from Princeton, a B.Litt. in economics from Oxford (where he was a Rhodes Scholar), and a PhD in economics from Princeton. Prior to going to Cornell in 1962, he was a lecturer at the University of Maryland, held various positions in the U. S. Bureau of the Budget, and, from 1957 to 1962, was associated with Princeton University. At Princeton, he was director of the undergraduate program of the Woodrow Wilson School of Public and International Affairs from 1958 to 1962, and was the first director of Experimental European Summer Research. Since 1963, he has been a consultant to the Ford Foundation on the Latin American program in its Overseas Development Division.

with AID support, in a collaborative effort with the Faculty of Administrative Sciences of the Middle East Technical University in Ankara. Some of my observations are based on that project. The greater part, however, of the "evidence" on which I shall rely is drawn from my work as a consultant in connection with five or six foundation-supported efforts to strengthen or establish new schools of business, or business and public administration, in Latin America. I have no direct knowledge of the Asian or African situations, but I suspect they may differ in important respects. Let me register the warning, therefore, that my comments should be regarded as applying primarily to the current Latin American scene.

Let me also note a certain ambiguity in the statement of the topic for this session. Quite appropriately, the term "challenges" is employed, but the matter to which institutions must respond in facing these challenges is not made explicit. Should we be addressing ourselves to the issues facing a particular university? Or the university community as a whole? Or the agencies—foundation or governmental —which provide the necessary financial support? Our mandate is unclear. That being the case, I intend to exploit this ambiguity and refer, on occasion, to all three of these parties.

With these cautionary notes sounded, let me now take up what I would tentatively suggest are five of the more important challenges or problems involved in assisting in developing institutions of management education overseas.

I.

First is the problem of establishing an effective relationship between what is done to assist an overseas institution and the objective of strengthening the U. S. university or universities involved. This challenge, which too often has been neglected or underestimated, takes many forms.

It first manifests itself when a U. S. university is considering taking on a commitment to assist in the development of a management education program overseas. From my vantage point, the vague desire to be of service, or the unfocused feeling that it is a "good thing" to be in the assistance-rendering business, is not a sufficient justification for such a step. Rather, I would argue, the faculty and administration of the U. S. university should properly ask, "What benefits can *we* realize? Which of *our own* institutional needs can better be met if we take on such an assignment?" And they should agree that there is a sound justification for proceeding only if the proposed overseas commitment holds promise for producing needed improvement in the faculty, curriculum, research, or doctoral programs of the U. S. university. This approach may first sound a bit cold-hearted as a response to the needs of overseas institutions, but it is not unrelated to the likely effectiveness of the response. Unless the U. S. university puts a high value on the benefits which it is to derive from the overseas endeavor, its best administrative talents and its most capable faculty are not likely to be heavily engaged in the project. And unless its best talents are committed, I doubt very seriously that the job overseas will be well done.

A second manifestation of this challenge arises in connection with shaping the course and spelling out the ingredients of the assistance program. Here, I think, the relevant prescription is simple: The developmental program should be so constructed as to take into account both the needs of the overseas institution and those of the U. S. university as well. It is clear that tensions may arise in wedding these obectives. Many discouraging illustrations could be cited. I remain optimistic, however, about the attainability of the twin goals, if it is recognized that a good bit of thought and effort are often required to engineer the desired compatibility.

A third dimension of this problem arises in connection with the governmental and foundation structures which provide support for overseas programs. In the Federal government, responsibility for overseas assistance has been lodged in the Agency for International Development, while responsibility for strengthening the international dimensions of the programs of American universities is (or apparently is to be) vested in the Department of Health, Education, and Welfare. Similarly, at least until recently, a major foundation has operated with a structure in which overseas development activities have been organizationally divorced from efforts to strengthen the international training and research capacities of the American university community. Such organizational structures, it is abundantly clear, tend to exacerbate the problems of developing effective relationships between overseas endeavors and the needs of domestic institutions.

II.

The second issue arises when one asks, "With which overseas institutions should we collaborate?" Stated more elaborately, it might take the following form: "To what array of foreign institutions should our efforts be directed so as to enhance the likelihood of mutual profit, the prospects for permanent impact, and the promise of multiplied effects?"

When tackling this question, it must be recognized that management education, while relatively new in the developing (and for that matter, some of the developed) parts of the world, is assuming very large proportions and shows every sign of further explosive growth. It must also be recognized by all parties involved — the foreign institutions seeking help, the U. S. university community, and governmental agencies and foundations providing financial support—that the capacities of the U. S. university community for effective work overseas are limited. As deans of business schools will be the first to note, the supply of visiting faculty for overseas institutions, the availability of places in top-ranking U. S. graduate programs for training future teacher-researchers from overseas, and our collective capacity to advise and assist in other phases of institution-building are severely constrained. In fact, as the *EWA Report* suggests, only a very few schools can take on major commitments to be of help. There is, then, a critically important "rationing" problem.

The *EWA Report* suggests a number of criteria which are relevant to the selection of appropriate overseas partners. Leadership, stability, and prospects of local financial support for the overseas institution are important factors in the decision. From my own observations, I would also suggest that importance be attached to the presence, in the overseas setting, of opportunities for the business school to derive strength from, and lend support to, other relevant applied social science programs.

In light of the severe "rationing problem," however, I want to argue most strongly that our efforts be directed, primarily, or perhaps even exclusively, to a limited number of key institutions which hold promise for performing standard-setting and "breeder" services for other schools in their countries or regions of the world. More explicitly, I would urge that attention be focused on a very few programs which may be looked to for model curricula and which possess the capacity and commitment for preparing teacher-researchers for other institutions.

Looking back over the experience of the past decade, I must conclude that the several parties involved have too frequently scattered their shots too broadly. In special management education programs for foreigners in this country, students have been admitted from too large and diverse a range of institutions, with consequent delays in the attainment by institutions of a "critical mass" overseas. Similarly,

U. S. visiting professors have been placed in too broad a range of institutions overseas without apparent regard to the extreme scarcity of well-qualified candidates for such assignments. The U. S. university community can have only a very limited *direct* impact on the preparation of thousands of teacher-researchers in the field of management who are needed, and on the education of the tens, or indeed hundreds, of thousands of young men and women seeking university study in that field. What I am arguing, therefore, is that we must focus our efforts, necessarily limited as they are, where the multiplied impact is likely to be greatest.

III.

The third challenge on my list is to develop programs which, while reflecting the developmental needs of the U. S. institutions, will be truly responsive to the requirements of the standard-setting "breeder" institutions to which I have just referred.

Specifically, let me argue that U. S. assistance-renderers should not focus their efforts exclusively, or even primarily, on strengthening the practitioner-oriented dimensions of overseas programs. Instead, their efforts should be directed principally to the preparation of a cadre of teacher-researchers who, in turn, will produce effective teaching materials and prepare teachers for practitioner-oriented programs. In my judgment, we have placed too little emphasis to date on the development, in a limited number of overseas institutions, of a strong research environment. As a consequence, instruction is hampered by the absence of teaching materials truly relevant to the local situation, decision-makers in the public and private sectors are deprived of a much-needed information base, and the capacity for preparing faculty for other schools in the country or region is not yet in place.

To be sure, we have paid lip service to the need for a "research environment" in overseas institutions, but we have allowed our attention to be diverted. Accordingly, far too few of the staff members of the overseas institutions who have come to this country for study have enrolled in and completed studies at the doctoral level. Too often, moreover, potential contributions to teaching programs have been overemphasized, while research contributions have been neglected, when making judgments concerning the selection of U. S. professors for visiting assignments overseas and the timing and duration of their stays in overseas institutions.

On the matter of selecting candidates for visiting assignments overseas, let me add a further point, namely, a strong preference toward the relatively young, research-oriented scholar. This point may be regarded by some as little more than an individual bias, but it is related, I think, to the objective of fostering a research environment. The well-trained young scholar, in my judgment, is considerably more likely than his senior counterpart to possess the flexibility necessary for research overseas and to regard the overseas assignment as an investment in his own professional development. He is also more likely to integrate effectively with the often quite young and recently trained staff of the overseas institution and thus to enhance their reserach productivity. I am arguing, therefore, that providing a young visiting scholar may often be a particularly useful response to the needs of "breeder" institutions overseas.

IV.

A fourth challenge for our consideration is to determine an effective pattern, or patterns, for relating the U. S. academic community to developing institutions overseas. This issue, while of interest to all of us, is a matter of particular concern to the foundations and governmental agencies which provide support for collaborative efforts.

Perhaps the most familiar model for relating U. S. and overseas institutions is the one-to-one, institution-to-institution relationship. In such relationships, the overseas partner may be thoroughly indigenous, with a lengthy history predating the relationship, or it may be a newly implanted institution. An outstanding example of the first form of this relationship is provided by the AID-supported Michigan State contract with the Vargas Foundation's Business School in São Paulo; examples of the second type include Stanford's relationship with ESAN in Lima and Harvard's with INCAE in Central America.

The institution-to-institution relationship has certain advantages. It permits a clear delineation of responsibilities, and it highlights the importance of the venture to the U. S. institution involved, with the prospect, at least, that more thought and effort will be devoted to it. But this approach also has, or can have, several serious drawbacks. Too often, I think, it has resulted in an unhealthy limitation of the overseas institution's ties with the scholarly community as a whole. Frequently, this approach has been accompanied by excessive concentration of the students from the overseas institution in the graduate programs of a single (i. e., the allied) university in the United

States. It may also have unduly constricted the choice of U. S. faculty members for visiting assignments in the overseas institution. (It must be noted, however, that the U. S. institution has rarely demonstrated an in-house capacity to provide all of the visiting faculty from its own staff.) Perhaps the most serious problem with the institution-to-institution relationship, however, is the fact that, rather than focusing on common interests, it emphasizes (or appears to emphasize) disparities in the relationship, i. e., to place the receiving institution in a dependent status which is both unattractive and conducive to unproductive frictions. The one-to-one institutional relationship is, no doubt, appropriate to certain early stages or conditions of development in the overseas environment, but if the problems to which I have been referring are real, one must look for alternative models.

A second approach to the relationship between overseas institutions and the U. S. academic community involves the granting of foundation or governmental support directly to the overseas institution and allowing the institution to fend for itself. This approach may well generate a healthy degree of self-reliance in the overseas institution, and it may result in broad linkages with sister members of the scholarly community around the world. But there may be problems, too, with this approach. Decisions concerning graduate programs for staff members, hiring visiting professors, and developing libraries and research programs in the overseas institution may often be made with inadequate information, and the scarce administrative talents of the overseas institution may be dissipated in unproductive and counter-productive efforts. Moreover, this formula is not likely to produce programs which relate effectively to the needs of the U. S. institutions from which assistance may be requested.

Perhaps, then, a third, compromise model should be considered— one which involves making the grant directly to the overseas institution and establishing at the same time an advisory committee to assist that institution in developing its grant-supported programs. The advisory committee would be composed of individuals drawn from a number of different U. S. (and possibly foreign) institutions. Its mandate would be to offer advice, upon request, concerning the selection and placement of the staff of the overseas institution in graduate programs in this country, to identify and recommend candidates for visiting faculty posts, to consult on questions of curriculum and educational policy, and to advise the overseas institution on matters of academic administration. This formula is currently being tested in several instances in the development of management education in Latin America. The votes are not yet in, but preliminary results are encouraging, and it appears to be operating without the serious disadvantages associated with the other alternatives referred to above.

V.

The fifth challenge, and the last on my agenda, is to respond effectively to the needs of overseas institutions for counsel and assistance on institution-building problems.

In addition to their needs for improved professional competence in teaching and research in management, most developing institutions overseas (not unlike their U. S. counterparts) need to build stronger ties with their clienteles in industry and government, to expand and improve their libraries, to institute sound budgetary procedures, to rethink admissions procedures, and to introduce effective alumni programs. In many instances, I think, they can profit from assistance in these matters.

On occasion the U. S. academic community has performed admirably in providing such assistance. The excellent library that is now functioning at ESAN in Lima is a case in point. In other instances, we in the United States have discovered that we have much to learn from the accomplishments of overseas institutions, as from the admirably conceived special program for executives at the Universidad del Valle in Cali. As a general proposition, however, I would argue that the U. S. academic community has given too little attention to assisting in the range of institution-building problems to which I am referring here.

Looking at one of this array of problems, let us consider the needs of the staff member from an overseas institution who comes to the United States for advanced study. Often, I think, we would do well to recognize that he has two rather different objectives in coming to a U. S. university—first, to build competence as a teacher-researcher in management and his special field thereof, and second, to prepare himself for a career as an institution-builder and possibly as a senior administrator in his university overseas. If he, indeed, has these twin objectives, we must then ask whether there is anything we can do to promote the achievement of the second objective—to help him develop his institution-building awareness and skills.

Let me suggest, further, that that question be answered in the affirmative. In doing so, I am not arguing that U. S. universities possess a set of ready-made prescriptions for building schools of administration which will work, without adaptation, in other settings. But I am advancing the proposition, at least tentatively, that there are some aspects of academic administration and institution-building which can be fruitfully studied. Good research and teaching materials in the field of university administration are sparse, but there is, I think, a growing body of relevant materials which we should consider presenting in courses, seminars, or summer institutes in which at least some of the foreign students who come to our campuses might enroll. Such courses or institutes, let me add, would enrich the experience of foreign students not only in the field of management but in a broader range of disciplines as well. To date, I think, we have given too little thought to this dimension of our opportunities and responsibilities.

With that hesitantly advanced suggestion, my agenda has been covered. But the set of questions associated with our topic for this session has by no means been exhausted. Let me pass the baton, therefore, to my colleagues. I am looking forward with interest to their comments and to the panel sessions which follow. Thank you.

W. WARREN HAYNES
Harvard University

Institution-Building in Management Education:

SOME HYPOTHESES

The Sloan School of Management at Massachusetts Institute of Technology and the Harvard Business School are about to start a research project on institution-building in the area of management education. The project will be international in scope and will concentrate on projects receiving foreign aid. We are as yet undecided about the inclusion of projects in Western Europe; we are also uncertain about covering projects which lean in a technical direction, such as national productivity councils and the efforts of the International Labor Office. We plan to study a selected group of these institutions in depth and to survey the remainder.

You should not expect that I will try to present the findings in this paper. The grant is only a few days old and we are just beginning our study.

OBJECTIVE OF THE STUDY

The objective of our study will be to learn from experience how to do a better job of planning for the creation of new institutions.

W. WARREN HAYNES is Visiting Professor of Business Administration and Chairman of the International Teachers Program, Harvard Business School. He has MBA and DCS degrees from Harvard. From 1948 to 1963, he was on the economics faculty in the University of Kentucky business school. From 1963 to 1965, he was project director of the Ahmedabad project of the Harvard Business School at the Indian Institute of Management. In 1966-67, he was Director of the Division of International Activities, Harvard Business School. He is author of *Nationalization in Practice: The British Coal Industry* (HBS, 1953), *Managerial Economics: Analysis and Cases* (Irwin, 1963), and co-author of *Accounting in Small Business Decisions* (University of Kentucky Press, 1963), among other works. Together with Thomas M. Hill, he recently began work on a study of the process of institution-building for management education, with the initial emphasis on India.

Some projects succeed. Others fail. Some produce far-reaching effects and others have a minor impact. Unfortunately, few of us have taken the time to learn from these successes and failures. We thus violate one of the basic precepts of management, which is to follow up on past results before planning for the future.

The study will make use of models but will not be a mere exercise in model-building. We do hope to make a contribution to the theory of institution-building, or to the construction of models about the institution-creating process. But we also have some immediate and pragmatic goals in mind. We want to learn how to do a more effective and less costly job. We want to exchange ideas with others engaged in this process in other universities, in the Ford Foundation, in the U. S. Agency for International Development (AID), and other bodies engaged in overseas projects in management education.

BUDGETING FOR MANAGEMENT EDUCATION

One might argue—and I think I have heard this said openly—that any effort in management education, at least any effort in the developing countries, will produce worthwhile results. The shortage of managers is a serious bottleneck in most of the world. Efforts at development are clearly retarded by the shortage of managers who can plan, organize, decide, and implement. Any effort to break the bottleneck would appear to be to the good.

This kind of thinking is a luxury that the developing countries cannot afford and which the developed countries should reject. In the developing countries, one can identify a wide range of bottlenecks—shortages in raw materials, in foreign exchange, in capital equipment, in basic education, in electric power, and so on. The problem of planning in these countries is one of setting priorities. The returns from breaking the bottlenecks are high, but the resources to do so are scarce. It is a crime to sacrifice high-return projects in favor of those with low or negative returns.

In fact, the basic idea in development planning is simply the setting of priorities—of placing high-return projects ahead of those with low returns. We may call it project evaluation, capital budgeting, cost-benefit analysis, or program budgeting, but the basic idea is the same.

Institutions in management education are not exempt from such analysis. A project which fails has used up resources which could have been applied to the improvement of health or, in some cases, the prevention of starvation. A project which costs more in foreign exchange investment than it contributes in foreign exchange savings adds to the balance of payments problems of the countries concerned.

Our formal study has not yet begun, but my impression is that while many projects have produced returns which justify the investment of time and foreign exchange, others have failed to do so. I wonder, for example, whether all the projects in management education being planned for Great Britain can be justified in view of the shortage of faculty inputs. We need to learn more about how we can set the right priorities in the planning stage and how we can increase the returns in the implementation stage. We need to apply our understanding of management to management education itself.

THE NEED FOR MANAGEMENT EDUCATION

The first step in planning an institution is estimating the requirements of the market for its product. Merely estimating the numbers of managers required five or ten years hence is not enough. We often plan the details of our overseas programs to meet our own interests and our own capacities without giving enough attention to the requirements of the situation. Do we plan a heavy dose of operations research because we know it meets the needs or because of our intellectual satisfaction in the subect? Do we put on a three-day conference in PERT for top managers because we know their problems run along those lines or because we wish to show off our competence in PERT? Do we foster the case method because it is well-suited to the educational needs abroad or because it is part of our heritage?

I am not one of those who believe that cultural differences make the transfer of knowledge unprofitable, but I do think we need to examine what can and cannot be transferred and what will produce results. And let us keep in mind that projects with long-term payoffs must be discounted heavily before they can be compared with those having immediate results. Faculty who like to educate for the year 2000 might try to compute the present value of such efforts in countries in which the social cost of capital is 15 percent.

ENVIRONMENTAL CONDITIONS

Suppose we have found that there is a need for management education and that we do have a competence on our side to make a contribution. Next we need to determine whether the environmental conditions are suitable for such an effort. Again, I think we don't examine this question carefully enough. Dean George Robbins, at the University of California, in Los Angeles, did a magnificent job in sizing up the environment in India, and his report of 1959 contributed greatly to the efforts made there by MIT and Harvard. He saw clearly that the Indian university environment in the early 1960s would not be favorable to efforts in management education, but saw also that private industry would benefit greatly from efforts outside the universities.

Last year I was asked to comment on a plan for an effort in management education in another country. The need for such an effort seemed clear. But the particular setting under consideration was one which was most discouraging. My first reaction was that it offered a great challenge—it seemed cowardly to call it quits before making a try. But we need to be tough-minded about these matters. In the particular country involved—which I prefer not to identify—there must have been a large backlog of other projects where the likely returns were higher, and even in the area of management education less risky ventures were possible. I have learned during this Conference that the institution involved has undergone some enormous changes which would have wiped out any effort started a year ago.

These points may be obvious. All of us want to fill a clear need in an environment which is supportive. My question is whether we think hard enough about where and when a project is appropriate. Bad plans are screened out and good plans usually succeed, but we should be able to improve our analysis of projects that fall between these extremes.

By the way, part of the environment abroad is created by the institutions at home which are considering overseas projects. Some of the AID offices are much more difficult to deal with than others; some may make it impossible to spend funds effectively. Some of our American universities are eager to engage in overseas activities, only to find that they have been overly optimistic in estimating their own faculty resources which might be available. I am willing to offer the hypothesis that almost all universities are overly optimistic about their resources until they have been burned several times. My experience is that you are lucky if twenty expressions of interest in going overseas at the early planning stages result in one firm commitment to go in the implementation stage. The foundations and government agencies have a right, I think, to be critical of our inability to implement our optimistic staffing plans; but our error is an honest one which we can correct by more careful forecasting.

DETAILED PROJECT PLAN

The big decision is the one to go or not to go. Once the decision to go has been made, a program of action must be devised. I do not have enough time to develop this subject fully but would like to offer some tentative ideas.

(1) I wonder whether a short planning horizon is not preferable to a long one. I have heard officials in the Ford Foundation say that it takes ten years to create an institution. I would like to suggest that in the field of management education the second or third years are the crucial ones, and that if at the end of the third year you have not built a faculty and a fairly full range of educational activities, you are in trouble. I feel uncomfortable about projects which start slowly and grow by bits, though I have heard strong arguments for this kind of progress. Slow growth gives time to train the overseas faculty, to send them to degree programs, to test out educational ideas, and so on. But I am impressed with the excitement, momentum, and high morale which can be created under tight schedules. This question requires careful research.

(2) In planning an overseas project, all the issues which arise in the planning of domestic educational programs are present. I was startled to find that one institution in Asia is working on a curriculum design very much like that of American undergraduate colleges of commerce in the 1920s and 1930s—even to the inclusion of shorthand and typing and a heavy dose of straight economics. Perhaps such a plan is warranted in the particular setting, but I doubt it. We need to decide whether the curriculum will offer an integrated approach or a cafeteria selection of specialties—I'm afraid my wording has exposed my preference. The issue of mathematics is a more pressing one in some developing countries, but clearly less pressing in Europe, where, in fact, the temptation may be to build too heavily on a mathematical and theoretical base. One of the most pressing issues, for which there cannot be a single answer for all projects, is the relative emphasis between research at the frontiers of knowledge and practical training for general managers. If we haven't resolved this issue at home, we cannot expect it to be answered clearly in new institutions overseas. Each institution must, however, define its own objectives and decide on its own product mix in terms of those objectives.

(3) Some of us are inclined to improvise as we go along to permit the maximum flexibility and scope for imagination and spontaneity. But this may be merely a lazy way out. I have seen at least one case in which each step in curriculum development, course de-

velopment, and faculty development was carefully thought out in advance. Control charts were drawn up to reflect the progress made. In this case, at least, the pace of accomplishment was clearly accelerated by this kind of planning. It is a myth, I am convinced, that the best way to build a program is to gather a group of independent scholars and let them go their separate ways. That was fine for medieval Oxford or Cambridge, but is hardly suitable for a specific task in management education today.

THE CULTURAL INTERCHANGE

Many of these projects involving foreign aid run into conflicts among three groups: the outside "consultants," the host-country administrators, and the host-country faculty members who must eventually take over full responsibility. I suspect that some projects have failed completely for such reasons. I don't think we know yet how to deal with this problem.

The difficulty is partly that the problem is not clearly defined, and that we have not tried to learn from experience. One might think in the abstract that all one needs to do is to train the outside "consultants" in the culture they will enter; thus their deeper understanding will clear away all issues. The consultants will supposedly learn to respect the values and traditions of others and modify their behavior accordingly.

Such a view, so appealing in the abstract, turns out to be hopelessly naive in actual practice. Certainly it is desirable to learn as much as possible in advance about the other culture and to remain open for further learning. (By the way, I personally found reading novels set in the foreign country the most useful approach; unfortunately novels on most countries are not as available as they are on India.) But the issue does not present itself in a clear confrontation between American values and traditions and those in the host country. Within the host country itself one will find a conflict in values. Some persons will be mainly conditioned by the traditional culture, others will reflect their European or United States education, and still others will be in the process of shifting values even though they have never travelled abroad. In Asia and Latin America, a strong tradition of family hierarchy comes into conflict with the very idea of professional management.

We do need to achieve perspective on our own values, it is true. Some recent studies on institution-building seem to assume that the chief objective is to transfer norms. An American who goes overseas believing that the objective is to convert others to our way of life is not likely to be effective. If he thinks his mission is to spread the gospel of free enterprise and to combat socialism, without taking the time to understand how irrelevant those terms become when one faces the real issues, he is going to convert a manageable problem of ends and means into an unmanageable one of ideological conflict.

Normally we know enough to avoid these major conflicts of values. The really serious problems are much more subtle. Suppose, for example, that nepotism influences the appointments to important posts in the foreign institution. Do we accept this fact because it is a traditional feature of that society? Or do we fight it as a clear obstacle to sound institutional development? Do we align ourselves with the host-country nationals who oppose nepotism, or do we support the values of the hierarchy with which we are supposed to cooperate? I don't have the answers to these questions; I merely suggest that the questions aren't even being asked in the right way. The subject of cultural tensions in international collaborations certainly needs more research.

ORGANIZATIONAL PROBLEMS

Some institutions are from the outset entirely host-country institutions, with nationals of the host country in positions of authority. This is perhaps the least difficult type of organization to analyze, for here the outside consultant clearly must fit himself into the existing structure. My impression is that this pattern is often successful in spite of possible resistance to change and inertia. Sometimes strong leadership on the host-country side can make remarkable use of the help of advisors and foreign faculty members.

A second pattern is to permit the foreigners—Americans or whatever—to start up the institution and gradually turn it over to host-country nationals. I doubt that this pattern occurs in a pure form— usually host-country nationals are fitted into some parts of the structure from the outset. The main thrust comes from the outsiders, however, and they are responsible for the initial design and most of the early implementation.

A third pattern—perhaps the most common—is a mixture of the two, in which the two groups of different nationalities share responsibility, with a shift to the host-country nationals over a period of time. My remarks will now concentrate on the second and third patterns, both of which involve changing mixes of responsibility over a period of time and an eventual withdrawal of the foreigners.

I have some hypotheses on the organizational arrangements which are appropriate as these shifts take place. But perhaps these should be left until we have been able to test them. I feel safe, however, in making one generalization: Too few of us plan in detail for these organizational shifts, nor are we prepared for the changes in responsibility and authority which follow. Phasing out a project is almost like giving up an adopted child; it seems easier in the abstract than it is in practice. I think we could avoid a great deal of misunderstanding and tension if these issues were discussed openly and rationally. Most of us find it difficult to let go, yet the very nature of institution-building under discussion requires a process of letting-go in the later stages. We ought to study how this can be done effectively and with a minimization of personal cost.

The process of phasing out is also strenuous for the host-country participants. They want to take over. They may suspect that the others are reluctant to give up authority, whether true or not. A mere disagreement on plans at this point may be interpreted as interference.

The resolution of these misunderstandings is not easy, for they are almost inherent in the situation, unless an unusually high level of communication has been achieved. Communication at long distances across cultural barriers is hard to achieve.

A radical solution to the phasing-out problem is for the advisors to divest themselves of authority, abruptly and completely, as soon as they think the new institution can survive. They can do this by changing the contractual arrangement to one in which the host-country institution decides completely what services it will buy from the advisors. I have seen this done in one case, and was amazed at how well it cleared the air and improved communication between the two parties. It would, of course, be a dangerous approach if the institution were not yet ready to stand on its own.

THE FACULTY DEMOCRACY ISSUE

One of the most sensitive issues in parts of the world where hierarchical leadership is traditional is faculty democracy and academic freedom. If the institution is new and the host-country faculty relatively inexperienced, it can be an explosive problem in which the advisors are easily caught.

The problem may arise in this way. A large part of the host-country faculty may have been exposed to Anglo-American traditions of academic freedom and faculty control over the curriculum, but they have not had a large enough exposure in practicing these traditions. If they have not been members of a Western faculty, they may not understand how many issues of this sort are resolved by tradition. Most British and American faculties do not care to become involved in administrative details. They are willing to accept a dividing line between administrative decisions, which can be decided by administrative authorities without reference to the faculty, and academic issues. My impression is that the more mature the faculty the fewer issues it wishes to consider—but the more strongly it will fight on the big academic issues.

In faculties with less experience, these traditions are unknown in a practical way. Faculty members may rightly be in a state of semi-rebellion against the authoritarian and antiquarian administrations they have observed in their own countries. They may, therefore, be extremely sensitive on these issues. The result, which I'm afraid I have observed and know to be a real problem, is that the faculty may engage in a continual battle with the administration over every detail—and over what is and is not an academic issue. Such faculties fail to realize that this approach threatens their control over the really important issues of academic policy and, in fact, threatens academic freedom itself.

It is easy for outside advisors to become caught in this issue by taking sides with one faction or the other. The advisors are supposed to report to the hierarchy, I assume, but do they have any obligations to the academic traditions they know and understand? I don't know the answer, but hope to have more insight when our study is completed.

In Latin America, or at least parts of it, this issue is complicated by some rather extreme ideas on student democracy which I do not yet fully understand. I don't know the solution to such problems—in most cases they will be resolved by time, but at a great cost. This represents a practical problem in the meeting of cultures which we need to study in greater depth.

CONCLUDING REMARKS

I have several misgivings about this talk. First, it states conclusions on matters which we have not yet studied systematically. All my generalizations should be taken as hypotheses requiring systematic research. Second, my talk is very spotty—it covers some issues and neglects others, even some of the most important ones. For example, I have said nothing about staffing the institution—about recruiting and selecting the faculty. I have said little about curriculum design, since I think I have little that is new to say on the subject.

My last apology is for the methodology on which this paper is based. There is nothing more contrary to the scientific tradition than generalization and theory based on personal experience. Most of you are familiar with the various so-called principles of management which were developed in this way in the early part of the century. I hope that we don't produce a similar set of principles of institution-building based on a narrow set of observations and personal rationalizations. I do hope we can arrive at some dependable generalizations and useful prescriptions based on an objective study of a fairly broad sample of institutions in various parts of the world. When our study is completed, it should no longer be necessary to rely so heavily on the kinds of personal impressions which have made up this talk.

REINALDO SCARPETTA
Universidad del Valle, Colombia

Technical Assistance Abroad:

VIEW FROM A HOST SCHOOL

It is indeed a great pleasure to be here today, for among you are colleagues, former professors, and close friends who have worked with us in Latin America.

It was suggested that I refer my comments to "presenting reactions to the overseas activities of U. S. business schools from the point of view of the host school."

Knowing this in advance, I took the liberty of asking several deans of Latin American graduate schools of business to give me their thoughts on the subject and to comment on my views. Therefore, what I will try to express here will be a recollection of what they have said plus a few points held by us at del Valle.

As a first premise in analyzing those reactions, let me state what I consider to be the mission of the business school in social and economic development.

Social and economic development require an institution which provides efficient coordination of developmental efforts, understands variables involved in such development, and provides the leadership

REINALDO SCARPETTA is Dean of the División de Ciencias Sociales y Económicas of the Universidad del Valle, Cali, Colombia. He has a BS in industrial management and industrial engineering from Georgia Institute of Technology, and worked several years for W. R. Grace & Co., Colombia, and Industrias Metálicas de Palmira, also in Colombia. In the early 1960s, he was one of the founders of the management development program offered through Universidad del Valle for Cali business executives. Later the program was made available to younger executives throughout Colombia. He also was a founder of the Comité Latinoamericano de Decanos de Escuelas de Administración, with members in eight Latin American countries.

to bring about organized creative change. This, in my opinion, is the role of management as an institution, and the business school is the place where the people who manage tomorrow can become acquainted with management's tasks, philosophies, and tools.

Therefore, the business school has to be a cornerstone in the creation of intellectual capital for a society's management. Its research, service, and educational functions should extend to all levels of management—and hopefully to the management of most of society's major enterprises. To do this, the scope of intellectual activity and technological involvement must be widened. The professor of management, as the manager himself, must maintain an "overall" view of development in order to be able to accomplish his task of training new managers and continually retraining old ones.

The business school must then be able to create and interpret change as a challenge to entrepreneurial and managerial spirit. It must help create or rapidly understand new tools that make management more efficient, and it must develop educational strategies to constantly update and stimulate managers to improve their performance.

To help produce at the university, or within the enterprises themselves, managers capable of managing creative change in society's institutions, is in my opinion the role of the business school in social and economic development. In any case, the business school will have a growing role in society's education and may well become the place at which the professions meet the community to study and solve organizational problems.

Latin America is a continent where the scarcest resource is entrepreneurial ability. Trained managers for industry, commerce, and government are few and generally overworked. It is also a continent in which countries are in different stages of organization and economic development. Social mobility is limited. And large, complex social problems keep on growing.

Among the limitations under which a Latin American manager must work are: scant human resources with which to work; inefficient and, in cases, rudimentary government mechanisms; rapidly changing patterns of societal behavior which vary substantially from country to country; growing unrest caused by growing population and the need to feed, clothe, house, and provide education and employment for it; established social and economic rigidities limiting the power of individuals to accomplish things; competitive pressure from without for local markets and resources; and overwhelming competition in selling his products in international markets.

To these, one could add limitations coming from the nature of national economic structure, such as unavailability of credit, poor communications, expensive transportation, and very limited information on which to base decisions. The Latin American manager must operate under these conditions and must also be capable of improving them.

The Latin American manager is deeply immersed in the life of his community. He cannot be a simple spectator in his country's development. He must be a principal actor. He must take a part in business and governmental leadership. As a businessman and citizen, he will undoubtedly be required to do so.

What I am saying is that a graduate of a Latin American business school will be required to be a promoter of change, a motor for development, truly a leader in fashioning the society in which he lives. The business school will have to provide him with the tools to be just that.

The training must be given in many cases in less time than is required in a more advanced society. The economic and social pressures that society exerts on a young and able professional to start working at once mount rapidly in our countries. The business school will also have fewer resources, such as libraries, teaching materials, research and extension facilities, and in many cases will also lack strong links with the business community. Finally the graduate business school, in the majority of cases, receives a man poorly trained for business subjects and not possessing the basic technical skills required to accept, understand, and utilize modern concepts of management.

In our business schools, in spite of limitations, we must develop a curriculum broad enough to give a young man more than a glimpse of international economics, enough information to get a feel for his government's problems, and access to social scientists who will acquaint him with the changing nature of the people for whom and with whom he will work. He must also understand the nature of world power philosophies, their political struggles, and their goals, so that he may analyze his own country's interests and opportunities in relation to these forces. And then, of course, he must acquire the tools with which to manage and control an enterprise.

In learning these, he must be taught to teach, for quite probably most innovations in his enterprise will be started by him. He must train his subordinates to execute those changes as well as convince his superiors of their value.

The job of training people for business in various countries in Latin America is further complicated by the political and economic nature of our universities and by the fact that the university and business worlds have grown very far apart. Some of the best graduate schools of business in Latin America have been created outside of universities, because there was no local university which offered even modestly auspicious conditions for the development of a business school. This unfortunate situation gives our schools an additional challenge, that is, to bring together the university and business worlds through the medium of the business school.

To achieve the results sketched above, we have asked many of you in American universities, schools of business, and other institutions to cooperate with us in developing our programs. But we have invited you also to help us create much more than appropriate curricula. You have joined us in building our institutions, in training our professors, in planning our research, and in financing our efforts.

Your government and your private, multinational companies have substantially affected the nature of our economy and our business practices. I would venture to say that some of the best professors of management in our countries have been American businessmen who, possessing great ability, initiative, and leadership, have understood and improved our business world.

A point made several times by my colleagues, which is relevant to the general theme of this Conference, relates to the impact which the professional management of your international companies makes on our own managers and on the future of our private sector. Your international enterprises bring to us the power of American technology, organization, and business methods. You combine the skills of science and modern management with world-wide organization, possessing tremendous decision-making power. You attract our best young men to your organizations, purchase control of many of our companies, and gradually become a creative force within our society.

This, of course, is good. It has greatly contributed to our development. But it can also be disastrous for us unless we are able to understand and acquire partial control of the new business world you are creating. We must understand and control this new business environment in our countries, or we will find ourselves faced with serious political and economic consequences.

The challenge before us is nothing short of creating a new approach to international affairs and management, in and out of government. Our business schools, our universities, and our technological institutions must take an active part in structuring this new environment.

If education for international business is a matter of emphasis in your schools, *it is a matter of survival in ours.*

Over the last several years, North, Central, and South American business schools have begun to make efforts towards training young Latin Americans to meet the above challenges. I would ask the people in our governments if there ever has been a better investment of resources. In spite of the short time of their existence, the impact on our societies made by Getúlio Vargas, in Brazil; Monterrey, in Mexico; INSORA and Católica, in Chile; and ESAN, in Peru, to name a few, is more than evident.

For instance, it is quite possible that INCAE, through its several seminars for Central American businessmen, has been a major contributor to Central American integration, promising to produce just the type of manager required to make the Central American common market an economic reality.

Your personal and institutional cooperation has been essential in most of the projects mentioned, and continuing relations strengthen our hope for improvement in the future. For the help you have offered us in the past, as well as for your interest in our future, we are sincerely grateful.

If there is evidence that we have succeeded in doing some important things, there is also evidence that we have made several mistakes. Or at least, this is my feeling and that of many of my colleagues. Having learned from them, we hope to make our future relations better and more efficient. I will try to mention some of the most important aspects in making future relations more successful.

The first point to be made is that a business school must answer a recognized need of the community and must receive its unconditional support. Starting a business school in Latin America should be a decision taken at the request of the local people, and only when they unequivocally pledge support to making it a reality—and financial support alone is not enough. This, of course, applies to helping an ongoing program as well as to creating new projects. The time invested in developing a proper atmosphere will produce growing returns once the school or program starts functioning.

An obvious corollary is that the leadership and a major part of the decision-making responsibility must be in the hands of nationals. This, sadly, is a point very often overlooked, especially when financial aid is required to produce measurable short-range results. In such cases, problems of split authority arise because parties seek different goals.

When we ask you for help, it should be because we cannot do something ourselves. Asking you to help us do something we can do ourselves results in mutual frustrations. We must ask you for help when we need it—and for those things which we can best do together.

Once we have defined the area and purpose of the help we require from you, we must make sure that we utilize it wisely and effectively. This means creating conditions which maximize the transmission of knowledge. We must be able to receive knowledge from you, and must have the capacity to translate that knowledge into our own frame of reference.

This requires efforts from both sides. The recipient institution must have properly trained staff to take maximum advantage of the outside resource. The man coming from outside must have someone with whom to work: a colleague who is desirous to learn. Between them must exist excellent communications so as to maximize the usefulness of the visitor. The local man must commit himself to a continuing self-education effort in order to permanently update himself. It will be his duty to keep the institution abreast of developments in his field.

The institution providing the help also must meet certain requirements. It should enter into association with us for the right reasons, a very important reason being, for instance, that both parties gain. It is very important also that the project be part of future developments solidly planned by that institution. It is not advisable to send someone to Latin America for whom there is no institutional base to which to return.

You must send us the right man—one who is able to teach and anxious to learn. Such a man is expensive. He must be properly motivated, technically competent, truly a professional in his field. He must be able to teach, to teach how to teach, and to inspire creative research. This man should be chosen jointly whenever possible.

Finally there are things we can do together. We must work out suitable financial arrangements with budgets flexible enough not to limit the program unnecessarily or submerge its administrators in a sea of red tape. We must not find ourselves committed to doing the wrong thing, no matter how sensible the same action would have seemed years before when we designed the project.

We must recognize that when working together for common goals, there are few things we cannot do. But we must be patient and flexible. Professional ties and mutual affection link us, and the same objectives motivate our work.

Last year we founded CLADEA—the Committee of Deans of Latin American Schools of Business Administration—embracing twelve institutions which have common features, such as a full-time faculty with master's and PhD degrees, students having degrees from other disciplines, and a graduate program that culminates in the awarding of an academic degree.

The purposes of the Committee are to promote the international dimension in business education in Latin America (which is especially important in the light of Latin American integration and the creation of the Common Market), and to achieve an efficient operation by pooling academic resources among the schools.

I sincerely hope that through CLADEA and other older ties, we can work out long-range programs between our institutions and yours.

CLAUDE Mc MILLAN
University of Colorado

Experience With the
Michigan State Project in Brazil

REFLECTIONS, SEVEN YEARS LATER

I was pleased to be part of a thoroughly successful experiment in institution-building: the Business Administration program in Brazil, coordinated by Michigan State University (MSU). I left that project as Chief of Party, in September, 1960. It occurs to me now that had I been asked to reflect on that experience before a group of this sort in September, 1960 rather than today, I would have been less temperate in portraying some of my more vivid impressions. Things have changed. We found ourselves chiding our Brazilian counterparts, as we worked together to build a viable school of business administration, for the disposition of their students to arrogate unto themselves a proprietary interest in the administrative affairs of the school; for their disposition to protest and to strike—practices then extremely rare in the U. S. educational system, in which students focus their attention on study and personal development. We were critical of the disposition of the developing Latin American nations to build and maintain costly steel industries, auto assembly plants, and national airlines, when the economic justification was elusive—sacrificing economic propriety for national pride. We counseled against costly foreign military adventures to oppose real or imagined

CLAUDE Mc MILLAN is Professor of Management, School of Business, University of Colorado. He has an MS in business from Colorado and a PhD in business administration from Ohio State University. From 1956 to 1960, he was Chief of Party of Michigan State University's Technical Assistance Mission, São Paulo, Brazil, as a result of which he co-authored *International Enterprise in a Developing Economy* (MSU, 1964). After serving on the MSU faculty for five years, he joined the Colorado faculty in 1965. He has written numerous articles based on his work in Brazil, including "The Swap as a Hedge in International Exchange" (*California Management Review*, Summer, 1962). He is co-author of *Systems Analysis: A Computer Approach to Decision Models* (Irwin, 1965).

enemies, in the face of agonizing social problems at home. Since leaving Brazil, I have noticed that Berkeley, the race to beat Russia to the moon, and Vietnam have become American enterprises. If these be manifestations of social progress, then we clearly lag behind our Latin American neighbors in the process of social evolution.

THE CHANGE AGENTS IN THE BRAZIL PROJECT

The principal change agents in the Brazil project were: (a) the Getúlio Vargas Foundation, a quasi-governmental organization concerned with improving the processes of administration in government and industry; (b) the AID of the U. S. Government; (c) Michigan State University; and (d) the Brazilian faculty at the University of Bahia, the University of Rio Grande do Sul, and most of all, the faculty of the Escola de Administração de Emprêsas de São Paulo (EAESP).

Of these, it is my belief that the Brazilian faculty of EAESP and the leadership of the Getúlio Vargas Foundation (GVF) were the most important. The environment within which these change agents functioned was a hostile one, as I will indicate shortly. Dealing with this hostility was chiefly the responsibility of the Brazilian faculty of EAESP and the leadership of GVF. The discipline of business administration would eventually find its way into the Brazilian university system, but without the initiative of GVF, under the leadership of Simões Lopes, a highly respected man of great personal integrity and public prestige, its advent would have been much delayed.

None of the Brazilian faculty of EAESP were professional educators at the beginning of the project. All of them became educators following their affiliation with the School. This was the intent of GVF. It was recognized that bringing off substantive changes in the Brazilian university system would be an exceedingly difficult task. Required was a school outside the system, staffed with a newly created faculty which would be free to innovate. In retrospect, this was a wise decision indeed. Today the discipline of business administration exists in several other universities in Brazil, but its existence is tenuous. The chief thrust in this new discipline continues to reside at EAESP in São Paulo.

THE ENVIRONMENT

(a) The business community

The need for formal educational programs in business administration was not recognized by Brazilian industry in 1953, at the beginning of our program. Much of the leadership of Brazilian industry lay in the hands of the owning families, and there was no dirth of family members to carry on. The respected fields for study were law and medicine, with engineering just becoming respectable. Business administration itself was not regarded as a prestigious pursuit. While much of Brazil's industrial success could be attributed to a growing class of entrepreneurs, many of Italian, German, and Portuguese ancestry, when an enterprising immigrant achieved success he was prone to want for his children the more prestigious life of those in whose ranks he was only partially accepted: the non-commercial aristocracy.

A handful of leaders of the American business community in Brazil performed useful functions in the early life of the School: providing advice and counsel, serving at times on the Board of Trustees of EAESP, and in rare cases providing modest financial support in the form of student scholarships. Both Brazilian- and American-dominated industry supported the School by sending to its 13-week management development program promising managerial personnel from their firms. By 1965, Brazilian and American business in Brazil contributed to a revolving, interest-free student loan fund. But at no time has industry in Brazil been much more than a customer of the School's product. Yet without industry's ready acceptance of the graduating students, the School could not have survived, and the significance of this acceptance should not be underrated. However, considering the monumental financial problems which the School has faced and its efforts to raise financial support from industry, it is surprising that such support has been so negligible. Today about half the resources required to operate the School are raised through student tuition and fees, a practice which stands in strong contrast to the general practice of free public university education in Brazil.

(b) The Brazilian university system

Like universities in general, including those in the United States, Brazilian universities have exhibited little disposition to change. The *catedrático* system is deeply entrenched. Great importance is attached to the credentials a graduate obtains upon accepting his degree, including the federally-sponsored "status" which he receives. Graduates in economics had come to feel that their certification as economists qualified them for the nation's positions in administrative leadership, and saw the emergence of a degree program in business administration as a serious threat. Ultimately, the degrees of graduates of EAESP did receive federal recognition, but only after continued pressure from the EAESP faculty, the students themselves, and support from GVF. Continuing hostility from economists impedes progress in business administration in the existing university system.

UNEXPECTED PROBLEMS

(a) The graduate program

It was the original intent of GVF that EAESP should conduct a graduate program in business administration patterned after that of the Harvard Business School. Via a graduate program, it was believed, the quality of Brazilian industrial leadership could be improved and Brazilian professors of business administration could be produced for spreading the discipline. This plan was set aside when it was recognized that graduate programs, as such, do not exist in the Brazilian educational system, and if an impact was to be made on the existing educational structure it would have to be via a program comparable to those prevalent in Brazil. The initial degree program, then, was a four-year undergraduate course. A serious problem then arose when, subsequently, a graduate program was introduced. Those students with an undergraduate degree in business administration from EAESP felt insecure alongside their colleagues with graduate degrees. For those having received federal recognition as business administrators, what was the implication of this new breed with graduate degrees in the same field?

(b) The expanded program

In 1958, five years after EAESP came into existence, GVF, AID, and MSU began to address themselves to expanding the program of EAESP to the University of Bahia and the University of Rio Grande do Sul. We grossly underestimated the prestige problem associated with this thrust. The Brazilian faculty of EAESP was well-prepared scholastically to help these existing institutions, much as MSU had helped EAESP. In general, the Universities of Bahia and Rio Grande do Sul recognized the quality of EAESP and its ability to perform an advisory function in the design and implementation of curricula in business administration. However, it was quite another thing to admit this publicly. These institutions were proud and deeply sensitive. Ultimately, the Brazilian faculty was accepted and programs were begun at these institutions, substantially through their own efforts.

THE NATURE OF THE INVOLVEMENT OF THE MSU STAFF

I've tried, above, to portray some aspects of the project which are perhaps less known. I have the impression that all of you are somewhat familiar with the MSU program in Brazil, but perhaps not so aware of the non-structural aspects of that program—aspects which involved the MSU group, and aspects for which nothing in our past experience had really prepared us.

We were never detached, objective analysts of the School's problems. We were deeply involved in the actions and passions of the School. We were intimate partners of our Brazilian colleagues, and as partners generally do, we frequently disagreed. At times we were, I think, quite obstinate, domineering, and unyielding. On questions of a purely academic character, I think we generally found complete agreement with our Brazilian faculty counterparts. On questions of administrative policy, student relationships, and new innovations, we frequently disagreed with the Brazilian administration of the School. We generally felt that the administration was indecisive and passive. With some justification, I think, the administration of EAESP felt that we were unappreciative of the unique attributes of the Brazilian scheme of things academic, and unprepared to compromise.

None of the members of the MSU staff had any particular experience to recommend him for the Brazilian assignment, in my view. Like our counterparts in American-controlled Brazilian industry, we were sent to Brazil largely because we had functional skills which were needed there. In all honesty, I believe we, on the MSU staff, did not represent the best academic competence in our various areas of specialization. One essential attribute we did share was complete dedication to the purposes of the School. We genuinely believed that the programs to which we had addressed ourselves, as partners with our Brazilian counterparts, were important, and we were proud to be identified with them.

FACTORS WHICH MAKE FOR SUCCESS

Essentially, I believe the factors which contribute to success in institution-building of the sort I've described are:

(a) freedom to innovate;

(b) a sense of mission;

(c) considerable team unity among the Americans;

(d) freedom to maneuver in terms of administrative relationships with one's home organization, the U. S. Government, and funding groups; and

(e) adequate financial support.

The Ford Foundation has contributed significantly to the Brazil project. The contributions of the U. S. government are well known, and GVF has supported the program from the start. Resources, however, continue to be a major problem. If the promising programs at the Universities of Bahia and Rio Grande do Sul fail, the cause will most likely be a lack of financial resources. Educators in developing nations must come to recognize that professors of business administration compete in a larger market than those in many other areas of teaching. Professors are badly paid in Latin America, at best. Those at EAESP are among the best paid in Brazil. Unless administrators in the existing university system can reward those teaching business administration more appropriately, the discipline of business administration may not survive in those institutions.

Some way must be found to obtain great support from the industrial communities of the world for the development of business administration education. Considering the magnitude of U.S. business involvement abroad, and the importance to U. S. business of improved management education, surely U. S. business must become a major source of funding for education in business management. Perhaps those of us here today have a responsibility to help make this apparent and to conceive of ways in which the needs and rewards can be made apparent to business leaders in this country.

For those among you who would like a detailed chronicle of the Brazil project, be advised that the Bureau of Business and Economic Research, Michigan State University, will publish shortly a book by Don Taylor entitled, *Institutionalizing the Discipline of Business Administration in the Brazilian University System.* I've read the manuscript and recommend it highly.

STERLING D. SESSIONS
Escuela de Administración de Negocios
para Graduados (ESAN), Perú

The Rewards and Tribulations of Establishing a Business School Overseas:

THE ESAN EXPERIENCE

BRIEF HISTORY OF ESAN

ESAN (Escuela de Administración de Negocios para Graduados) is the Peruvian graduate school of business administration located in Lima, a city of over 2,000,000 people, called the "City of Kings" because of its close relationship with Spain dating back to the early 1500s. The school was founded in 1962 as the result of a request from a group of Peruvian businessmen to the Agency for International Development (AID) in Lima to produce a feasibility study which might lead to the establishment of a school of business administration. The feasibility study project was awarded to the Stanford University Graduate School of Business by AID; and after an intensive on-the-spot investigation of available and future resources, Stanford agreed to administer the contract for the Peruvian and U. S. governments for at least five years. After that period it was hoped ESAN would be "Peruvianized," with continued modest support from Stanford.

Stanford initially sent a team of nine men to Lima to launch the school under the direction of Dr. Alan B. Coleman. The necessary problems of locating a building, establishing a curriculum, initiating

STERLING D. SESSIONS is Dean of the Escuela de Administración de Negocios para Graduados (ESAN), Lima, Perú, and Visiting Associate Professor of Business Administration, Stanford University. He has an MS from New York University and a DBA with an emphasis in marketing from Harvard University. Prior to assuming the ESAN post in 1966, he was Associate Professor of Business Management at Brigham Young University. He has held marketing positions with several retailers. He is a member of the Board of Directors of CONAPROPE, the organization of North American businessmen in Perú.

a library, and the important factor of determining which students should attend, filled the months of this first year.

Some of the universities in Lima were vying for ESAN when it was first founded, but since it did not appear wise to establish a working relationship with any one school it was decided to have ESAN completely independent. It does, however, have full degree-granting authority and maintains close contact with existing universities in Peru through its Board of Trustees. Representatives from each of the major universities serve as members of the board, along with delegates from industry and government.

The first class of 43 students entered ESAN in March, 1964 and graduated 11 months later with a master's degree which is roughly equivalent to the first year of a two-year MBA degree program at the Stanford Business School.

ESAN PROGRAMS

The master's degree program provides the major emphasis at ESAN, but in addition the school has three other educational directions. The first of these is our evening executive program which has attracted middle management employees of firms in two different types of programs: one being involved with general management concepts of accounting, finance, marketing, production, business policy, and organizational behavior, and the other in specialized areas such as marketing management and industrial relations. The second is an advanced management seminar which is held on a full-time basis for three weeks in August at a pleasant resort in the Andean foothills east of Lima. Last year five professors from the U. S., four of them from Stanford Business School, were brought to Lima. This advanced management seminar emphasizes problems which confront top executives in Peru, such as the economic considerations of balance of payments and international trade, management uses of the computer, and some of the newer concepts in marketing, production, and organizational behavior.

The third direction is akin to the off-campus extension courses held in the United States. These courses are taught, over ten weekends in the smaller communities outside of Lima, by successful ESAN alumni, in terms of their previous academic performance and business qualifications, along with some members of the ESAN faculty. This venture is not designed to treat the various aspects of business administration in an exhaustive manner, yet it is perhaps the first time some businessmen have been exposed to such rudimentary concepts as cash flow analysis. To reinforce this program the Peace Corps has cooperated in providing volunteers with MBA degrees to be in the classrooms during the weekends and then work with the businessmen during the week in implementing some of the concepts and methods learned.

The master's curriculum at ESAN has been developed to correspond to the needs of the country. The sophistication and needs of Peruvian business at present do not demand a specialized two-year MBA degree. The program lasts 11 full months instead of the usual 17 or 18 months for an MBA degree in the United States. The students are in class 18 hours a week, and it is estimated that another 40 or 50 hours outside of class are required for class preparation, written reports, and studying for examinations. Exhibit 1 provides an idea of what is taught during the year.

Exhibit 1

ESAN PROGRAM OF STUDY — FIFTH ACADEMIC YEAR

April 1968 - February 1969

April 1 - June 14	June 24 - Sept. 6	Sept. 16 - Nov. 22	Nov. 30 - Feb. 28
Accounting 1	Accounting 2	Accounting 3	Policy
Economics 1	Economics 2	Industrial Relations 1	Industrial Relations 2
Statistics	Production 1	Production 2	Quantitative Methods
Organization	Finance 1	Finance 2	Finance 3
Marketing 1	Marketing 2	Marketing 3	Business and Its Environment
Written Analysis of Cases	Written Analysis of Cases	New Enterprise Development	Research Project

ESAN STUDENTS

We are frequently questioned about the composition of the student body in the full-time master's degree program. In some schools of this type, where the $750 tuition is high in terms of South American standards, the student body is primarily composed of sons of wealthy merchants, landowners, etc. To the contrary, we have found that many of our students have not had the opportunities afforded by wealth, as evidenced by the 55 men of the present class of 73 who have received grants-in-aid from a private sector loan fund. This loan fund is developed and administered somewhat the same as in the United States where a student borrows on the basis of demonstrated need while he is going to school, and then begins to repay the loan after he starts work.

Our students come from different backgrounds, as will be seen in Exhibit 2. Although the number of observations is not enough to infer much statistically, it is apparent that an educational or intellectual elite is being developed at ESAN as indicated by the shift from public to private high schools, professional occupation of the father, and the educational levels attained by the father.

The average age of the student body at ESAN in 1967-68 is 28 years, which might indicate that many of them have had working experience since earning their undergraduate degree. However, the curve is skewed to the right because of a number of men in their late thirties who have come from military and business careers to earn their degree.

Exhibit 2

ESAN

Personal Data — First Four Classes

CLASS	HIGH SCHOOL		WORKED WHILE AT UNIVERSITY		FATHER'S OCCUPATION			FATHER'S EDUCATION			MAR-RIED
	Public	Private	Yes	No	Profes-sional	Owner	Em-ployee	Univer-sity	High School	Elemen-tary	
1st	55%	45%	*NA	NA	30%	20%	50%	NA	NA	NA	NA
2nd	58%	42%	65%	35%	27%	25%	48%	30%	52%	18%	NA
3rd	43%	57%	55%	45%	31%	48%	21%	41%	51%	8%	28%
4th	28%	72%	33%	67%	41%	22%	37%	57%	31%	12%	24%

Note: **Total number of students:**   1st Class **43**
                                         2nd Class **50**
                                          3rd Class **81**
                                          4th Class **76**

*NA = not available

We seek at least 15% of our students from other countries, and during the past four years have attracted them from most of the countries in South America, Europe, and the United States. For instance, we have a woman student at ESAN now who has a most interesting history. After receiving her degree from Vassar she joined the Peace Corps, came to Peru, and was sent to a small colonial city named Ayacucho, which is located at an elevation of 12,000 feet, approximately 300 miles southeast of Lima. She learned Quechua, the original language of the Incas, and in turn taught Spanish to many Indians. She married a man from Lima who owned a large ranch in Ayacucho, where they are now growing potatoes. One evening a graduate of the Harvard Business School suggested she obtain more knowledge of business administration to improve the efficiency and profitability of the ranch. She applied to ESAN, was accepted, and will be graduated in March, 1968 with a master's degree.

Students are admitted to ESAN on the basis of (1) an admissions test which we have obtained from the University of Chile and which has demonstrated a high degree of correlation between test results and classroom performance, (2) a careful appraisal of their grade-point average, and (3) personal interviews for marginal applicants.

At the present time we are working with the Educational Testing Service in developing an aptitude test in Spanish. We have concluded an agreement with ETS to establish a pilot project for such an examination. The first stage will be completed by the latter part of November. As more graduate schools of business develop in Latin America, there will be a greater need to establish comparability among students applying for these schools. A reliable aptitude test in Spanish will aid in solving this problem.

FINANCING OF ESAN

ESAN is financed at present by three sources of funds. Money is given by the Ministry of Education of the Peruvian Government to pay for all Peruvian faculty and staff. Funds from the U. S. Government through the Agency for International Development pay for the U. S. faculty at ESAN, the acquisition of library books and periodicals, and ESAN graduates who are in advanced degree programs in the United States. The balance of the operating income is derived from tuition and fees which defray operating expenses such as rent, utilities, and the purchase of equipment.

We had planned to ask the private sector for money beginning November 1, 1967, but the recent economic downturn precipitated by the devaluation of the Peruvian currency has delayed this particular campaign until, perhaps, next year.

ESAN's strategy is to aid in the education of competent business executives who in turn will spread their influence in their respective companies. As a consequence we have not planned to ask for private funds until the value of our product was demonstrated. In light of the favorable comments we have received from executives in Peru, and the expressed desires to help financially, we believe that when we begin soliciting funds we will be able to achieve the necessary income from the private sector to offset the anticipated expenses of increasing the size and number of our programs. Our influence with the business community is rapidly expanding, as evidenced in Exhibit 3.

Exhibit 3
Expansion of ESAN Faculty and Student Body

	1964	1965	1966	1967	1968 (est.)
U. S. Faculty	*9	*9	6	5	2
Peruvian Faculty	0	3	4	5	7
Peruvian Staff	15	20	24	33	28
Master's Degrees	43	50	71	66	80
Master's Degrees Cumulated		93	164	230	310
Graduates — Executive Training Programs	110	149	190	223	335
Graduates — Executive Training Programs—Cumulated		259	449	672	1,007
Total Alumni	153	352	613	902	1,317

*includes two research associates

FUTURE PLANS

Our future plans involve the construction of a new building since we are in an overcrowded condition in our present location, which formerly housed the Canadian Embassy. We also plan to increase the size of our student body and faculty to meet the demands of Peruvian management, and to initiate computerization, including systems analysis and design, in our curriculum in the immediate future. We intend to establish an international research center in business administration and economics which will serve as a research platform for scholars from universities in other countries undertaking research in Peru. In this regard, we are working with professors from the University of California, Kalamazoo College, and Cornell University, who are now in Peru conducting research.

Ideally if a school had "everything in its favor," it would have the following:

1. Faculty commitment at the cooperating institution, including a willingness to spend time overseas for periods longer than six months. (See letter from Stanford's Frank Shallenberger in appendix to this paper.)

2. Intelligent and calm administrative coordination at the sponsoring school, including a competent, patient campus coordinator. Parenthetically, to do it over again, I would want Telex-communications in order to have immediate two-way dialogue between the campus and the overseas installation, since the time lags imposed by international mails frequently distort the issues involved and on the other hand create a scarcity of data for decision making.

3. Sufficient money to buy U. S. faculty who are intellectually gifted, research oriented, superb teachers, fluent in the foreign language of the country involved, understanding of the problems created by cultural differences, psychologically stable and mature, in possession of a sense of "mission," and enjoying a rock-solid marriage. (These people are obviously hard to find.)

4. Sufficient money to obtain faculty from the foreign country who are intellectually gifted, research oriented, bi-lingual (knowing English extremely well), superb teachers, patient with the U. S. faculty, well trained in the U. S., preferably with a terminal degree, and willing to devote their full time to the school. (These people are rather hard to find.)

5. Complete cooperation from the facilitating organizations, be they AID, the Ford Foundation, or the host Government, including the immediate payment of contract funds when due and payable.

6. Complete support from the business sector must be a reality.

7. The administrators of the school in the foreign land must not be prone to frustration.

8. There must be a total absence of hostility and jealousy from competing institutions in the foreign country, including the opposition party in Congress.

9. The location and cultivation of a student body which is: intellectually gifted, mathematically competent, humble, politically neutral, not given to student strikes, not given to desires to dominate the board of trustees, willing to work at least 60 hours a week on their degree, and understanding of the peculiarities of the U. S. faculty. (These people are rather hard to find.)

The pitfalls and problems of establishing an overseas campus are laced through the preceding "factors for success." I will dwell no more on this truism. If any of the preceding factors are missing, you have problems!

THE OBJECTIVES OF ESAN

At ESAN we are attempting to incorporate many of the techniques, concepts, and processes that are used in the United States, into the Peruvian economy subject to its being ready for, and needing, such functions, not only now but within the next five years. For instance, there is no need in our curriculum to dwell at length on the public ownership of corporations and the development of a stock market, since these vital factors in the United States economy are hardly evident in Peru. We emphasize the local scene in our case-development process, where our director of research and four research associates have developed 65 business cases of considerable length which attempt to explain the workings of a number of Peruvian businesses.

Looking at our product more philosophically, we are attempting:

1. To establish an educational environment where there is little veneration for the status quo. That is, we try to cultivate the seeds of change in the sense that there must be a more effective way of doing things. We are also trying to reinforce those characteristics of a culture upon which our civilization is built, such as integrity, honesty, hard work, and a number of unmentioned social institutions which give life and well being to the existing social order.

2. To develop a sense of urgency by incorporating into our curriculum the teaching methods and case materials that express, "now is the time, and here is the place, let's go!"

3. To aid in the care and feeding of democratic systems which make it difficult for any one person to build an empire for personal gain. We believe that decisions should be based on merit and abilities, not just beliefs, names, and social station. In a real sense, we are trying to avoid a cultivation of *personalismo*, that is, "I have a friend."

4. To establish an educational environment where vigorous study and patient inquiry into relevant matters of business administration develop personal discipline. In many cases ESAN is the first exposure to difficult, demanding, intensive work in the classroom.

5. To cultivate initiative and leadership through individual and group research projects leading to frequent interaction with the business community, guest speakers from the United States and Peru who highlight the rewards of

entrepreneurship, and the opportunity of getting acquainted with successful alumni who are applying some of the concepts enumerated here in a financially and socially rewarding manner.

6. To aid our students in coping with an environment of uncertainty which is created both by lack of data about the economy and by constant political and economic instability. For instance, the manager of a U. S. automobile assembly plant who has lived 26 years in Argentina, Venezuela and Peru, recently told me: "In the U. S. we may make one major decision a week. It will be based on vast resources of statistical data and qualified manpower to implement the decision. Here, we make seemingly hundreds of decisions a week because we must wear so many hats. These decisions are too frequently guesses, because we do not have the operating data we need, nor a detailed awareness of what is happening to the economy. Consequently, we have far more confidence in the quality of of our decision when it is made in the U. S. in contrast to a similar one being made here."

I see our role in this most exciting venture as one of aiding the development of a middle-income group where social class, family name, or childhood background will not determine salary levels, titles, and advancement. As I think about it, you might call this effort revolutionary.

.

APPENDIX

To: FACULTY [of the Stanford Graduate School of Business]

From: FRANK K. SHALLENBERGER

Subject: OVERSEAS PROGRAMS

When I think of the great satisfaction and benefit our family got out of a year and a half overseas, and when I hear others comment on what they, too, have gained, I wonder if we are all accurately appraising the advantages and disadvantages of such an assignment. Here, for what they're worth, are my own observations:

Clearly, there are sacrifices involved. "Out of sight," tends to be "out of mind." For the younger men, an overseas assignment can well mean a break in their climb up the academic ladder. It's all wrong, in my opinion, but it's true—professional advancement is based primarily upon research, publication, and professional contacts. Overseas, you do tend to lose touch with what's going on in your field, and you have little time for writing or opportunity for research of the type which earns you professional recognition.

You may lose ground at the School—your promotions may suffer, you lose contact with colleagues (many of whom will think you're a fool to go—and some will even tell you so), etc. Even the older faculty, who have tenure, are vulnerable in terms of curriculum, courses, school policy, outside contacts.

And there are other, non-professional sacrifices. The living in Latin America or Asia or Africa is certainly not as comfortable as in Palo Alto. You will find taxis, meals, liquor, and cigarettes (at the Embassy) a good bit cheaper, and your wife can have lots of help—but many things cost more and the help is untrained and the water is questionable and you have to "halizone" the lettuce, and a really good piece of steak is hard to get, and the plumbing won't work and the plumber won't come, and these frustrations become highly irritating when compounded by the language problem.

You miss your friends and worry about what the tenants are doing to your house, and if you are older and your children are in school in the States, you worry about what they are doing and why they can't write and you miss them very much. If they are with you, you find the schools quite poor by California standards. And the poverty is unbelievable and sickening and frustrating because it's so widespread and there's so very little you can do about it. You miss the outside consulting income you might have earned at home. And the big, non-taxable overseas salary you get disappears down the drain in cables, phone calls, extra expenses, and bringing the children down because your wife can't stand not seeing them.

But what's more important? Life is very short and there are many, many things to see and do, and nowhere near enough time to do it. So we have to make the most of the brief period we have allotted to us—have to live every minute, have to cram into it all we can. When we stay at home, particularly if we remain on our academic island, we miss the best of it, we become terribly provincial, terribly protected and isolated from all but a minute fraction of the world and life.

There is a great, big, wonderful, exciting, turbulent world out there and it's going places and you can't feel it, you can't appreciate it, you can't understand it unless you go out and see it for yourself.

An overseas assignment opens up whole new vistas, the world begins to mean far more to you and your family, and especially to your children, who gain thereby a treasure for their whole life. The language is a chore and a frustration, but it's also a challenge, and, ultimately, a thrill and satisfaction of accomplishment and, again, something you can treasure forever.

Your teaching has to be fundamental and practical, and this is good for all of us. Your impact is far greater than at home. You see the "multiplier effect" at work in abundance and for a long time after you have returned home. You are not teaching people who would have "made it" anyway—there is no gilding of the lily. You are teaching people who deeply need what you have to offer and who would have had nothing if you hadn't provided it. You have the thrill of hearing, "You have made us *free men*—the knowledge you have given us has freed us from the social and economic bonds that would have kept us and our children shackled. Now we can do anything." A little flowery, perhaps, but sincere—and satisfying.

You become, I believe, a far better teacher. The emphasis shifts to what the students need, not what the faculty member knows. The language problem forces you to communicate more clearly and more forcibly. Great teaching doesn't come from technical competence. It comes from inspiration, dedication, breadth of experience, perspective. If our mission is to broaden the intellectual horizons of our students, isn't it appropriate that we broaden our own horizons first?

You gain other dividends. One is an opportunity, free from the distraction of committee work, faculty politics, social affairs, magazines, newspapers, TV, and so forth, to stand off and look at your life and your career and your direction in a new perspective, to decide what counts, what is important and what isn't. While you may not come home richer, or higher up the academic ladder than you would have been if you hadn't gone, inevitably you will come home a little wiser—and, I think, a little happier—and more at peace with yourself.

And finally, you get the great thrill of "being in tune," of being a participant instead of an observer, of playing a significant part in the greatest drama of the 20th century, in mankind's greatest achievement, the development of the underdeveloped world.

F. K. S.

EDGARDO REYES SALCIDO

Instituto Tecnológico y de Estudios
Superiores de Monterrey, México

Some Attributes of Effective Technical Assistance Programs in Less Developed Countries

INTRODUCTION

Our experience in Monterrey, Mexico, has been of double value, for we have received as well as given technical assistance. Perhaps in this sense, a few explanatory words of what our school is and the role it plays in Latin American development may be pertinent.

The Institute of Technology and Superior Studies of Monterrey was founded by private enterprises in the City of Monterrey, in response to the urgent demand for human resources in an unlimited, expanding market. In 1942, the most important businessmen of the industrial area of Monterrey gathered in order to contemplate a two-dimensional phenomenon. On the one hand, the technicians who in another era came from the United States and Europe were no longer available to Monterrey industry by virtue of the war; and on the other, the market for products from Monterrey was growing to unlimited dimensions in view of the contraction of peacetime industry by the United States in order to dedicate its forces to the war effort.

EDGARDO REYES SALCIDO is Dean of the Escuela de Graduados en Administración in the Instituto Tecnológico y de Estudios Superiores de Monterrey, México. He has an LLB from the State University of Nuevo León and an MBA from the University of New Mexico. He has been with the Instituto for 12 years. Prior to becoming graduate business school dean three years ago, he was director and later dean of the undergraduate business program at the Instituto. He has participated in numerous management development programs in México and other Latin American countries, and has delivered more than a score of papers before international meetings in Latin America on the subjects of management training, industrial relations, and business education. He has also written extensively on these subjects.

To solve the problem, they decided to found a university with full-time professors and full-time students, away from the national and international political movements and where study and dedication would be the principal determinants of progress and success.

To finance this educational project, more than 90 percent of the enterprises in the region contributed 1.5 percent of their total assets. Thus, on September 6, 1943, the new Institute of Technology and Superior Studies of Monterrey was born. Through the years this Institute has become one of the principal universities in Latin America.

Even though at the beginning the Institute followed the models of American universities, as the years passed the need for adaptation became so pressing that today we have among us a university which has learned to tailor the scientific and technological improvements of the principal American sources to the culture and the accompanying socio-economic environment of Latin America.

Today, the Technological Institute of Monterrey has more than 250 full-time professors, a little more than 5,000 students, and enjoys a well-earned prestige throughout the continent. Nevertheless, although proud of our development and success, we are deficient in many respects.

In the progress of our 25 years we have received aid from a great many universities north of the Rio Grande, and in the last 10 years we have given our modest contribution to the universities of Central and South America.

WE HAVE RECEIVED TECHNICAL ASSISTANCE

Since the Technological Institute is located in an under-developed country, it is easily understood that the eyes of the founders would be directed toward our northern neighbor and that the request for aid would be presented to the major universities of the United States. Universities like Wisconsin, Texas, Houston, Stanford, Harvard, etc., have advised us, have visited us, and have granted scholarships to our faculty members. On occasion, they have sent professors to teach on our campus.

Also, IDB, AID, OAS, UN, and the governments of our neighboring countries to the South have enriched our student body by sending students with scholarships in increasing numbers every year. Furthermore, Stanford, Case-Western Reserve, and Wisconsin have "Junior Year Abroad" programs on our campus.

Our experience as recipients of technical aid is no different from that which has been described at this meeting, and furthermore it fits in perfectly with the description given to you by Dean Reinaldo Scarpetta, of the Universidad del Valle, in Cali, Colombia.

Perhaps it may be of value to mention that my colleague on this panel, Dr. George Simmons, spent one semester with us as visiting professor in the area of Marketing Research; also, our great friend, John Fayerweather, spent a semester with us, in his field of specialization.

In the light of our experience as a recipient of technical assistance, I wish to make six critical observations.

1. *Institutional Relations* We firmly believe that institutional relations should be given priority over relations between individuals. We believe that the best programs are those that establish a tie with an institution in the under-developed world for as long a period as possible. With sorrow, we have seen lamentable incidents of sporadic ties or of poorly-planned ventures, designed at times to take advantage of a grant or to benefit from the opportunity of a contract approved with hastiness and without much thought.[1]

2. *A New School* We believe that under no circumstances can we justify the creation of a new university or a new school with the excuse that in the receiving country there exists none of sufficient caliber to be developed by the institution giving the aid. Institutions created "from scratch" in an underdeveloped country by U. S. universities rarely give good results. They are seen by the local community as foreign entities, like strange beings that do not respond in any manner to the needs, urgencies, and demands of the country in question. We believe that in every case, a careful study of the existing institutions in the receiving country would result in the selection of a deserving institution that can capitalize on the outside help. If it is believed that a country does not have a local institution capable of receiving outside help, the likely explanation is that, at the moment, the country does not need such help—it isn't opportune.

3. *The Need to Adapt* I do not believe that we should view an under-developed country as an "Under-developed United States" or in any case as an "Under-developed Mexico." The slogan of AID, "adapt but not adopt," is very often forgotten in field decisions. Each of our countries has a different culture that makes it more or less receptive to some kind of technical help; a measure of revenue per capita or any other statistical figure does not in itself constitute an

---

[1]All technical aid is a great responsibility to whomever is receiving it; and not all technical assistance is constructive and desirable.

index of the likely degree of receptivity, capacity—and thus success—of technical aid. Without getting into anthropological arguments, we know from experience that each country has unique cultural variables that deserve serious study in a genuine effort to achieve adaptation. Of course, adaptation is not the responsibility only of the giver, or only of the recipient; both must make a sincere and intensive effort to understand the elements in question so that the assistance can have the desired success.

4. *The Able Professor*   After having listened Thursday evening to Dr. Costanzo, Vice President of the First National City Bank, setting forth the personal characteristics that businessmen going overseas on work assignments must possess, I don't understand why similar characteristics are not required of the professors sent forth to our universities by the more developed nations. The task of "cultural fertilization" that the professor accomplishes is just as important, if not more so, than the task with which business executives are entrusted in foreign countries. The intrinsic capacity of a professor in his particular academic field is not enough to guarantee success in such an experiment. If there were a table of values which should be followed in choosing the proper candidates, I think we ought to prefer at all times a less academically prepared person, but with more flexibility and enthusiasm, than an inflexible "high scholar" filled with a sense of self-sufficiency.

5. *The Choice of the Receiving Institution*   I firmly believe that in each country only the best and most capable institutions should be chosen to receive technical assistance. Political factors should not be taken into consideration. It is our experience that contamination by political factors is present to a greater degree in countries being developed than in countries already developed. Nevertheless, the need to rid ourselves of these contaminating factors is essential to the success of the program. A modest and sincere attitude on the part of the professor coming from developed countries is absolutely indispensible to complement the preparation of the local professors. As the visiting professor should be trained for his mission abroad, it is no less important that the professor who will be his colleague in the host institution should also be prepared and trained. Perhaps in the future, new study programs and new techniques will be developed by the universities in both parts of the world, developed and under-developed, to promise more favorable results from technical assistance.

6. *Capacity to Receive Assistance*   In preparing professors and

administrators to receive technical assistance, we should insist on obtaining the approval of the rector or president of the university and all administrative authorities prior to requesting, or accepting, a technical aid project. Only with the sincere and enthusiastic consent of the persons charged with directing and administering the recipient institution can we be assured of a necessary condition for success. A frank evaluation of our capacity for receiving assistance should be made before a project is accepted, if only for the sake of public relations or political exigencies.

There are many other factors that, for lack of time, I will not be able to express during this meeting, but I should like to endorse and agree with the viewpoints presented by other participants.

On the other hand, as I stated at the beginning, the Technological Institute of Monterrey has not only been the recipient of technical assistance through the years, but it has, during the last decade, provided technical aid to our neighboring republics in Central and South America.

WE HAVE GIVEN TECHNICAL ASSISTANCE

One of the programs best known in the United States under which the Technological Institute has given technical aid to other institutions is that provided by a contract that was signed in June of 1959 between Enseñanza e Investigación Superior, A. C. (a non-profit Mexican corporation sponsoring Monterrey Tech) and the International Cooperation Administration (now AID) for the training and guidance of professors and students in universities from other countries in our region. Hundreds of students and nearly 100 professors have come to Monterrey Tech during the nine years of the contract to specialize in a field or to continue a program of training.

Moreover, in July of 1960, the contract between EISAC and AID was extended to cover direct programs of technical assistance and "consultative services," given by Monterrey Tech to many Latin American universities. During the summers, dozens of professors from different departments and schools of Monterrey Tech have visited their neighboring countries to discuss with their colleagues such matters as the formation of curricula and the development of professors, techniques of instruction, and concrete programs consisting of assignments, classes, or courses.

Some other contracts have been signed with international organizations and others directly with Latin American universities; as an example we may cite the contract that for six years existed between the Universidad del Valle, Cali, Colombia, and the Technological Institute of Monterrey for the training of professors in the field of mechanical engineering. We also receive students from Panama in a similar program with the university in that country.

Our experience in these and other programs has brought us to similar conclusions as those presented here, but I would like to refer in particular to several points which are of singular relevance.

1. *School of Administration or Program for Management* It is our experience that the majority of requests for help that we receive from countries being developed, including requests from cities in our own country, specifically request a "School of Administration," yet in most instances the solution is a "Management Course." We believe that the existence of good and productive courses for executives is an essential condition for the subsequent existence of a School of Administration. If after several years an atmosphere has been developed, a market has been created, and the community has been convinced of the need for educating administrators in an academic environment, then is the time that outside technical assistance is opportune for the creation of a School of Administration, whether graduate or undergraduate.

2. *The Authenticity of the Demand* We have found, through the years, that it is difficult to evaluate an authentic need for a new institution, and even more difficult for a Management Course. Very often the demand arises from the good intentions of a person trained in the United States who has detached himself more or less from his home environment. On occasion, political factors detract from the value of a request for aid, making it difficult to assess its justification. We believe that a thorough study should be made to test the presence of an authentic need before measures are taken to plan and execute technical assistance projects. We also believe that additional funds are needed from the foundations and international organizations to support adequate studies of the evaluation of the need for technical assistance in this field.

3. *Availability of Resources* Once the need has been evaluated in the light of the local factors in the host country, we are left with the grave problem of evaluating our own resources. We are opposed to the practice of certain universities which contract instructors for the sole purpose of sending them abroad to boast of the title of a temporary professor at one or another university. A careful assessment of our talents and capacities will very often convince us not to embark on a technical aid project. While the backing of the presi-

dent or rector of the prospective host university is indispensible, it is nonetheless important that we do not damage our own resources to benefit neighboring institutions in other countries. It is true that our institution benefits from all projects of technical assistance, but the cost involved may be too great.

4. *Orientation and Training* I would like to insist once more on a point which we very often refuse to admit. We all need special training to teach and help universities in other countries. Success in the United States does not guarantee a parallel success in countries beyond its borders; our capacity as professors must be complemented by a capacity to understand and appreciate values indigenous to other cultures. In this role, the wife and family of the professor play an important part for which they should be oriented and trained.

5. *Ad Hoc Programs for Foreign Professors* To conclude, I would like to say a few words in opposition to the programs designed especially for foreign professors. It seems to me that the existence of special doctoral degrees for foreigners as offered by some European universities are offensive and violative of academic standards. It is inefficient to design non-credit programs for foreign professors in the United States. I think our colleagues from other countries should be governed by the same regulations and the same rules, and accorded the same dignity, as we would treat our own national colleagues from other institutions. The favors and privileges are needed to facilitate the process of adaptation to the new surroundings, and they should be relinquished by the visiting professor after a relatively short period of time. We should bear in mind that we are working with developed professors even though they come from under-developed countries.

Even though this narration of points could continue indefinitely, I think the main objective of this panel is to seek a greater participation on your part and not to have this turn into a monologue. I would like to conclude by thanking Tulane University and Education and World Affairs for their courtesy in inviting me.

GEORGE B. SIMMONS
University of Massachusetts

Problems in Assisting in the Development of a Business School Abroad

It is obvious, as we have seen, that business schools in the United States have much to offer the process of economic development through technical assistance to developing business schools and management training institutes in the less developed countries. Participation in these technical assistance contracts not only confers, at least in potential, great benefits on the country and the educational institution receiving this assistance, but it also provides the granting institution with an opportunity to realize obvious direct, and perhaps more subtle indirect, benefits. Most of these are well known: foreign travel for the faculty, the development and refinement of course material exposed to a new cultural setting, the stimulation of foreign students on the campus, expanded opportunities for research in economic development and international business, etc.

With, however, so much to be gained from participation in technical assistance, we cannot help but note that many of these ventures have failed to come anywhere close to their initial expectations, and many others have, rightly or wrongly, been considered failures, even though the criteria for evaluation are sadly lacking in operational terms. We should therefore look at this problem in terms of what

GEORGE B. SIMMONS is Director of the Center for Business and Economic Research, and Associate Professor of Business Administration, School of Business Administration, University of Massachusetts. His MBA and DBA degrees are from Indiana University. Prior to joining the U-Mass. faculty, he was on the Columbia business faculty for four years. In 1965, he served as Chief of Party for the Columbia University program at the Universidad de Buenos Aires. In 1962, he taught a seminar in marketing research at the Centro de Productividad de Monterrey (México), and in 1964 he taught marketing management at the Universidad de Buenos Aires. Together with Charles F. Stewart, he wrote *A Bibliography of International Business* (Columbia University Press, 1964).

the contribution of the U. S. school can, and should, be. What benefits from participation in the program can the assisting school most reasonably expect? What problems may develop? What understanding should the several parties to the agreement have in order to minimize conflict and maximize the likelihood of substantial accomplishment?

The optimal contribution of the established business school will, obviously, vary with the type of arrangement and the environment in which the development process is intended to operate. If, for example, the U. S. school is asked to come into a situation in which there is a clear commitment to modernization in this direction, and in which the principal decision-makers in the developing institution are reasonably sophisticated about what type of end product they desire, the assisting school might very well restrict, if that's the proper word, its contribution to the more technical aspects of course materials, program organization, case collection techniques, and a reasonable supply of teachers and books. Here the assisting institution attempts merely to make available to the host school the same type of educational program that it offers at home. In this setting it hopefully does not have to come to grips with the problems of adaptability to a different culture, this process of translation being taken care of within the host institution. Most business school faculties who have had experience in these programs would, I believe, find this arrangement, whether or not they consider it desirable, to be something of an "ideal." Clear separation of responsibilities, calling on each of the cooperating partners to operate in his own realm of competence, does not usually square with the complexities of interpersonal relations and organizational realities that are magnified in a cross-cultural setting.

A more common situation, and one that may lead to a more or less permanent state of frustration, finds the assisting school in a position of supplying not only technical detail, but also shaping and promoting the goals of the developing institution. In this case the host faculty is not prepared to receive assistance in its most technical form. Rather, it requires an analysis of its own mission and the development of a program suitable to the goals so derived. This poses a most interesting problem for the business school having an assistance contract, particularly if it is new to this area of activity. How, for example, is finance to be taught meaningfully to students in a country with a poorly developed capital market and a chronically high (by U. S. standards) rate of inflation? Obviously, there are rules of behavior appropriate to any environmental setting, but the instructor and his text books, oriented as they are to the U. S. domestic setting, may be particularly inappropriate to this task. Thus, developing the most meaningful course content may require extensive research into the pattern of economic activities of which the developing institution aspires to be an influential part. This may, indeed, be a much larger task than the contract envisaged, but it clearly is one that must be accomplished if the project is to make any sense.

From this type of observation we may derive a general statement that the assisting school must, if it is to make an effective contribution, analyze in some detail the system in which its counterpart school is going to operate, and thereby form a basis for designing its proposed pattern of operation. This is certainly not a hopeless task, but it does require more time and work than may be expected by many schools embarking on this mission.

We should not expect to find continued, and enthusiastic, support at home (by, say, the faculty, administration, and other interested parties) unless the benefits to the assisting school are widely understood. To become so understood they must be articulated in terms that are interesting to various parties on the home campus; specifically the technical assistance programs should offer some good prospects for substantial research as well as contributions to development of programs on the U. S. campus. Very often, assistance work may be expressly linked with programs in international business administration. This may or may not be realistic, depending on how each is handled and the nature of the relationship between the two. Quite clearly, sending U. S. professors abroad for a two-week lecture tour on their favorite topic is not going to turn them into authorities on the way business is conducted in the host country. Even worse, it may cause them to form narrow and naive ideas on how hopelessly great the gap between domestic and foreign culture and business practice appears to be. On the other hand, if the tours are generally of a longer duration and allow, or specify, that the teaching function will accompany or follow systematic research into the local environment, the program may contribute substantially to the professional development of individual faculty members in new and useful areas of competence.

From another point of view the development of an instructional program away from campus may provide an opportunity to experiment with new aproaches and materials that may be more difficult to introduce in the established procedures at home. This should not suggest that the developing institution should be used as a guinea pig for poorly reasoned, though novel, ideas; the problems of cross-cultural transfer of information are too great in themselves to permit such carefree experimentation. The challenge of developing a new program may, however, provide a very nice setting in which new pedagogical techniques, as well as new patterns of organizing course material, may be introduced. When the faculty see the overseas program in terms of this more pervasive configuration, its attraction hopefully will assume a form substantially exceeding that of the diversion of tourism combined with occasional speaking obligations. If this state can be realized, the program may then count on the continuing and enthusiastic support of the interested and important groups on the home campus.

The most significant problems have arisen in technical assistance contracts and have had their roots in two oversights:

1. Failure to develop, prior to the commencement of the project, a sophisticated analysis of the system in which the developing institution will function, as briefly discussed above, and

2. Failure to determine a set of operational goals that can be used to develop policies and procedures, and most importantly, to evaluate the progress of the program on a continuing basis.

It is obviously not very helpful to state the objectives of technical assistance in such terms as "helping the less developed country to progress economically" or "assisting in the development of a strong system of higher education." These are, of course, related to the end goals of the activity, but they are not very helpful in reaching the types of decisions that will have to be made as the program progresses. At the other extreme, it is hardly more realistic to express objectives in terms of operating details (e. g., number and names of courses to be given, amount to be spent on books, size of resident staff, number of foreign students to be trained, etc.) without relating these activities, in operational terms, to the impact they will have on the system that represents both the environment and the object of technical assistance. The setting of specific goals in these programs must follow the analysis of the environment, and they must be so stated that they relate individual program activities to a state of "terminal behavior" that is acceptable, and meaningful, to the higher aspirations of the technical assistance agreement. Thus, the process of goal-setting must look ahead to the termination date (which should be very clearly understood), developing a description of what the developing institution should be at that date. The attainment of this description within the time allowed thus becomes the basis for setting lower-order goals, policies, and procedures. If the direction in which the program is to move is not understood and accepted from the beginning, the already obvious problems of cross-cultural communication can be magnified to the point that little progress can be made toward a mutually satisfactory end.

Attendant to the process of goal definition is the necessity of allocating various responsibilities to the cooperating parties involved. Primarily these would be the school offering the technical assistance and the developing institution; however, in many cases, an equally important partner may very well be the sponsoring agency. The most likely difficulty relating to the allocation of responsibility would be the prospect that more than one of the cooperating institutions might claim jurisdiction over the same area of decision. A commonplace example might be the question of who decides which students from the host institution are to be sent to the United States for graduate study.

Perhaps a more dangerous area of oversight, however, would be the failure to allocate exhaustively all of the areas of responsibility that must be covered. This can have a most debilitating effect, when, say, each of the schools believes, or acts as if it believes, that decisions on program content should rest with the other. The U. S. school may, for example, feel that it is in no position to outline the overall program, being more suited to supplying specific information when specific needs have been articulated. At the same time the host institution may feel that the assisting school is doing less than a complete job if it fails to come up with solutions to some of the more difficult policy problems.

Obviously there cannot be a clear-cut set of general rules for the successful management of a technical assistance project for the development of a business school that will contribute substantially to the development of its economy and society. Each situation must be evaluated in terms of the inputs that each cooperating institution can provide, and the effect that these inputs, when combined, can have on bettering the system in which the developing school will operate. Furthermore, as is well known, the attitudes and motivations of individuals influencing the contribution and activities of participating schools may vary over a wide range, thereby introducing an even greater degree of uncertainty as to the form the outcome will take.

EDWARD L. ELLIOTT

University of Illinois

Some Guidelines for the Conduct of Overseas Activities

Participation of the U. S. Government in world affairs is not of recent origin. As a Latin American, I shall refer to the Monroe Doctrine, issued in 1823, by which the United States indicated its intention to participate actively in the affairs of the nations of the Western Hemisphere. U. S. citizens, however, have only recently begun to realize that world affairs is something in which they, as individuals, should also participate. This recent awareness can be attributed to the fact that improvement in transportation and communication methods has led to an effective narrowing of the world's dimensions, thus making it necessary for nations situated thousands of miles apart to become aware of each other's problems. The recent global political climate has also increased the degree of interdependence. The economic competition for friends in the world political arena is a present and significant fact of the contemporary international scene.

Improvement in transportation and communication methods has

EDWARD L. ELLIOTT is Assistant Professor of Accountancy in the College of Commerce and Business Administration, University of Illinois. He has MS and PhD degrees from the University of Illinois. In 1960-61, he worked in the cost accounting department of Creole Petroleum Corporation, Maracaibo, Venezuela. In 1965-66, he served as director for economics and business administration at the University of Guayaquil, Ecuador, and set up a School of Business Administration and Accounting which began to function in 1966. During 1966, he was an economic advisor to the government of Ecuador under a USAID contract, working directly with the Minister of Finance on budgeting, accounting, and fiscal policy. In 1966-67, he was economic advisor to the Dominican Republic, also under a USAID contract, with similar duties as in Ecuador. His dissertation, 'The Nature and Stages of Accounting Development in Latin America," will soon be published by the Center for International Education and Research in Accounting, at the University of Illinois.

also exposed the inhabitants of less-developed countries to the higher standards of living of the more advanced nations. In an effort to "reach the Joneses" they are no longer willing to accept "ignorance, poverty and disease as the natural course of events" but instead are looking for ways and means to obtain economic advancement.

Economic advancement, however, depends to a large degree upon education. Human resources must be capable of administering, in an efficient manner, the material resources of nations.

At this reunion we are concerned with Education for International Business. This topic, however, could be broken down into two major areas:

1. Education for U. S. citizens in the U. S. A. and/or abroad.
2. Education for foreigners:
   (1) In the U. S. A.
   (2) In their home countries.

Our task on this panel is to discuss strategies for overseas activities. This task is, therefore, directly related to sub-classification (2) of education for foreigners.

The word "international" at the present time appears to possess a degree of magic or prestige which makes involvement in international affairs a type of special goal to be attained. As a result, many U. S. universities are actively engaged in the pursuit of contracts to help educational institutions in the developing countries, and I believe that we are in agreement as to the desirability of helping these foreign institutions to develop programs in the business area (our topic today).

Within the developing nations a stress on education for the "noble" professions (medicine, law, and engineering) has not fostered the advancement of a group of professionals capable of meeting the business needs of a developing economy. In fact, in many of the countries, business as a university program is of very recent origin. In the past, business knowledge was acquired through experience in the tightly controlled family enterprise, and access to this knowledge was limited to the sons or family of the proprietor.

If we accept the idea that business growth will be a necessary factor in economic development and that the evolution of a capable managerial class is a prerequisite for business growth, then it follows that high priority must be given to the provision of courses relating to business education, preferably at university level.

The gaining of knowledge through experience is too time-consuming to meet the pressing needs existing in many of the countries. U. S. universities have had long experience with business education and are, therefore, well-qualified to assist in the development of business programs in other countries.

Contracts to assist other universities should not be undertaken, however, for the supposed "prestige" involved in international activities. The signing of contracts and reports on foreign activities makes "nice" articles in the home-town newspaper and may even serve to enhance the standing of the university in the local community, but these selfish motives should not be the reason for "going international."

The following are some of my opinions on the conduct of overseas activities:

1. The program abroad should have the full support of the administration.

   (a) It should be an integral part of the university's activities. Faculty members on foreign assignments should have the same opportunity for promotions and salary increases as those who remain at home.

   (b) Timely decisions must be made on all problems which occur in conducting the program. The use of a coordinator for administering foreign programs is quite common. This individual, however, must be available for visiting the host country on short notice. Solutions to urgent problems cannot and must not be deferred until the coordinator can find time from his normal duties. Such a delay may compound the lack of coordination and thus result in further problems for the administration to handle.

   (c) Materials requested by the faculty should be shipped promptly. Anyone who has been engaged in foreign operations can testify to the importance of this point. Materials for classroom use are almost non-existent and have to be secured in the United States. Delays in the acquisition of requested materials coupled with delays in mail delivery frequently lead to receipt after the period for which they are required.

   (d) At times it will be necessary for the administering institution to spend some of its own money on the program. On signing a contract, efforts should be made to include all costs involved. Frequently, however, "hidden" costs occur. Programs should not be allowed to deteriorate because the contract did not provide for these "hidden" costs.

2. The administering institution should consider capable students from the host country for fellowships and assistantships at the U. S. campus. In other words, contract funds should not be the only source for enabling capable students of the host institution to pursue graduate work in the United States. In this connection, I believe that schools offering undergraduate as well as graduate programs are in a better position to offer financial assistance since the student can often be utilized in the undergraduate program.

3. The administering institution should utilize the same criteria for admitting students of the host institution as those used for admitting other foreign candidates. "Inside knowledge" of the host institution's programs should not be used in evaluating the candidate. The use of "inside knowledge" has created some embarrassing situations. Candidates accepted at the administering institution have been placed on "special" programs, while other graduates of the host institution have been accepted for full graduate study at accredited U. S. universities. The student on the "special" program, upon learning of these differences, resents the "preferential" treatment which he receives.

4. Faculty assigned to the host country should be individuals who would be considered for similar employment on the home campus.

Frequently, contracts are accepted without adequate consideration being given to staffing requirements. The difficulties involved in getting qualified individuals to accept teaching positions are underestimated, and as a result, the administering institution often finds itself in a very awkward position. To meet its obligations many undesirable practices are used. Two of these follow:

(a) Faculty members are hired on a first-come basis without adequate screening procedures.

(b) Graduate students are sent to the host country as "professors," and are not properly supervised in carrying out their duties.

This is one of the biggest problem areas in overseas programs. The damage done by unqualified personnel is frequently irreparable and continues to occur throughout the contract period.

5. Professors assigned to a project should have a *working* knowledge of the language.

Before being sent to the host country, a professor should be required to demonstrate proficiency in the language. This does not imply fluency, but it does mean that complete ignorance of the language should not be tolerated.

Language classes in the host country involve a considerable loss of time from contract activities and in most cases do not result in future benefits since the individual generally does not acquire a working knowledge of the language until his tour of duty is nearly completed.

Simultaneous translation is, in the opinion of the author, a poor substitute for personal communication. It places too much reliance on the ability of the translator, especially where a technical vocabulary is in use.

6. Contracts should be clearly drafted so that all interested individuals can determine:

(a) what will be provided by the administering university.

(b) what will be provided by the host institution.

(c) what counterparts will be assigned,

(i) to take over teaching duties,

(ii) to assist in program administration.

Moreover, each department of the host institution in which contract activities are performed should receive a copy of the sections of the contract with which it is concerned. This is necessary since contracts covering activities to be performed in several departments are usually signed at the top-administration level. Unless the individual departments are conscious of their responsibilities under the contract, problems will frequently arise.

7. Finally, we should always try to cooperate with an existing institution in the host country. This may present numerous problems which could be eliminated through the establishment of one or more separate schools under the direction of a U. S. university. It is evident that such schools would be able

to initiate rules, standards, programs, etc. without the opposition frequently encountered at existing institutions when proposals for changes are presented. However, these "separately administered" schools often create friction between the U. S. university and the local institutions. This friction affects the students as well as the administration, and may even be reflected in the employment market, where preference has sometimes been given to graduates of local institutions who according to the employers are more easily assimilated into the local business environment. Moreover, I feel that the development of programs within an established institution would better ensure the continuing success of the program after the departure of the administering institution.

THOMAS A. GRAVES, JR.

Harvard University

Lessons Learned from Stanford's ESAN Project

Dean Grayson referred earlier to the thirty-four strategies enumerated in the *EWA Report*. I shall focus on No. 34, the Acceptance of Technical Assistance Contracts to Establish Schools Abroad. This is the top of the grand strategies.

The *EWA Report* presents a very clear warning to those who are considering this level of involvement:

> The grand strategy should be considered only by the most affluent schools . . . . If only because a school's span of attention and span of control have finite limits that are not known until they are exceeded, more difficulties have arisen out of participation in programs abroad than in any other activity.

> If a school is to become engaged in an institution-building effort abroad, it should do so gradually and only after full exploration and inquiry at home and abroad. . . . Many schools currently feel pressured to *do something* in international business. The most visible activity consists of technical assistance programs abroad. But they are easy to turn on and hard to shut off. (pp. 61-63)

With this warning in mind, I am going to focus my remarks on the experience we have had during the past five years at Stanford

THOMAS A. GRAVES, JR., is Associate Dean for Educational Administration, Harvard Business School. He has MBA and DBA degrees from Harvard. During most of the 1950s, he served in numerous administrative capacities at the Harvard Business School. In 1960, he became director of the IMEDE Management Development Institute, Lausanne, Switzerland, leaving in 1964 to join the Stanford University business school as Associate Dean in charge of the school's international activities, including directorship of the International Center for the Advancement of Management Education (ICAME). He returned to Harvard in 1967. He has written articles for several professional journals on business education and management development.

University, in accepting a technical assistance contract with the Agency for International Development (AID) and the Peruvian Government for establishing a graduate school of business, ESAN, in Lima, Peru. For the past three years, until this fall when I moved from Stanford to Harvard, I was Campus Coordinator under the contract at Stanford for the ESAN project.

ESAN is now five years old; it is a strong, healthy educational institution, making good progress toward becoming a fully Peruvian graduate school of business of high quality. In reaching this stage, we have faced just about every problem in the book, and we have been fortunate to have found some of the solutions.

I shall try to suggest the major pitfalls and problem areas we have been able to identify in administering this contract at ESAN and Stanford, and perhaps these problems will suggest some of the factors for success. I hope that these remarks may have some relevance to the strategy decisions which your schools may be facing. But let me warn you that each situation and experience is unique, and it is difficult and perhaps dangerous to generalize too far.

Now to the pitfalls and potential problems. First, before you consider seriously entering into a contract to take responsibility for establishing a major school like ESAN overseas, look carefully at this opportunity in terms of the resources and interests of your own school and faculty. "International" is "in" these days, so don't be misled by superficial enthusiasm. Is your faculty really internationally minded, in terms of man-years abroad, not in terms of the guide trip? Is the reward system at your school, for faculty recognition and promotion, geared to work overseas? The answer is very likely "No" to this second question, so can you and your faculty really live with this fact of academic life? Do your faculty members have some real competence for this particular opportunity—in terms of language, cultural understanding, experience? Living and working in Lima, under the best of circumstances, is a lot different from Palo Alto! Can you staff this program with your top faculty members, without hurting at home? The opportunity costs are very real. You may not find complete answers to these questions before you move ahead, but let me simply suggest that it is important that these questions be raised and answered to your satisfaction before you move into the first stage of the project.

And this first stage should be a careful, realistic, feasibility study. It is essential that before you sign the contract, you determine as well as you can if the project is do-able in the local environment. Does the local government really want to support this new school, and will the government have the stability and longevity to continue to support it during the school's early, tenuous years? Is the business community behind the school, in terms of demand for its graduates and in terms of the eventual financial support from local business firms? Also, is the local academic community interested in cooperating with this new school intruding from the outside, whether it is to be affiliated with an established institution or to be independent? Finally, is the basic plan for the new school realistic, in terms of the local culture, relationships, demands, and problems? To get honest answers to these questions before the contract is signed, it is important that the feasibility study be thorough and careful to the extreme, conducted at least in part by objective faculty members from your own school who can relate this opportunity and its pitfalls to the resources and interests of your school. A feasibility study conducted by a too-enthusiastic proponent or advocate of the project can get you into trouble.

So now you are at the contract stage. If you are contracting with AID or the Ford Foundation, remember that you are negotiating with very experienced and competent people; they would expect you to be represented by equally able men. Be sure that the contract provides for enough money and enough time. The project is going to take much more of both than you think. And even more important, the contract should be flexible, should provide for the unknowns and the unexpected; no matter how good your crystal ball, you are going to be amazed at the unforeseen events which are going to arise, sooner than you think! Also, be sure that all parties to the contract, especially the local government and the local university, understand their responsibilities under the contract. Finally, get to know your contract administrators well, at AID, at the Ford Foundation, in the local government; these men are important and you are going to be working very closely with them for weeks, months, and years ahead.

A fourth area for serious attention focuses on the importance of starting the school with your top faculty and administrators. The director of the new school and the campus coordinator are key men, and those whom you choose set the image of the new school at home and abroad, and they set the stage for success or failure. At ESAN and Stanford we were very fortunate indeed to have Professor Alan B. Coleman as the first *Decano* of ESAN and Professor Gail M. Oxley as the first Campus Coordinator: They made the difference. At the same time, make every effort to involve your own faculty, both at the start and on a continuing basis, in the school. Every faculty member at the new school you are administering need not be one of your own, but there must be enough of them, at a high level of competence and status, to provide an image for the new school, at home and abroad, which will greatly enhance its chances for success.

If you choose your faculty wisely, you do not need to be concerned about the next pitfall—trying to transplant the United States overseas or talking down to the local nationals. The new school, to be successful, must respond to local needs, problems, opportunities, and resources. Take your time to find out what these are, on the spot, before you open your doors to your first students. And based upon this study, make your curriculum relevant, applicable, and meaningful for the students that the new school is to serve. Then be ready to change this curriculum at any time; you are inevitably going to make a lot of mistakes, and your faculty must be flexible in responding to the environment as they come to know it better. Just because a particular approach worked well at Stanford is not necessarily an argument that it will work well at ESAN. Respond to the interests of the local nationals; they may well know what is best, better than you do!

Then there is the question of standards and performance, which may be very difficult. State-side standards and expectations of performance may well have little relevance, if applied rigidly, in the new school, especially if it is in a developing country. At the same time, it is very likely that you are going to be under pressure to lower the teaching and learning level of the new school to a point where you can no longer live with your own view of professional conduct and where you are no longer making a contribution. Remember that the chances are good that your school has been invited to start a new school because existing standards in the local academic community were too low. So somehow, through what will be trial and error, set standards and expectations that are reasonably and realistically high, taking into account both the culture in which you are working and your own mission in being there.

Just as soon as possible, involve the local community in the new school—business, education, and government. Your job is to get in there and then get out as soon as feasible. This is their show, and the sooner and more completely the local businessmen, local government officials, and local educators become involved in a responsible and active way, the better your job will have been done.

The other side of this coin, of course, is not to move too fast. Institution-building is a long, slow, hard, and frustrating process.

You wouldn't have been asked to undertake it if it were easy. So you can only hope that the faculty members you have out there (and their wives) have patience, wisdom, tolerance, and like to live overseas for extended periods.

Finally, in a project like ESAN, communications between the new school and the home campus are critical. These communications must be frequent and clear. Problems loom a lot larger thousands of miles from home in a strange environment and what seems at times a peculiar culture. Little problems can all too easily become crises. It is the essential job of the Campus Coordinator, working with the director of the new school, to avoid these crises by keeping communications wide open at all times, by letter, cable, telephone, and not-infrequent visits. Handholding by transcontinental phone is not an unusual occurrence.

So the new school is progressing well; the major problems have been solved; the local nationals are really starting to take over in a responsible way; and your faculty members feel good because of the individual experiences they have had overseas. So what does this really mean to your school? What feedback has there been to your curriculum, your research, your teaching and learning? It is important that there be substantive and positive answers to these questions if you are to judge this experience in institution-building overseas on contract a success.

Let me briefly summarize the factors for success which may be suggested by the examination of the pitfalls and potential problems discussed earlier:

- A faculty at home that is ready for and interested in internationalism, at the grand strategy level.
- A careful, objective feasibility study.
- A realistic and flexible contract.
- A top faculty and administration in the new school, from the start.
- A faculty and curriculum in the new school that responds to local needs, culture, and resources.
- High standards of performance that are also reasonable and realistic.
- Early and continuing involvement of the local community, business, government, and education.
- A realistically slow pace in light of the job to be done.
- Clear and continuing communications between the new school and the home campus.

— Feedback and contribution from the institution-building experience to the home institution.

Despite the very real warning set forth in the *EWA Report*, there are tremendous opportunities for American business schools to assist in the development of education for business overseas. Institution-building is a difficult but rewarding role, as we have found at ESAN. Dr. Alan Coleman says that if he had known in advance of all these pitfalls in starting ESAN, he might not have accepted the job. But he and his successor, Dr. Sterling Sessions, were ready to give ESAN the leadership it needed, and the Stanford Business School was ready to support ESAN to the extent necessary to assure its success. If you feel your school is also ready, go ahead. It's an experience that has significant benefits, both here and abroad.

THOMAS M. HILL

Massachusetts Institute of Technology

Institution-Building in India

In accepting the assignment of panelist, I agreed to make some brief opening remarks. Knowing that this panel discussion would be immediately preceded by three prepared talks, it seemed quite unlikely that my comments would be needed as a basis for discussion and quite likely that they would be to some extent repetitive. Having listened to Messrs. Carmichael, Haynes, and Scarpetta, I now know that I was right on both counts.

I find it interesting, however, that the questions raised by Dean Carmichael on the basis of his observations of management education institution-building in Latin America are strikingly similar to those which I had intended to present as arising out of my observation of the same process in India. This suggests that there are in fact certain culturally independent problems generic to the institution-building process and/or to the utilization of foreign professional assistance in connection therewith. Let me, therefore, comment on the relevance of his comments to the Indian situation.

Excluding such indirect (but by no means trivial) assistance as has been rendered through teacher-training programs – ICAME at

THOMAS M. HILL is Professor of Management in the Alfred P. Sloan School of Management, Massachusetts Institute of Technology. He has an MBA from Harvard University. From 1961 to 1963, he headed the MIT Advisory Group to the Indian Institute of Management, Calcutta. He has been a consultant to various industrial enterprises, principally in New England. He has written two books and several articles, mainly in managerial accounting. In the last few years, he has continued to advise the Indian Institute of Management as well as the Indian Institute of Technology, Kanpur. In collaboration with Warren Haynes, he is beginning a study of the management education institution-building process. In its initial stage, the project will consist of a number of in-depth case studies of Indian institutions, as a basis for generating hypotheses as to some of the critical variables.

Stanford[1] and ITP at Harvard[2]—American technical aid to India in respect to management education has been heavily concentrated on the national Institutes of Management in Ahmedabad and Calcutta. The cooperating American universities have been, respectively, Harvard and MIT, and the source of dollar support has been the Ford Foundation. I have worked with the Calcutta Institute since 1961, have followed closely concurrent developments at Ahmedabad, and, to the extent possible, have kept in touch with the activities of other Indian institutions concerned with management development. My present opinions, which I recognize to be somewhat impressionistic, are based on these observations.

Dean Carmichael's criticism as regards deficiency of feedback from overseas to domestic programs is clearly pertinent to both Harvard and MIT in respect to their Indian affiliations. While working in India has no doubt had some "internationalizing" effect on those faculty members directly involved, in neither case has there been any significant integration of foreign and domestic activities. The nearest approach to this has been limited utilization by MIT of the Calcutta Institute as a base for doctoral research. As a result, participation in these institution-building projects continues to be generally regarded by the Harvard Business School and Sloan School of Management faculties as a form of social service, probably desirable but sharply divergent from the main stream of professional activities conducive to either personal or institutional development in the domestic context.

If I correctly interpret Dean Carmichael's second point, he suggests that the capacity of the American university system for effective technical aid is probably less than has been implied by our past efforts, and that we might maximize the impact of such assistance as we can render by concentrating future efforts where they can be expected to have a substantial multiplier effect—that is, by helping to develop a smaller number of very strong, strategically located institutions which would ultimately propagate their own kind. I agree.

The Indian Institutes of Management were intended to be, and continue to show promise of becoming, precisely this kind of institution, and my only present regret on this score is that there are two rather than one. Had there been but a single faculty, or were the present two merged at this juncture, the resulting institution would

1[A discussion of the International Center for the Advancement of Management Education (ICAME) appears on pp. 240-44 of this volume. — Ed.]
2[A brief discussion of the International Teachers Program (ITP) appears on pp. 253-54 of this volume. — Ed.]

have, I believe, very nearly the requisite capacity to provide effective development assistance to others. It is at least intuitively plausible that such indigenous capacity could be more efficiently utilized than can American aid.

It is, I think, of some interest and relevance to note that, as of 1959, the plan was for a single such institute to be located in Bombay and "backstopped" by an American university which was neither MIT nor Harvard. The difference between the 1959 plan and the 1960 actuality can, I suspect, be attributed largely to inability of the Ford Foundation, which had been actively engaged in selling the American management education model, to start imposing restrictive conditions immediately after completion of the sale. Such loss of control at the critical initiation stage may be a normal concomitant of a strategy whereby any development aid agency is cast in the dual role of promoter and financier.

I agree also that our technical aid objectives have been too limited (Dean Carmichael's third point) if we have in fact been generally satisfied with helping new management schools to develop only to some level of capability inferior to our own. I am unwilling to admit to any such deliberate mal-intent in the Indian situation, but I will concede that neither Harvard nor MIT appears, in retrospect, to have sufficiently emphasized the research component of the teaching cum research mix—which fact bears heavily on their aforenoted failure to integrate their activities in India with those at home.

In this connection, Ford Foundation policy should be mentioned. While giving a certain amount of lip service to the need for research, the Foundation has not been—and, to the best of my knowledge, is not now—at all anxious to support the training of Indian faculty to the doctoral level—which is probably a generally necessary, although obviously not sufficient, condition for the promotion of management research in India.

As to Dean Carmichael's criticism of the one-to-one institutional relationship strategy, my hearty concurrence is a matter of record. In an unpublished discussion paper entitled "Management Education in India",[3] I have said that such pairing arrangements seemed to me to have the undesirable effects of: (1) making faculty membership in the affiliate so important a criterion in the selection of American advisors as to result in the occasional waiver of what are really much more vital considerations; (2) encouraging, at least in the Ahmedabad

---

3An excerpt from this paper is included in an appendix.

case, a form of faculty in-growth by excessive reliance on a single source of training, and (3) creating an unhealthy, excessively personalized junior-senior relationship conducive to inter-institutional friction.

I should add that, presumably in recognition of these deficiencies, all four institutions are currently seeking to broaden the contacts of the Indian Institutes with the larger American management education community.

Finally, in support of Dean Carmichael's argument that more attention need be given to the development of administrative "know-how" in institution-building, I can say that the principal internal difficulties encountered by the Calcutta Institute (you are perhaps aware that the political situation in West Bengal poses some rather interesting external problems) appear to have been very largely attributable to administrative deficiencies. I am now convinced that we need be much concerned with the management of education, as distinguished from and as an essential prerequisite to the education of managers— which concession I would expect to be well received by an audience composed largely of deans.

APPENDIX

Management Education in India: American Aid in Retrospect*

The task assigned to the two Institutes was that of introducing to India a field of postgraduate study not only new to that part of the world but also peculiarly dependent on educational methods radically different from those employed in the Indian universities. The necessity for relying on the country of origin for both organizational models and faculty cadres familiar with those models was therefore unavoidable, and the relevant question was not as to the need for American aid but as to the means for obtaining it. The mechanisms elected for this purpose—specifically, a pair of one-to-one American-Indian institutional affiliations—have not proved entirely satisfactory. The difficulties experienced can no doubt be attributed in part to normal human fallibility, but stem more largely, I believe, from weaknesses inherent in the support system itself.

---

*Excerpt from unpublished paper, "Management Education in India," by Thomas M. Hill.

The critical needs have been for (1) American advisory service in India and (2) Indian faculty procurement and/or training in the United States. Satisfaction of the first of these logically calls for the careful selection of individuals who are qualified by age, experience, professional status, and, perhaps most important, interest and temperament for the specialized task of constructively influencing the development of an organization from a non-authoritative position in that organization. The second requires, ideally, creation of an Indo-American management education community by establishing direct channels of communication between the Indian Institutes and the largest possible number of their American counterparts.

The institutional-pairing arrangements here employed served to encourage the presumption that each of the new Institutes should tie itself closely to, and model itself exactly on, its American partner. As regards the selection of advisors, a natural consequence was that faculty membership in the affiliate was seen, on both sides, as an important criterion. Given the shortage of persons otherwise qualified, coupled with the fact that the job afforded no generally recognized opportunity for professional advancement, this highly restrictive requirement could not always be met without waiving others probably more vital. The general effect has been to promote replication in India of the Harvard Graduate School of Business Administration and the Alfred P. Sloan School of Management. Indian interests might, I now believe, have been better served by efforts to reproduce selected characteristics of both these and other American institutions, coupled with greater emphasis on educational experimentation.

In respect to faculty development, the direction of effort has differed in the two cases. The Calcutta Institute has relied heavily on MIT help to recruit in the United States Indians holding American doctoral degrees, and it has so far done relatively little in the way of training. Until recently, the Ahmedabad Institute had recruited largely within India and had sent most of those so recruited to Harvard for a year of further study. Both methods served reasonably well to meet initial staffing requirements, but neither is a suitable means of satisfying continuing development needs.

Foreign recruitment alone is clearly insufficient and, moreover, because the recruiting agency function is incompatible with other academic activities, is both inefficient and burdensome as heretofore practiced. On the other hand, such group training as any single American school can feasibly offer to any foreign affiliate is deficient on two counts: (1) because training up to the doctoral level is now wanted for an increasing number of younger men and (2) because uniform exposure of any large segment of a given faculty to any single pedagogical system has come to be seen as a form of undesirable in-growth.

A more subtle but nonetheless real cause for criticism is a certain artificiality in the inter-institutional "partnership." Despite any individual intentions to the contrary, the group attitudes that emerge are not, as presumably intended, those normally found in an association of peers. They seem, in fact, much more like those commonly present in the parent-child relationship. The senior is well informed concerning the junior's affairs, feels personally responsible for the latter's actions (which are seen as reflecting on the senior), and is therefore under compulsion to criticize any unacceptable behavior; but the junior is not in a position and is not expected to reciprocate in kind. In the institutional situation, the consequences are, on the one hand, a frustrating sense of responsibility unsupported by any real authority and, on the other, an annoying consciousness of ill-defined inferiority. The tensions thus created cannot but adversely affect the more vital inter-personal relations of the Americans and Indians who must work closely together to achieve the common goals.

Two desirable characteristics of the one-to-one support plan probably explain its adoption. On the one hand, it is administratively simple, and was therefore quickly and easily put into effect. On the other, it contributed, perhaps significantly, to initial acceptance of the Indian Institutes by identifying them with established educational institutions of some international repute. Whether or not these essentially short-run advantages justified the original decision, they are now largely irrelevant and, to my mind at least, heavily outweighed by the aforenoted disadvantages. An alternative arrangement which appears to meet some of the stated objections is the consortium mechanism currently employed for pooling the resources of nine American engineering schools in development support of the Indian Institute of Technology at Kanpur. There are, however, other possibilities which might serve even better.

❀   ❀   ❀   ❀   ❀

First, there is need for the formation of a voluntary association of those Indian institutions desirous and capable of operating in this new field of professional study. The immediate purposes of such an association would be, on the one hand, mutual reinforcement in the pursuit of such common and presumably non-competitive objectives as development of teaching materials and university teacher training

— 191 —

and, on the other, achievement of economies of scale and benefits of diversification by drawing as a group on the resources of an increased number of American schools.

Given such an association, I think it would be feasible to establish a communication network linking these Indian affiliates with a substantial cross-section of American management education. As previously suggested by reference to the Kanpur case, an institutional consortium might serve this purpose. I believe, however, that given institutional endorsements in lieu of contractual commitments, it could be equally well accomplished by a more flexible and economical organization of strategically located individuals. This conclusion is based on observations (1) that performance on inter-institutional aid commitments usually depends on the efforts of a very small number of interested persons and (2) that analogous arrangements have worked well, albeit on a smaller scale than here contemplated, in support of certain European educational ventures.*

The proposed system, by substituting a several-to-several for two or more one-to-one relationships, would greatly enlarge the resources potentially applicable in any given period to a similarly expanded set of needs. As a result, the probabilities of successfully matching available resources—specially qualified advisors, Indian faculty recruits, openings for faculty trainees—with concurrent needs would be significantly increased. At the same time, certain wasteful duplication of effort—as in the multiple screening of the same universe of Indian faculty prospects in the United States—would be eliminated.

While such a system might be promoted on a purely "service to India" basis, widespread dissatisfaction of American universities with the contributions of their prior "technical aid" activities to domestic programs suggests that its marketability would be considerably enhanced by high promise of useful feedback. The key to achieving the mutual benefit probably essential to any highly effective and long-continuing Indo-American educational association is, I am convinced, markedly increased emphasis on the research component. There being no dearth of relevant problems associated with economic development (including the rapid development of managerial capacity), the principal requirements for encouraging international collaboration in research appear to be those of (1) making opportunities widely known and (2) providing financial support.

---

*IMEDE in Lausanne is one of several examples.

RODERICK F. O'CONNOR
Georgia Institute of Technology

Mutual Benefit in Overseas Activities: The del Valle Program

In his talk on strategy for overseas programs, Dean Scarpetta pointed out several keys to success. One was the need for both parties to gain from the relationship. This is a crucial point, for unless an overseas education program is rooted in the healthy soil of self-interest at both ends, it is unlikely to develop the strength and spirit necessary to sustain it.

Steve Zeff has asked that we discuss specific overseas experiences. The School of Industrial Management at Georgia Tech has, for several years, worked with the leadership group in Colombia's Cauca Valley through their university, the Universidad del Valle.

The program had its beginning in an invitation by the Colombians to study with them their region's developmental needs and opportunities. The aim was to discover if management education might contribute to the solution of their problems.

Fortunately, as in many developing areas, their situation was

RODERICK F. O'CONNOR is Professor in the School of Industrial Management, Georgia Institute of Technology. He has MS and PhD degrees in psychology from the University of Delaware and Vanderbilt University, respectively. He conceived and helped originate the Cauca Valley Development Program in Cali, Colombia, including the Graduate School of Management for policy-level executives from Cali and other parts of Colombia. The program was established in the Universidad del Valle, Cali. From 1948 to 1953, he was engaged in practice and graduate study in clinical psychology. Since 1953, he has been a management consultant to approximately 60 organizations, including private industry, public, educational, and religious institutions. He is head of the Latin American program of research and teaching at Georgia Tech, and is author of "This Revolution Starts at the Top," (*Columbia Journal of World Business*, Fall, 1966), which discusses the development and concept of the Cauca Valley program.

extraordinarily viable. The problems were staggering and increasing daily. The leadership group was open-minded, competent (though few in number), and searching for answers to their own and their country's problems. In addition, the Universidad del Valle, already distinguished by a world-renowned medical school, was searching for direct ways to help in the economic development of the region.

This opportunity came to us at Georgia Tech at a time when we, too, were searching for new answers. Like most management schools, we were in a process of fundamental change. Not only were we revolutionizing our own curriculum but we were also searching for a new purpose, for new objectives to meet the challenges of the 1960s.

In the United States, however, it is extremely difficult to see the way clear to major institutional changes.

The great strength of the United States was made possible by a high degree of institutionalization. Our institutions on the whole are strong and securely established, staffed with people well-trained in existing systems and procedures. In these days of catastrophic change, however, we pay somewhat of a price for this strength and stability. We have lost a measure of reactibility and viability. The institution that serves society well in one decade may become a drag on progress in a few short years. In the face of massive environmental changes it is difficult to know how major reorientations of purpose, of policy, of structure, of systems and procedures might be conceived and carried out.

Business and management education is certainly not immune to such danger, as the Gordon-Howell and Pierson reports[1] pointed out several years ago.

The very hugeness and complexity of our society poses many additional problems—through obscuring the manner in which different types of institutions interrelate, through making difficult the link between cause and effect. For example, how can we be sure whether, in our business courses, we are training or mis-training our students for their future careers? It is quite possible that their success is due more to the fact that our students are generally made of good stuff and the companies they go into typically have training programs. The very strength of our society, and the difficulty of securing an answer, make it appear unnecessary to ask ourselves that painful question.

In societies which are smaller and in the process of development,

---

1[For full citations to these reports, see footnote 6 in the **EWA Report.**–Ed.]

where institutions are still in the formative stage and error is not obscured by existing strength and stability, it is much more feasible to ask such questions.

The nature of the interrelation between sectors, the connection between cause and effect, the relevance and validity of educational programs—all are easier to determine. (College graduates who have been mis-trained immediately join the ranks of the unemployed.) What is more, it is much easier to set up experimental solutions to serious problems and measure the results.

In the Cauca Valley, there were factors which created an unusually viable situation. There was no established management school. The need for new answers was urgent. They had a university committed to the development of the society. There was an eagerness to learn by those at the decision-level in their society. Thus there was a marvelous laboratory for ideas, for innovations, for testing out new objectives and approaches to management education. The Colombians, having direction and control of the program, had the power to direct the effort toward their own goals and purposes, so that they would benefit first.

The result of this fortunate coincidence of needs was the creation of a new kind of graduate program in management at the Universidad del Valle, with the leaders of the society as the students. Since October, 1964, one hundred and twenty individuals have enrolled, including the chief executives of most of the important businesses, agricultural leaders, three ex-ministers in the national government, the Minister of Public Works of the present administration, the Mayor of Cali, the Rector of the University, and the deans of the Schools of Medicine, Engineering, and General Studies. In January, 1968, another class will begin for which forty leaders have already been accepted. The classes are held from 7:30 to 10:00, two mornings a week at the University. Studying is done at nights and on weekends, with written exams given each quarter. The students also formulate and turn in projects during the course. These projects serve as evidence that the academic material has been learned in such a way that it can be realistically applied to operations (they are also a test of relevance of the academic content). The projects also serve as plans of action to be actually carried out by the enterprises, with the goal of directly bringing about development.

The course is oriented around the developmental mission. Concepts and modern management tools are stressed. The course areas are: the management task; Colombian economic development; the development of markets, of financial resources, of physical resources, and of human resources.[2]

Only the Colombians can say whether our participation has been of value to them, but we at Georgia Tech can say with certainty that the Colombian experience has enriched our own School of Industrial Management.

What were the specific opportunities we saw for ourselves in Colombia?

Management education is best seen as a field in the process of evolution. There is little resemblance between the courses taught in most universities in 1960 and those we teach today. Fundamental changes have occurred. We have seen the emergence of an intellectual base in the field. Descriptive and technique-based courses such as Personnel Administration and Production, among others, are being replaced by analytical, conceptually based courses.

This dynamism is continuing, of course, and seven years from now, we in management education hopefully will be able to state again that our courses bear little resemblance to those we taught in 1967.

What we at Georgia Tech were searching for was an approach through which we could make a significant contribution to this effort of renewal. To this end, we were given the opportunity in Colombia to add to our knowledge and capibility in at least six major areas.

The first was in the integration of management knowledge. We saw the chance to develop a curriculum which overcame the tendency toward over-specialization and fragmentation. By having the professors continually analyze with the student-managers their enterprises, and counsel them on their projects, it was possible to achieve a view of the enterprise as a whole and bring to the teaching of the functional areas a vision of purpose and objectives common to the entire enterprise.

Second, since most enterprises in the Cauca Valley are relatively new and since we were working with the entrepreneurs themselves (from whom we could learn a great deal), we saw the chance to build into the course areas the creative or entrepreneurial dimension.

Third, having the enterprises as well as the managers as part of the program, we would be able to bridge the gap between manage-

2See Roderick O'Connor, "This Revolution Starts at the Top," **Columbia Journal of World Business,** Fall, 1966, pp. 39-46.

ment education and actual operations, and thus impart the vitality and challenge of real life to the teaching process.

If an organization is to keep up with the quickening pace of change, it has become crucial (in the United States as well as abroad) for the top-level managers not only to be the chief executors of action in their enterprises but the chief learners as well. The fourth challenge we saw was to build a management education program which would so stimulate and benefit the executive that he would be motivated to make the difficult, sustained effort which both rigorous, formal learning and true self-development require.

The student-executives had much to teach the professors. To build Colombian courses (since U. S. courses obviously lacked relevance in Colombia), we had to learn from the executives the distinctive reality with which their enterprises were faced. The Colombians had selected as students only those executives who had proven themselves as competent managers, and we had much to learn from their experience and knowledge. This created a natural setting for accomplishing our fifth objective—building an educational effort not as a program of instruction but as a process of discovery in which both student and professor participate in the learning process.

The sixth opportunity we saw was to build a management education program that would be relevant and valid not only for business management but for all types of organized activity. To this end, leaders from other sectors were invited to join the course, and they accepted. (The fourth group, starting in January, 1968, will include labor and military leaders.) The manner in which the executives from the agriculture, government, and education sectors have put the concepts and analytical tools learned in the course into action with tangible results, gives evidence that this goal, at least in part, has been accomplished.

In conclusion, an important base for strategy in overseas education programs, if they are to have the strength which mutual self-interest provides, might be to start by asking ourselves the questions:

> How can we use this opportunity to bring new viewpoints, new structures, new kinds of curricula to management education?
>
> What are we, in our own school in the United States, trying to accomplish?
>
> What do we, ourselves, need to learn?
>
> What should be our role in our own society?

The developing countries offer the opportunity to gain some new and unexpected insights into these key questions.

Discussion Comments
Overseas Activities

Panel A: Mc Millan-Sessions

REPORTER: Hugh B. Carnes

The discussion was essentially descriptive rather than analytical. Emphasis seemed to be on asking questions, rather than answering them. Major interest seemed to turn on the financing of such activities. Availability of continuing financial support to insure viability of projects already launched seemed to be the major concern. Questions directed to panelists dealt largely with sources of financing.

Dean Brown described Columbia's participation in Argentine education for business students. Students rioted against U. S. participation, and the final outcome was a series of six-week seminars for the faculty of the University of Buenos Aires. Written off at its conclusion as a failure, later activities of the group which was trained have since caused Columbia to regard it as a success.

Much of the discussion reiterated ideas presented by the speakers at the general session, urging degrees of emphasis or de-emphasis. It was pointed out by Sá e Silva (São Paulo) that the United States is to a great degree the sole source of doctoral degrees in business.

Panel B: Reyes Salcido-Simmons

REPORTER: James T. Murphy

There was extensive discussion on the problem of convincing U. S. professors that overseas activities are worth the effort. A strong attitude exists that one falls behind by going overseas; colleagues are not necessarily sympathetic; articles are neither read nor written. The full professor who may not have to worry about publication is either engaged in something else he prefers or is not suitable for an overseas assignment. Thus a big problem is to find a system of rewards. At Michigan State, the reward structure for overseas activity is very much like the structure at home: a professor is encouraged to teach, consult, and engage in meaningful research for the local area. Any evaluation of published research must be in terms of its contribution in the overseas environment, not to be compared to a similar article or book in a U. S. context. While consulting is sometimes discouraged and sometimes disallowed because of a government contract, every attempt should be made to gain more flexibility in this matter so that constraints on consulting will not prevent a desirable professor from accepting an overseas assignment.

In an overseas assignment, there exist a number of problems of allocation of effort as well as potential conflict: (a) Foreign institutions should not depend on U. S. schools to send only teachers. U. S. faculty should be used to train local people, not to fill slots. If the U. S. institution has not agreed to this goal, conflict can easily arise. (b) It seems inefficient to send U. S. faculty elsewhere for the purpose of training others; a better approach may be for U. S. professors to define meaningful research goals and let the research output be used for training of foreign nationals. For this to be appealing, the home institution must understand the nature of a professor's research, and the professor must treat the activity as an investment in himself. (c) Building on Point (b), above, Franck (Syracuse) argued that we tend to export knowledge based on our own values and experiences. Such knowledge may not be adaptable to the local foreign environment, nor may foreign students trained in the United States subsequently re-adapt well to their own environment. Conflicts are easily possible in such cases; therefore, the U. S. professor *must* be involved in research at the local level in order to properly contribute. Building on these remarks, Scarpetta (Colombia) commented that there are many ways of solving problems; the institutions involved (host-U. S.-sponsor) should spend a lot of time in defining the problems. A small group of highly motivated and involved people will probably define problems more appropriately and will establish better programs than will relatively disinterested persons.

The discussion also turned to the question of possible incompatibility between goals of the U. S. and sponsor schools. What are the goals of the U. S. schools? Are we so affected by international developments that we want to understand them and build up adaptability by seeking foreign contracts? Is it purely altruism, or philosophic goals? What are the goals of the foreign schools? Mainly to make their product more competitive with Americans!

One conclusion which seemed to have a significant impact on the group was that overseas programs which have failed have really had no basis or reason for being in the foreign locale. Opportunism does not often lead to success in this context.

Panel C: Elliott-Graves

REPORTER: Eric W. Vetter

Of primary concern during the discussion was the seeking of information on several key aspects of assistance programs.

Two schools of thought emerged on the question of whether an American business school engaged in establishing business education in a foreign country should work with an existing foreign college or university or whether it should attempt to establish an entirely new institution in that country. Stanford was urged not to affiliate in its venture in Peru because of a need for independence and autonomy in its approach. Most ventures, however, have been paired with existing institutions despite the problems of traditionalism in the foreign host institution. This appears to be especially important in European countries where the products of business management programs may not be accepted by the community if they lack credentials (school tie) from an established institution.

The University of Southern California experience with the University of Karachi followed this pattern, and acceptance and cooperation of the business community was probably greatly increased because of the University of Karachi's established position in the nation. This pattern also enabled USC to draw upon the entire Karachi faculty in building a curriculum, and permitted better administrative control because the entire resources of the university were available to the new business program.

The separate approach by Stanford at ESAN, in Lima, was aided by the simultaneous establishment of two management development programs for Peruvian managers. These have helped to seed the Peruvian business community with managers possessing a modern outlook, and has meant a high degree of acceptance of ESAN graduates by both the Peruvian and U. S. business firms in Peru.

A serious concern over creating a new independent institution is what happens to the institution when the American funding of its program runs out. ESAN's long-run success will depend on the support of the business community and the general situation in Peru. The Karachi program has had strong government support since its inception, and this relationship will be a key factor in its long-run welfare.

The question of whether to affiliate with an existing institution may be academic at times, because the prospective host country may not have a school suitable for a joint venture in business education.

After a decision is made with respect to affiliation or non-affiliation with an existing school, the major problem of developing a faculty arises. It is probably not possible to have the necessary stockpile of U. S. professors for a large-scale program at the time the program begins. But some capacity must exist, and the consortium approach now being used by Big Ten schools in the Midwest deserves attention. Success in a consortium may rest on how well the schools and professors know each other before entering the venture.

The need to include a major provision for developing local nationals as faculty members is an important aspect of any assistance contract. Stanford trains MBAs from Peru at Palo Alto so they can return to Lima and teach at ESAN. Columbia hosted a program which trained 36 Argentines at the master's and PhD levels for the University of Buenos Aires. A difficult aspect of the faculty question is how to integrate trained local nationals into the faculty to replace the visiting American professors. One approach is to have the local national study with the American professor and then take over his course work. The pitfall in this approach arises when the local national is not adequately trained in U. S. methods or academic criteria in business education. This person may turn the course around after taking it over and resort to an obsolete local teaching tradition, or he may not be able to continue to develop the course because of a lack of in-depth academic training. Because of this problem, it appears desirable to train local nationals in the United States, or perhaps at third-party locations such as ESAN, in academic methods and criteria.

Another problem in the faculty area arises over the salaries paid American professors abroad versus those paid the local national instructors. U. S. faculty members are typically much higher paid than the local nationals, and when this occurs within an existing institution it can create conflict situations and administrative problems. Getting the host institution to amend its policies is a solution—it was used by IMEDE in Switzerland to attract faculty members they wanted. In some countries the morale of local national instructors is affected by the much higher salaries the graduates of the business program command relative to theirs.

The length of involvement of the American school with its overseas counterpart is an important strategic consideration. Maintaining momentum in the American school is difficult when the contract period extends for a considerable length of time (e. g., five years or more). Contracts for shorter periods have greater incentive for developing the capability of the local nationals to take over the program.

This capability-development is perhaps best accomplished when time pressure is felt at the inception of the program. Related to this is the idea that the American team abroad should not consider itself as the best judge of the type of future assistance, including extensions of the program, that should occur. It is important to remember that the initial call for assistance came at someone else's request and that it is integral to any decisions regarding follow-up assistance.

Evaluation of assistance programs has been conducted primarily after completion of the contract. Nonetheless, it was suggested that provision in an assistance contract for an on-going independent evaluation may be a potentially useful exercise. The need for independent outsiders in such an approach is important, because the program-builders are not likely to have unbiased perceptions of their activity and evaluation data. Even the evaluations that occur after completion of the contract are frequently not in clear cost-benefit terms. The benefits to faculty members and the costs to administrators are difficult to define, but added effort in this area appears warranted by all parties associated with assistance programs.

Panel D: Hill-O'Connor

Reporter: Eugene T. Byrne, Jr.

The two panelists delivered opening remarks that served largely to acquaint the group with the nature of the overseas operations directed by each.

More than at other sessions attended by the reporter, this session gave most attention to a single topic. Specifically, the group discussed the kinds of attitudes that should prevail for both the host and guest institutions. It appeared as if this session received great impetus from the comments delivered earlier by Deans Carmichael and Scarpetta.

Although by no means unanimous, there was a consensus that institution-building projects should stem (almost) entirely from selfish motives on the part of both the host and guest institutions. From this consensus, it developed that paternalism has no positive role in institution-building. In fact, it could be identified as a major factor leading to possible failure. This position was not ruled inconsistent with a mutually-determined welfare motive. Where institution-building is successful, it will often have a substantial effect on the economic development of the host nation. This effect should not be overlooked by self-seeking participants since it can be used as a motivator for each.

Self-interest on the part of an American university can rarely be defined independently of the university itself. A desire to promote an international business program may provide only temporary motivation to faculty. The successful efforts will require continual motivation.

O'Connor recounted the thinking leading up to Georgia Tech's acceptance of an invitation from Dean Scarpetta, of the Universidad del Valle in Cali, Colombia. Prior to the invitation, a number of the faculty at Tech were quite concerned with the basic assumptions of U. S. business education. They felt that, in many ways, industry and education had institutionalized and crystallized to the point where it might no longer be possible to think constructively about the needs of industry and how business education can satisfy these needs. Such conditions do not exist in Colombia, and Tech eagerly accepted the invitation. It was viewed as an opportunity to experiment in new ideas in a rather transparent environment, where results of experiments could be more easily seen.

Most participants agreed that this view established the motive of self-interest. However, two major concerns were expressed by the group. First, could the host institution be expected to accept the basic motive? Second, with the particular national economy so far behind the U. S. economy, tremendous educational benefit should derive from transplantation of existing management ideas. Why was this not done?

On the question of motives, the specific questions that Tech proposed to examine were judged to be relevant to the educational problems faced by the host institution. If answers to the questions could be obtained, the educational goals of the institution would be advanced. The second question was answered by noting that neither institution was perfectly satisfied with current U. S. business and educational practices. Nor were they confident that current concepts and practices would best serve the needs of the host institution as educational goals.

Returning to the general case, the welfare motive was established as the eventual development of a cadre of teacher-researchers. Opponents suggested that most host countries could benefit more from the development of faculties whose primary function is to teach practitioners. While many participants could accept the validity of this view, there appeared to be a consensus that this was more a short-run than a long-run goal.

Despite the emphasis on long-run goals, there was general agreement that community support must be established very early in the process.

Evaluation of institution-building efforts was judged as totally inadequate. Except for comments like: "Nothing seems to be happening," or "When things do happen, they take too long," neither the panelists nor the participants suggested any methodology for evaluation. A possible reason for the lack of methodology is that institution-building efforts have been largely unpublicized. Whatever reporting does take place is usually suggestive and experiential. All agreed that a more orderly approach, one that is designed to seek and reveal commonalities, is required.

Hill provided the only comment that was directed toward the matter of faculty rewards. He is certain that the home institution provides insufficient recognition of the purely administrative tasks required of faculty at foreign institutions. One reason for this is that the home institution does not make arrangements to obtain feedback from the foreign institution. More than likely, a faculty member is considered on an educational vacation when he accepts a foreign appointment.

PAUL A. FABRY
International House

Remarks

Good evening, and welcome to International House.

To explain simply why International House is here: we thank our existence to the *lack* of education for international business. More than 24 years ago, this organization was established by leading citizens of Louisiana because the business community of New Orleans—in fact, the entire southern area—lacked the type of education that you are trying to give this and the next generation.

They didn't know how to go about broadening international business or international relations—in fact, they didn't even know how best to organize their own port. The port was in a difficult situation at the end of World War II, and some 1,000 people got together to make it an important trade outlet to the world. They formed International House which today has a membership of nearly 3,000 leading citizens from the southern part of the United States, seeking to give the community the education for international trade and to give the port a facility to promote its services around the world.

Today New Orleans is unquestionably the Number 2 port in the United States, second only to New York. I do not say that this happened only because of International House, but we have probably played an important part in keeping the port in its leading position.

PAUL A. FABRY is Managing Director of International House, New Orleans. He has studied in Budapest, Paris, Basel, and Vienna, graduating with doctorates in international law and political science. From 1950 to 1954, he was head of one of the information and publication divisions of Radio Free Europe, in New York City. For more than six years, he was public relations advisor for E. I. du Pont de Nemours, Inc., in Wilmington, Del., where he was concerned chiefly with the company's international operations. He joined International House in 1962, and has since organized seven large trade missions for business delegations to Europe, Asia, and Latin America. In his 26 years in diplomacy, journalism, business, and administration, he has traveled to over 40 countries on all continents.

International House is dedicated to "world trade, peace, and understanding." We are still much needed, perhaps because the fine institutions you represent still do not produce the necessary result in the business community [LAUGHTER] — although Jack Grayson mentioned my academic degrees to show that I can go into the academic field in case International House folds. [LAUGHTER] However, I don't intend to do so because I feel that there is a need and opportunity for trade organizations such as ours in giving the people in business the necessary "education" for international business, which they didn't get in school.

To do this, our association maintains an excellent library and a trade development department; we also conduct trade missions, receive foreign delegations, publish directories, and do the type of work on a community level which you are trying to teach executives of small and large corporations to do for themselves.

We speak many languages in this building. We have a staff of about forty people, half of whom speak two or more languages. Our efficient library is used by businessmen all over the South. We have representatives in 50 countries abroad. Our club facilities are open to visitors from all over the world. We do translation work, conduct trade seminars, arrange exhibits at home and abroad, and help the businessman in many ways to become and stay interested in foreign commerce.

I hope, gentlemen, that your cities and your universities will be instrumental in building a new sophisticated business community—consisting of business diplomats, the type of internationally minded executives that we try to develop for better and bigger world trade.

MARSHALL A. ROBINSON
The Ford Foundation

Remarks

Jack Grayson asked me to make a few remarks. I think he stressed "few" because he knew that this would be a gathering of business school deans, and in recent years there has been far too much talk and not enough money from the Ford Foundation. [LAUGHTER AND APPLAUSE]

I would like to speak about a couple of things that are on our agenda these days and see if I can relate them to what is going on here. You are exploring two basic questions in these meetings: first, what must be done to prepare students for business careers in an environment that is multinational in character? Second, what can be done to improve the level of business administration knowledge in other countries? In a sense, you are asking one another: what-do-you-do-here and what-do-you-do-there?

As many of you know, this is the way that the Ford Foundation has dealt with the problems of teaching and research in business administration. I will say a word first about what-you-do-here.

The Ford Foundation spent about 35 million dollars—a figure that many of you have come to recognize as a statement that "we

MARSHALL A. ROBINSON is Officer in Charge of Higher Education & Research in the Division of Education and Research, The Ford Foundation, New York City. He holds MA and PhD degrees in economics from Ohio State University. From 1950 to 1960, he was associated with the National Bureau of Economic Research and the Brookings Institution, and was on the Tulane economics faculty and the business school faculty at Dartmouth College. In 1960, he became Dean of the Graduate School of Business, University of Pittsburgh, leaving in 1964 to join the Ford Foundation as Director of the Program in Economic Development and Administration. He was given his present duties in 1966. He is senior author of *An Introduction to Economic Reasoning*, a Brookings publication which has been translated into ten languages.

aren't going to do it anymore"—on what-you-do-here. Within this, a few million slipped into the field of international business education and research. I think these international business dollars were some of the best the Foundation has spent. I can say that because I didn't have anything to do with it. As a matter of fact, my first contact with this part of the Foundation program was when I was a hopeful supplicant—when I was a business school dean during what we call the boom phase of the Pittsburgh business cycle. [LAUGHTER]

The real inventor of this component of the Foundation's work in international business administration was a man who is now an executive for one of our co-hosts, Education and World Affairs—Irwin Sanders. Sanders, and others, insisted that the professional schools be included in any overall Foundation approach to universities that had to do with the development of the university's international dimension. As a consequence, many universities, exploring their international activities, found that there was some lively stuff going on in the business schools, and business schools found that there were people and ideas in the rest of the university that could help them do a job. Internationalism is a leading element in some of the structural changes now under way in universities; and business schools, through this work, are in the thick of these structural changes. This is why I think it was one of the most important things that the Foundation did in this field.

We all know that the war between the business schools and the rest of the university campus has not disappeared because of these efforts. But it is clear that when the business school demonstrates a concern for international affairs, or urban affairs, or, to pick another tough one, the moral dimensions of leadership, it is closer to what the rest of academe believes is the job of those who are in a university. What this means, then, is that the field of international business is becoming something more than an additional functional area in the business school's realm of interest; it is another important intellectual link between the business school and the university.

Now a word about the other half of the agenda—that is, what do you do for the overseas institutions? I have already said that we put $35 million into domestic business schools and in their people and research. And then, about 1965, we stopped, but it wasn't an abrupt stop; our trustees called it "the most extended terminal program in Ford Foundation history." By 1965, we had also spent for overseas business administration programs about $10 million—and, in the past two and a half years, we have about doubled that.

Business administration is catching up, it's catching on, and it's spreading. In some respects, it is regarded as a panacea for a lot of problems: the balance of payments, the technological gap, and everyone's economic development problem. I expect someone soon will say that business administration will solve the population problem. Yet it is being demanded, and these needs are going to be met.

Most of the money that the Ford Foundation has spent overseas in this field has gone to the so-called developing countries. And most of the discussions this afternoon had to do with the developing countries. These are the areas in which AID, the Ford Foundation and the Rockefeller Foundation are interested, and, not unexpectedly, these are the areas in which academics are most interested. Today the developing countries have some of the world's best business schools— and many that aren't the best now are clearly on their way. How many of you, for example, have heard as clear and precise a statement of the mission of the business school as that of Dean Scarpetta of the Universidad del Valle?[1]

Tremendous progress has been made in management education in many of the developing nations; enough progress, perhaps, to warrant a suggestion that we should not lose sight of the so-called developed world, which remains relatively impoverished with regard to the field of business administration. More specifically, I suggest that we recognize that Europe has perhaps the most backward collection of management education resources you can find anywhere in the world this side of China. Indeed, where else but in Europe do we find the only 20th century industrial society to permit a full-fledged business school (IPSOA) to disappear?

The cultural barriers to management education work in Europe are enormous. In many respects, they are more obstructive than those in the "eager to learn" and poor societies. But that portion of the world's problems that has its roots in the inadequate performance of European enterprise, in East Europe as well as West, is just too important to shrug off. Interest within Europe is growing, and the opportunities for you and your colleagues to help will grow correspondingly. What I want to say is that my colleagues and I see this as a new development job—one which is important, difficult, and likely to take a long time. It has our deep and continuing interest, and I hope it will have yours.

1[The paper referred to appears in this volume on pp. 136-42. —Ed.]

HERMAN B WELLS
Indiana University

Strategies for Education in International Business:

THE BUSINESS SCHOOL IN THE UNIVERSITY CONSTELLATION

Dean Grayson, ladies and gentlemen, in the light of all that's been said yesterday and today, it seems a pity to inflict a speech on you after a long day of work and a splendid dinner. But program planners always seem to be concerned with maintaining the sobriety of the crowd. Hence a speech is added to the dinner interlude to lengthen the period between the martinis and the nightcap scotch and soda. But I have listened so hard and so long today, that I'm frankly about exhausted, and I assume you are too. I'll try to be as brief as possible, though that's rather difficult. I am no longer a university president, but I must act like one tonight, because I'm going to catch a plane in a little bit.

It's been a long time since I've had the opportunity of attending a national meeting of business school deans and faculty. In my brief period of service as dean of the Indiana Business School, I enjoyed the meetings of the American Association of Collegiate Schools of Business tremendously, and I formed warm friendships that have lasted through the years. Some of my colleagues of that period fell from grace, as I did, and became presidents. It was a period in which business school deans were in fashion for presidencies. Some entered

HERMAN B WELLS is Chancellor of Indiana University and President of Indiana University Foundation. He has an AM from Indiana. After two years as Professor and Dean of the Indiana Business School, he became acting president of Indiana University in 1937 and president in 1938–a post he held until 1962, when he took his present position. He has advised and participated in numerous ad hoc commissions on education, particularly under UN auspices. He has been a trustee or board member of many educational, civic, and scientific organizations. Since 1963, he has been Chairman of the Board and Trustee of Education and World Affairs.

business to practice what they preached. Now most of my former colleagues have retired, and so it's increasingly difficult to keep in contact with them. Therefore, I especially welcome this opportunity to meet with you, and I hope this will start a new cycle of friendships.

I'm sure we all welcome the opportunity to visit this delightful, colorful city. It's an appropriate setting for discussing strategies for education in international business, for here such a topic becomes real—by reason of the boats that ride in the harbor, by reason of this building (International House), of which my old friend Rudolph Hecht was one of the founders, and by reason of the activity of New Orleans businessmen in the international field.

I'm especially pleased to have Tulane University organize this Conference. Tulane's professional schools have long been active in the field, and the entire university has an interest in comparative cultures. I readily admit being a bit partial to Tulane, because I have the honor and pleasure of serving as a member of the University's Board of Visitors. Being a member of the Board of Visitors is a glorious assignment for an ex-president. We are royally entertained at meetings, and we are taken into the inner sanctum of university problems. Our advice is asked, and we don't have to take any responsibility for the advice we give. You can't have it better than that.

Finally, on behalf of Education and World Affairs, I wish to thank Tulane for the excellence of its arrangements and to thank all of you for coming in such large numbers, thus assuring the success of this Conference. I, too, wish to thank the Ford Foundation for its special grant which made this Conference possible. I wish to thank Dean Grayson, Dean Shultz, and Mr. Zeff for their good service on this particular task force, the report of which we've been considering yesterday and today.

ACTIVITIES OF EDUCATION AND WORLD AFFAIRS

I've been asked to depart from my subject to say something to you about Education and World Affairs, because Bill Marvel couldn't get here. He expected to speak at the lunch today. I have been the Chairman of the Board of Trustees of Education and World Affairs since the organization was started, and I give it about one-fourth of my time. Actually, Herbert Longenecker made about as good a brief statement about the purpose and function of Education and World Affairs at noon today as I've heard. I shall try not to repeat his remarks. Instead I shall try to go on to say a few additional things about the organization.

We are essentially a fact-finding, research, and information-dissemination organization. We were organized as a result of the deliberations of the so-called Morrill Committee, which recommended the creation of an organization such as Education and World Affairs.[1] We were brought into being in 1962, and our basic financing has been underwritten by the Ford Foundation and the Carnegie Corporation. Certain of our special projects are financed by other foundations, notably Rockefeller and Danforth. You'll find in the back of the *EWA Report* on Business Administration a list of recent EWA publications. The Professional School Study is now in the process of being disseminated, so to speak, by six conferences held throughout the United States, of which this is one. This is the only one which concentrates on a given subject. The others are regional conferences discussing the whole range of professional education.

EWA from time to time makes policy statements. A recent statement attempts to give the guidelines for research carried on abroad in sensitive areas. It's had wide acceptance, and thousands of copies have been distributed. If some of you are having difficulty finding proper guidelines for the direction of overseas research by your faculties, I would recommend a reading of this statement.

We have two operating divisions in addition to the major research and publication function of EWA. One is the Overseas Educational Service, which attempts to place American professors in universities in developing countries, largely in Africa and the Middle East. OES provides, with the help of the Ford Foundation, the Carnegie Corporation, and others, "topping-up" money to equalize salaries for American professors paid by the foreign universities. In time, I think OES will be one of the important arms of EWA.

We likewise have fiscal and staffing responsibility for the Universities Service Center in Hong Kong. This is a research facility for scholars who wish to study the problems of modern China. It is operated not only for U. S. scholars, but also for scholars from the United Kingdom, Australia, New Zealand, and Canada. These other countries are included because they have good scholars in the field and especially because the Carnegie Corporation furnished the original money—Andrew Carnegie's bequest included the British Empire.

Perhaps that's enough about EWA. I will conclude by saying that EWA is a very lively organization, one in which I find great satisfaction in working, and with which I hope you will keep in con-

---

[1]The University and World Affairs, Report of the Committee of the University and World Affairs, J. L. Morrill, Chairman. Published by the Ford Foundation, 1960.

tact through the years as business schools go into ever higher levels of international involvement.

Now, a backward glance which throws light on the relevance of our meeting. When I became Dean of the Indiana University School of Business in 1935, our Indiana industries were for the most part concentrated in the American market. Now, even in the Hoosier hinterland, major industries are not only concerned with overseas sales, but are truly multinational, with plants all over the world. Today, when I call one of my friends—at Cummins, Eli Lilly, or Mead Johnson—it seems entirely natural to hear the secretary say, "Oh, he's not here, he's in London—or Paris, or Delhi, or Tokyo—and won't be home until next week." This did not happen three decades ago.

Recently I served on the National Advisory Commission on Food and Fiber. This commission was created to recommend a national policy for agriculture which would insure an adequate return for the farmer and at the same time enable us to supply our share of food needed to feed the world. And after a preliminary look at our assignment, we very soon discovered that a major part of our attention would have to be devoted to international questions. This would not have been true of a similar commission three decades ago.

THE BUSINESS SCHOOL AND THE UNIVERSITY

In inviting me to speak, Dean Grayson asked that I offer a few comments on the Business School and World Affairs as seen from the President's chair. Therefore, these comments must, of necessity, be personal, and I shall start by confessing my biases.

I believe that the international component in the American university has lagged far behind society's needs. I'm convinced that in the 20th century the American university must accept the entire world for its parish. It should, therefore, embrace the philosophy of the old Indian peasant who said, "The world is my village, and all mankind my kin."

I'm biased toward the comparative method in teaching. I believe that a comprehension of one's own culture is greater when it is seen in part through the eyes of others. Remember the Kipling line, "What should they know of England who only England know?"

In addition, emotionally I'm an old-fashioned, free-trading internationalist. Intellectually, I try to comprehend the complexity of the international dimension in education, economics, and government, and I know that we shall not have the "one world" envisioned by my friend and distinguished alumnus of Indiana University, Wendell Willkie. We shall not have "one world" overnight, yet I am convinced that we must work steadily toward that end, and that economic policy and business practice have an essential contribution to make to the search for world political stability and peace. Only out of economic growth and improved standards of living can the new nations develop conditions which will permit stable governments which are capable and strong enough to enter into cooperative political arrangements. Ever-widening areas of markets and trade can make a great contribution to these objectives. And finally, I believe with Emerson that, after all, the greatest meliorator of the world is selfish, huckstering trade.

So, as seen from the President's chair, in any attempt to meet a university-wide international commitment, I see the role of the business school as central.

In addition to my biases, my thinking is also conditioned by my personal observation of the development of the business school within our university system. I took my baccalaureate degree in business in 1924, when the national enterprise of business education was in its infancy. At Indiana University, courses were few and the content was thin. We bravely asserted that we were a professional school, but this required a bit of self-delusion. In that day, there were those who doubted that business studies could ever achieve true professional status. You know better than I that present-day course offerings at their best have become as rich and significant as those in any other professional field. All this has been achieved in four decades. The growth in enrollment, budgets, faculties, and research has been equally significant.

One of the most exciting features of this Conference, to me, is to be able to witness the process by which a professional specialty is created. Here we see a specialty in the making: Statements of needs and goals, sharing ideas about the content of specific courses, delineation of areas needing investigation, creatively sharing experiences —all this is going on. If one can judge from what has happened in the older areas of specialization in the past four decades, this specialty, now in its infancy, will reach rich maturity as a result of your patient and imaginative efforts.

In calling for a larger international role for the entire university in general and for the business school in particular, I am not insensitive to the scarcity of resources or the dangers of proliferation. As a nation we are at the present time engaged in an orgy of institutional proliferation, unnecessarily increasing the overhead cost of American higher education; and I fear that before it has run its course it will result in disastrous competition for many of our smaller private colleges and universities. Course proliferation is perhaps an even deadlier disease, for it not only increases costs unconscionably, but also tends to dilute and debase the quality of the offerings.

I am likewise aware that the business school is only one part of the total university and that universities are notoriously resistant to change. Yet the business school should not try to go it alone. It should ask for the help of other faculties and the general administration. The international component must receive a fair hearing in every priority decision.

Notwithstanding all of the dangers and difficulties, any dean, with the help of a few interested members of the faculty, can change the outlook and orientation of the entire school by seizing every opportunity, large and small, to emphasize through precept and example the importance of the international component.

In even the poorest schools the dean has many lines to pull. Ways can be found to promote study, travel, and research abroad. Men who display unusual interest can be rewarded in many ways. Visiting scholars and foreign students are a ready resource often too little utilized.

From the vantage point of the President's chair, I have always been astonished by the lack of faculty awareness of interdisciplinary resources and of any active interest in cooperation. Also I am always dismayed by the failure of students to take advantage of the extracurricular cultural offerings of the University community.

Little has been said in this Conference about the importance of the humanities in the background of the student preparing for life abroad. Art and music are international languages. The young man who expects to live abroad will find a knowledge of art and music tremendously helpful in establishing rapport with other nationals.

Perhaps there is not time in the MBA curriculum for formal study of the arts, but I dare say that your art historians would welcome an opportunity to talk informally with your MBA candidates, as would your musicologists. I am certain that gallery tours could be arranged. A careful viewing of exhibits in the college museums and attendance at college concerts could fill leisure hours with pleasure as well as profit, resulting in a better preparation for international life.

Look about you. I am sure there are unusual resources which you may have for the asking. I will wager that imaginative leadership can considerably internationalize the teaching content and outlook of any business school within five years, with little outside help.

The *EWA Report* speaks of several levels of business school involvement. For many schools the highest level is neither possible nor desirable.

But as I view the business school from the President's chair, I believe that a university with large resources has an obligation to undertake this highest level of involvement, including technical assistance to business schools in new universities in the underdeveloped lands.

I have seen the crying need of many of the new nations and new economies for business and entrepreneurial leadership. Dean Scarpetta put the matter forcefully this afternoon when he said, "For us training in business is a matter of survival." During the colonial era, business activity for the most part was carried on by the rulers—hence business activity has inherited a bad image in the recently liberated lands. Yet achieving political stability depends in large part in many areas upon economic growth, and economic growth simply cannot take place without business leadership. Business education, therefore, will deserve a high priority for a long time to come.

This is just as true in the underdeveloped socialist countries as it is in the free enterprise economies. I am sure you are all aware that the economic apparatus of the East European and Russian world is undergoing searching re-examination at the moment. My colleague, Irwin Sanders, at EWA, who played such an important role in these EWA studies on The Professional School and World Affairs, discovered a story in Eastern Europe a few months ago that is told over and over as one travels from capital to capital. The story, inspired by the struggle to achieve economic reform, is as follows:

The owner of a house of ill fame whose business was declining went to an old rabbi who was known to be a wise and shrewd advisor on all manner of problems. Said the owner: "My business is very bad. What on earth shall I do?"

The old rabbi replied, "Make some changes, freshen up the place, paint it, put in new carpets, new furniture, make it more attractive in every way."

The owner followed the rabbi's advice and waited patiently, but after a year had passed and business hadn't improved he went to the old rabbi again. "I did what you told me to do," he said. "I changed the carpets. I painted. I made the front of the house more attractive, and yet business still continues to decline."

"Ah, yes," the rabbi said. "I understand you did all this. But you failed to change the one thing that was all-important. You failed to change the girls."

This story would indicate that even in the socialist economies they have come to realize that old communist political bureaucrats are ineffective business entrepreneurs, and that trained managers are essential to the success of their economic enterprise.

Unless the business schools with sufficient resources accept the task of providing assistance in manpower development for the under-developed world, governments will turn to the private consulting firms and other sources. I happen to believe that the business school, in many instances, is not only a viable instrument, but is also the best instrument to perform this function. Once undertaken, however, the assignment must be taken seriously and not be allowed to receive second-rate attention merely because it is far away.

A few weeks ago there appeared in the *London Daily Telegram* a review of a new book by Max Nicholson titled: *The System: The Misgovernment of Modern Britain.* The review says:

> Part of the folklore of my generation was that we came into a lingering Victorian afterglow, swiftly dimmed by the Kaiser's war. Nicholson sees the Victorian effulgence differently.
>
> The disastrous change from triumphant economic expansion to stagnation was brought about, without any external difficulties to excuse it, in only a couple of decades between 1860 and 1880. Relative stagnation has reigned in the British economy ever since.
>
> The failure to expand education, training and scientific research; a Civil Service based on academic amateurism and not professional training—these, he says, were cardinal blunders.
>
> And earlier symbols of them were Arnold's Rugby and Benjamin Jowett's "backward-looking, anticreative, classics-oriented brand" of higher education at Oxford. This was when Britain got well and truly bent.

This book is one of many evidences of the recognition of the need for reform in English and European education.

But throughout much of the former colonial world there is a tendency to try to recreate their new universities in the nostalgic image of the Mother Country, long after the Mother Country has recognized the need for change. Technical assistance from our business schools can perform a vital service in helping to encourage realistic, modern, forward-looking policies in tune with local conditions and problems.

W. B. Donham was Dean of the Harvard Business School in my time. One of his several books was titled *Business Adrift.* It con-

tained an introduction by Alfred North Whitehead in which these
words appear, now more significant than when they were written:

> Mankind is now in one of its rare moods of shifting its outlook.
> The mere compulsion of tradition has lost its force. . . . We must pro-
> duce a great age, or see the collapse of the upward striving of our race.

In this era our nation has an awesome leadership responsibility.
All the world (except for Le Grand Charlie) so acknowledges it.
The implications for our universities are profound, and the role of
the business school is central, for truly business is a civilizer, and the
greatest meliorator of the world is common huckstering trade.

W. GEORGE PINNELL
Indiana University

A Critique of the EWA Report

I have never liked the word "critique." It's unfriendly. Despite all the protestations of Webster, or even Bennett Cerf for that matter, the word seems to convey the ominous tone of an impending disaster. To be on target, there is the implication that the speaker should vacillate between a little fault-finding with peripheral issues and a summary repudiation of the entire report. Consequently, I would like to begin by saying I think the section of the *EWA Report* dealing with business schools and education for international business is well done. The objectives of the *Report* were limited and were achieved. Were I not committed to hold forth for the next twenty minutes or so, I could, in all good conscience, commend the authors and sit down.

That, however, is not to be the case. Let's start from its being a "good report," and maybe I can generate a few further ideas or at least emphasize some of those already covered in the *Report* as a basis for future development of the topic. I must admit these comments were none too original when I wrote them, and each speech yesterday made them a little less so.

My first point is not of great consequence, but it does seem to me to be symptomatic of one of the basic problems in infusing the international dimension into the curricula of schools of business. The point is, ironically, that the Business Administration section of the *Report* appears to be an entirely domestic product. In fact, the first

W. GEORGE PINNELL is Dean of the Graduate School of Business, Indiana University. He received an MA from West Virginia University and a DBA from Indiana University. He serves as consultant or director for a number of companies, governmental units, and associations. He is a member of the executive committee of the American Association of Collegiate Schools of Business. In addition to participating in many international seminars and conferences, he has been active in the establishment and operation of his School's programs in Thailand, Pakistan, and Yugoslavia.

sentence in the introduction says that it is a *national* study. And a sentence on the second page of the same section issues a cogent warning to the effect that ". . . professional educators and practitioners often take a rather culture-bound view of their subject matter." Even though the blue ribbon group that prepared the *Report* is uncommonly well-grounded in international affairs, one cannot help but wonder whether further important insights might have been gained if someone from Western Europe or another part of the world had been included on the task force. I think we are inclined to forget that the air fare between Boston and London is only $95 more than from Boston to Los Angeles.

My point here, in addition to twitting EWA a little for not including a single international among the 36 members of the four task forces, is that it is almost common to approach international matters from a very national point of view.

A second point which plagues the reader of the *Report*, as I suspect it did the task force, is the uncertain meaning of the words "international business." The two words seem to embrace everything from the use of a non-domestic case in an existing course or a rather traditional course presented by an "international" teacher to a series of *intra*national courses on a nation-by-nation basis or *inter*national courses on a subject-by-subject basis.

Since international business is clearly not a discipline, and indeed the substance of the subject matter is very much up for discussion, the academic administrator has some very interesting problems. Those related to the curriculum are discussed in the *Report* at some length, and I want to comment on those in just a moment. But most administrators are *also* concerned with the selection of faculty for the international area, particularly when this step may well precede curriculum planning. What type of special preparation should he look for among the prospects? Or perhaps more important, what standards of measurement are available to the administrator in trying to find individuals who have the intellectual capacity and preparation to match individuals in established fields where standards of excellence may be better understood? Should he seek demonstrated ability in a traditional field with some international overlay? If so, what type of international experience is most useful?

If this type of question is difficult to answer positively, there are certainly warning signs that should be observed. As the *Report* points out, the international field appeals to "habitual nomads and picture-takers" as well as to competent, hard-working scholars. The international dilettante, who knows what a Scotsman wears under his kilt and has visited the source of the Nile River but who gleans little from his experience to enrich his courses, will hardly build a great program or a great school.

Because international business is as much an *attitude* on the part of faculty members as it is academic preparation, there is good reason for a school to try to develop a critical mass. This need to develop personal interchanges and cross-fertilization of ideas is one factor which justifies the formation of administrative arrangements which facilitate such developments. In short, the establishment of departments and areas or concentrations or majors is not bad *per se*. The formation of a meaningful unit for an aggressive and dedicated group of scholars, interested in exploring and improving the substance of international business courses, will not dilute the quality of any school provided—and I believe this is important—the school has the authority to use their talents in meaningful research and does not have to justify them by giving birth to an endless sequence of new courses. There is much to commend an arrangement by which a concentration of faculty members can be given the responsibility for the diffusion of the international business dimension throughout the curriculum of the school—both conceptually and pragmatically.

A third point which deserves mention is what seems to me to be the explicit emphasis in the *Report* on graduate programs. This may stem from the conviction that undergraduate programs will ultimately be phased out, or perhaps from the opinion that the analysis and recommendations are suitable in either program, or from many other good and sufficient reasons. In any event, we can be sure that, even if the decision were made tomorrow to phase out undergraduate programs in business, the influence of those programs would still be felt well into the twenty-first century. Regardless of the major, it is at the undergraduate level where a judicious choice of academic work could be most important in developing sensitivity to the fact that the world is one system. Given the time available and the demands made on that time at the graduate level, graduate programs in business are likely to underline the need to carefully structure the undergraduate program.

At this point I would merely express the hope that, building on the groundwork provided in this *Report*, further attention be given to the need for adaptation of international business to the heterogeneous constituencies served by the nation's schools of business at both the graduate and undergraduate levels.

A fourth question about the *Report* which I still have not resolved to my satisfaction is: Does it make the implicit assumption that the existing or traditional programs of business schools are national and consequently unsuited or of limited usefulness in international business? Without fretting about the answer, if there is any empirical evidence that this is indeed the case, it has not come to my attention. To the contrary, I have been briefed on a report which purports to show that basic U. S. management knowledge can be used successfully in many—perhaps all—of the countries of the world. That position undoubtedly claims too much.

To editorialize for just a moment, it might be useful to characterize the programs of U. S. business schools as being two-dimensional. On the one hand, they prepare a young person in concert with the rest of the university to accept a position in society. Hopefully, we sensitize him to his fellow man. Every businessman knows that individuals in the United States respond differently to different stimuli. The successful ones use the knowledge to generate the proper response from each person. There is no reason to believe he isn't equally sensitive to people from other cultures.

On the other hand, we attempt to equip the individual with as many analytical techniques as possible, based on such traditional disciplines as mathematics and economics. This is his kit of tools, and hopefully they will be enduring in their usefulness and versatile enough for international if not interplanetary fields.

Business schools go one step further and automatically fit a culture pattern to the student's knowledge and skill. Let me give this very simple illustration: A business school student is asked to do a study of the demand for razor blades. He starts with the assumption that most men shave every day because that is true of the only culture he knows. Further, his value system probably dictates that everyone should shave because the good people he knows shave every day and most of the bad ones do not. As a youngster he must have noted on television, for example, that the villain never shaves and the good guy never has any whiskers. Using culture-bound assumptions, he tries some very sophisticated techniques to determine the world demand for razor blades. It comes as a real shock to him to learn that only one man in seven around the world shaves every day. The recommendations would be disastrous, but the rest of the report would be pretty good. In other words, two dimensions of his education were good: (1) the preparation to become a sensitive member of society and (2) the infusion of fundamental knowledge and skills essential to his career field. In fact, it seems to me those two dimensions are truly international. The third dimension, however, is obviously incomplete. His culture is national and indeed his entire decision model may be truncated by national boundaries.

The development of the third dimension will require the most careful effort. The need gives rise to an obvious invitation to sprinkle the curriculum liberally with courses heavy with institutional and descriptive material based on experience. Schools of business are still attempting to recover from an earlier binge of just that type of curricular material but directed to the national dimension. Let's not subject ourselves to another report twenty years hence which recounts the overspecialization of business schools in the international field.

But I would like to agree with the *Report,* if I understand it correctly, on the idea that our students need a three-dimensional education. Many of us are still giving them two.

The nature of the third dimension occupied the sessions on curriculum strategy yesterday morning. It will occupy a lot more of our time before an acceptable answer evolves.

The *Report* at two or three points issues an important caveat which might be overlooked in the enthusiasm which comes with the possibility of a large grant. Any international involvement should be measured against the objectives of the school and the implications for the use of scarce resources. Can you spare your best people?—as Dean Carmichael said, "If you can't, don't get involved." By all means, remember that successful technical assistance programs have been two-way streets. Benefits flowed in both directions. Of course, the so-called threshold involvement developed in the *Report* would surely enrich the experience of students and faculty, regardless of the school's objectives. Anything less than that is not a wise use of existing resources. As the *Report* says, the opportunity cost of *not* doing so is high.

An important segment of the *Report* deals with a list of 34 activities in the international business field which would constitute an accelerating commitment to the field. Numbers 1 through 9 as a group represent a threshold range of strategies; numbers 10 to 16 represent the lower-intermediate range, and so forth. The case is so logical that it is possible to get the impression that 2 should follow 1 or certainly 12 should follow 8. I do not think the sequencing is that rigid or that important, and I suspect that the authors agree. As one man said here, if he had read the *Report* eight years ago his school would still be getting up to step 34. Not having that benefit, they jumped about 20 steps and it worked out well. I would just suggest that rules are never a substitute for brains.

Finally, let me say that I have no interest in a line-by-line nit-picking of the *Report*, and I am sure you do not either.

With its very limited objectives and the resulting need for breadth, the *Report* is not a deep, reflective document. It does not recommend an optimal curriculum in the international field. It doesn't even decide whether international business is the act of doing business across national boundaries or the process of doing business within many countries.

It does, however, tell you how some schools are approaching the problem.

It does not tell you how to get into the technical assistance field. It doesn't even tell you how to stay out.

But it does tell you what other schools are doing with other institutions around the world.

The same general comments could be made about research and continuing education. To me, the *Report* has several values but especially these four:

1. It is an up-to-date, if limited, survey of what is going on in the international business field.

2. It calls attention to the fact that many U. S. business schools are offering their students only two dimensions of a three-dimensional education.

3. It underlines the fact that the international business field is still very much in the formative stage, and

4. It is one more call to arms to find the substance and rigor that the field potentially has.

ROBERT Z. ALIBER
University of Chicago

Research Needs in International Business

Presumably those who established the program for this session wanted a prescriptive discussion about research in international business. Providing such prescriptions is risky—for what appears stupid or irrelevant will be laughed away or ignored, and what appears thoughtful, serious, and worthwhile might soon be on the way to a foundation—in someone else's briefcase.

Since research in business schools generally is directed toward problems, the sponsors of the program might have asked some international businessmen—the President of General Motors, the J. Paul Gettys, the Beatles—to suggest problems that seem to warrant researching. Given these problems—we might call this the demand side—the academics might suggest a menu—the supply side—of possible solutions or answers. But the entrepreneurs are not here, and so the demand side of the activity must be constructed as a collage based on speakers, reports, problems, cases, and personal testimony. Actually, my comments today are not directed toward specific problems, but rather

ROBERT Z. ALIBER is Associate Professor of International Finance and Economics, and Director of the Program of International Studies, Graduate School of Business, University of Chicago. He has an AM from Cambridge University and a PhD from Yale University. Before joining the Chicago faculty in 1965, he was staff economist for the Commission on Money and Credit (1959-61), staff economist for the Committee for Economic Development (1961-64), senior economic officer, Office of Program Coordination, USAID, and a lecturer in international economics, School of Advanced International Studies, Johns Hopkins University. He has published widely on international finance and monetary economics, including *The Future of the Dollar as an International Currency* (Praeger, 1967), *The Management of the Dollar in International Finance* (Princeton University Press, 1964) and "Gresham's Law, Asset Preferences, and the Demand for International Reserves" (*Quarterly Journal of Economics,* November, 1967).

toward a conceptualization of the uniqueness of international business.

One reason for this meeting is uncertainty as to what international business is all about, or what it should be all about. We agree international business is a good thing—even though we may not agree on what international business is. One approach is to say international business is whatever anyone does who says he works in international business—this standard is dangerous, for it denies any objective boundaries to the field. Another approach is to say that international business is the international counterpart to the domestic courses in the curricula of business schools—thus there is finance and international finance, marketing and international marketing, accounting and international accounting, behavioral science and international behavioral science, statistics and international statistics. Clearly, this criterion isn't enough; not all the curriculum offerings have an international counterpart, and there may be some desirable international courses which have no domestic parent. It seems clear that a generally acceptable view of the uniqueness of international business is a necessary condition before agreement can be reached on the direction of future research. And a considerable part of the explanation for the failure to join the issue is a lack of agreement on how extensive international business is. For some people here, international business is like quantum physics—it includes everything in the universe except sex.

At this stage, I don't wish to debate what research is, or the demarcation among research, journalism, and current events. In an applied area, the test of whether research is good is whether it increases our predictive ability. From the point of view of curriculum development—and I don't sense much disagreement with John Fayerweather's remark that more rigor is needed—research may help us develop sets of theories or behavioral relationships. It is worth a moment to consider whose research we're concerned with—our own, or that of our students. And if the research of doctoral students is deemed important, it seems appropriate to ask whether their theses should be evaluated primarily as a basis for entry into the teaching profession, or for their research content, or as an exercise in training for future research.

I raise this question because, to gain an insight into the current state of the art, I casually surveyed the doctoral theses in international business in the 1960s. Faddism is not unknown in the university—students tend to reflect the research interests, and even the research style, of their professors. This survey is not exhaustive; the sample size was about 100 from more than a dozen schools. My conclusion, based largely on the titles of the dissertations, is that these theses do not add a great deal to our understanding of what international business is all about.

Let me first speak to the types of research undertakings that are beyond the boundaries of international business. International business is not the study of the Wages Policy in Chile, or the Sources of Growth in Japan, or the Role of the Commercial Banks in the Development of Peru. These topics are interesting; they merit researching. But that the subject matter is abroad and the researcher is in the United States is not a justification for classifying the topic as international business. A study of French Planning does not become a study in international business because it is submitted to a U.S. university. The subject must be judged on its merits to determine whether it falls within the international business category; the country in which the study is done or who does it is irrelevant. The distinction is between foreign business and international business. Studies of various aspects of business may be useful to U. S. firms engaged in international business, but these studies are not international business. About three-fifths of the 100 doctoral theses, when judged by their titles, might more appropriately be considered foreign business rather than international business.

Similarly, a study titled A Comparison of Wages Policies in Britain, Netherlands and Sweden, or the Determinants of the Markets for U. S. Automobiles in Guatemala, Nicaragua, and Honduras, falls outside the boundaries of international business. These studies, too, are interesting and useful. Comparative studies of the market for Polaroid cameras in ten Latin American countries may be useful for predicting the markets in five or ten other countries. The point is that there is a meaningful distinction between comparative marketing and international marketing, just as there is a meaningful distinction between comparative law and international law. Some international studies are comparative studies, but not all comparative studies are international studies. Indeed, in some fields, comparative studies may have greater utility to business firms than international studies; from the point of view of curriculum development, comparative studies may add a great deal to our understanding of domestic problems. About one-fifth of the 100 theses might more appropriately be considered comparative studies rather than international studies.

By now, my thesis should be clear: the study of international business should be concerned with interactions among business and economic variables in different countries, and with the activities of firms as they cross boundaries. The uniqueness is in the term "interaction." You may think that I'm being precious about a definition. The point is not really where the boundaries are between international business and other subject areas; rather it is between what is central or critical and what is peripheral or tangential. In this sense no more than 10 or 15 theses in the sample of 100 theses can be considered to be in the relevant ballpark. These theses involve such topics as the international transfer of management skills, transfer prices, determinants of cash flows between home office and branches, and the financial practices of joint ventures.

One of the major elements in the study of international business should be the study of the relationship between similar economic and business variables located in different countries. Just as there is a world market for wheat and a world market for gold and the prices in each national center are tied together in a world-wide system, so a substantial number of economic and business variables in different national centers are components of a common international system. Few would argue with the proposition that price movements on the New York Stock Exchange are related to price movements on the Pacific Coast Stock Exchange. But how many will accept the proposition that price movements on the New York Stock Exchange have a meaningful relationship to price movements on the Paris Bourse? No one, to my knowledge, has demonstrated this relationship, yet it is a valid subject for research in international business. There are likely to be meaningful links between financial and business variables in different countries, for they are common elements in an international system. At the end of World War II, the phrase "When Uncle Sam sneezes, the rest of the world catches cold" may have been both simple-minded Keynesianism and poor history; but it projected a view of income-determination in the world. Few would deny that the Canadian economic variables of prices, incomes, and growth rates reflect counterpart U.S. economic variables—but how many believe that a similar relationship holds for U.S. variables and for similar variables in Argentina and/or Australia?

To say there are meaningful relationships among similar variables in different countries is not to say that there is one-to-one dependence. Nor is it to deny that local factors may sometimes dominate the international relationship. Our knowledge about these relationships is uncertain and imprecise; the point of research is to clarify these relationships. Let me give several examples. I believe there is a world central bank; its name is the Federal Reserve System, and this bank determines the world price level. Other countries can alter the local price level in their own currency but their impact on the world price level is marginal; if they inflate too rapidly, then they must devalue their currencies. Similarly the Federal Reserve System tends to set the level for interest rates abroad; other countries can alter their interest rates, but only within limits.

These remarks center on research about possible relationships among similar economic variables in different countries. This approach can be extended to involve relationships between different variables in different countries. For example, a change in EEC tariffs affects U. S. foreign investment, and a change in foreign investment affects foreign trade. Similar relationships may exist between a variety of variables in different countries—between exports and foreign investment, between changes in the price levels and changes in profit levels, between changes in interest rates and changes in profit rates, and between capital flows and changes in profit rates.

You may say that these problems fall within the domain of international economics. Certainly there is an overlap between what international economics is concerned with and what international business is concerned with, but the overlap is partial; international economics is concerned with a large number of welfare propositions that international business ignores. Moreover, international business should be concerned with the connections among national economic variables, especially a large number of price variables that international economics ignores. The fact is that international economics has given scant attention to the relationships between variables in different countries. But such attention is needed so that businessmen can better understand the environment in which they deal, and the strong links among the environments in different countries.

The second major element in research in international business should be the study of problems of firms which operate in several different national jurisdictions. In addition, firms may operate in areas which are differentiated on the basis of culture, taxes, tariffs, and scope for factor movements. The area of commonality may be only partially overlapping—the EEC countries may share the same tariffs, but they do not share the same taxes or the same financial structures and interest rates.

The problem for research is to determine the most efficient or effective ways the firm can mix its several activities in a variety of jurisdictions. In some grand sense, it is a massive linear programming problem—the firm must consider which factors to move to which production sites, which production sites should serve which markets, where income will be earned and where income will be taken. Viewed as a production problem, the firm must decide, given its estimates of demand in different jurisdictions, how it should organize its production. Viewed as a marketing problem, the firm must decide which products made in one country should be sold abroad. Viewed as an accounting problem, the firm must decide where to take its income, given the national differences in tax rates, depreciation, and in the tax treatment afforded to foreign income. Viewed as an organizational problem, the firm must decide how to organize so as to control and perhaps integrate the variety of its operations abroad—does it organize by function, by production, by area, or on some other basis?

These questions are much like those asked by firms which operate solely in a domestic market. At issue is whether the introduction of the international dimension substantially changes the problem. It is not enough to say that tax rates differ by jurisdiction, but to ask whether these differences introduce problems which are substantially different in kind or magnitude. The question at hand is whether there are systematic differences because of the international dimensions—differences because of the pull of national governments, because of time lags, restraints on choices, integration of staffs of different nationalities, integration of different national pay scales. It seems highly likely that American firms marketing in France encounter problems that French firms don't; the question is whether these differences can be systematized. The production problem for American firms in Germany may differ from that of a German firm, precisely because the former must cross a national boundary.

Several examples may help to clarify the point. Not uncommonly the managers of firms indicate that foreign investment must yield a higher return or have a shorter pay-out than the domestic rate. The usual explanation is in terms of a number of risks; these risks are generally unspecified, but might include exchange risk, nationalization, war, government constraints, etc. Some risks may be partly offsetting rather than additive and some may be correlated with domestic risks. What we need to know is the efficient way for the firm to evaluate these risks and to determine the appropriate yield differential.

The examples in these comments are drawn largely from economics, primarily because this is the material with which I feel most familiar. But clearly other disciplines are involved in the study of the firm in international business. The problems of exchange risk might better be studied by experts in finance. The structure of international firms might best be studied by organizational theorists. Experts in personnel management will be concerned with integration of staffs from different countries with different pay scales. Accountants will be concerned with the legal framework of business. Those in operations research would focus on the optimum location of activities. And experts in political science might be concerned with how international firms face national governments.

These comments have certain implications. The first is that obtaining meaningful insights into this range of international problems seems likely to involve individuals whose training is in a basic discipline like accounting or economics or behavioral sciences or in a functional field like finance. Perhaps the analogy is with regional economics: individuals are trained in other disciplines and then work within the applied field. The second implication is that relatively few individuals working in the applied field are likely to have the range of capabilities to deal with the many varied facets—the economic, marketing, production, organizational aspects – of international business problems. And this should not be surprising, for there are few expectations that any one individual should have the range of capabilities to deal with the domestic business problems. Perhaps team research provides an approach; whether this approach is productive is primarily an empirical issue.

SUMMARY

The first point is that the study of international business should be limited largely to the study of those activities which cross national boundaries; it should not be a catch-all for studies of one or more foreign dimensions. At the aggregative level, the focus of research should be the relationships among economic and business variables in different countries. At the level of the firm, the focus of research should be on the biases in understanding a particular functional area, because a firm operates in several jurisdictions.

STEFAN H. ROBOCK

Columbia University

Research Needs in International Business

That an urgent need exists for escalating and improving the orientation of research efforts on the international dimension of business undoubtedly is not at issue — particularly at this Conference. Therefore, without commenting further on the general need, I would like to focus my remarks on three specific research needs in the field of international business. They are as follows:

1. The need to make further conceptual progress in structuring the field, as a guide to both research and teaching.

2. The need to allocate more resources for integrating or absorbing into our educational efforts available knowledge and the increasing flow of research.

3. The need to better identify research needs and priorities in order to make rapid progress with the scarce manpower and financial resources available for research.

I

Defining the field of international business has become a popular

---

STEFAN H. ROBOCK is Professor of International Business, Graduate School of Business, Columbia University. He has MA and PhD degrees in economics from Harvard University. He joined the Columbia faculty in 1967 after six years as Professor of International Business and Director of International Business Studies at Indiana University. Since 1954, he has performed in consultancy capacities for the UN, U. S. Government, OAS, World Bank, USAID, and the Ford Foundation on overseas projects in South America (particularly Brazil), Africa, India, and the Philippines. He has published numerous works on regional and national economic development, including *Nuclear Power and Economic Development in Brazil* (National Planning Association, 1957), *Brazil's Developing Northeast: A Study of Regional Planning and Foreign Aid* (Brookings, 1963), and "Overseas Financing for U. S. International Business" (*Journal of Finance*, May, 1966). He co-edited the proceedings of the December, 1963 International Business Administration Conference, held at Indiana University.

parlor game, always enjoyable, sometimes spirited, and occasionally productive. I don't pretend to have an answer that will satisfy all present and potential players and, thereby, stop the game. But I find it useful for pedagogical and research purposes to separate three different concepts frequently and often indiscriminately used in discussing the international dimension of business. I refer to foreign business operations, comparative business, and international business.

Foreign business operations, as John Fayerweather has suggested, "are essentially domestic operations within a foreign country" in which "the U. S. manager's problems are not basically different from those he would encounter if he were to take a job with a company owned by nationals of the host country."[1]

Comparative business focuses on similarities and differences among countries and business systems. As the *EWA Report* notes, comparative business research "provides perspective for understanding" home institutions and environments. The *Report* also suggests, and I'm not at all sure what this means, that comparative research will "help to delineate the nature and contours of the institutional overlay which contains the truly international elements in business." (p. 52)

International business, or multinational business, emphasizes governmental and business problems particularly related to business activities across national boundaries, generally through the movement of goods, services, money flows, or personnel. The multinational firm which operates in more than one country is of major interest, as are the problems of governments in adjusting to the rapidly expanding phenomenon of international business operations.

The three concepts — foreign business operations, comparative business, and international business — are inter-related and may have overlaps. But even though the boundary lines cannot be precisely drawn, whichever of these concepts is adopted has great pedagogical and research significance. International business operations require knowledge on many aspects of foreign business operations and can benefit from many types of comparative business research. On the other hand, foreign business operations and comparative business do not have as a major focus of interest the inter-nation dimension of business activity.

---

[1]John Fayerweather, Jean Boddewyn, Holger Engberg, **International Business Education: Curriculum Planning**, Graduate School of Business Administration, New York University, 1966, p. 5.

I would endorse the suggestion made some time ago by Professor Raymond Vernon that, when dealing with foreign business operations, we are perhaps better off leaving the task of teaching (and I presume that he would include research) to our existing functional groups — to our production people, our marketing people, our finance people and so on.[2] As to comparative business research, I would hope that people in the functional fields can be stimulated to do their research on foreign business operations in a comparative way, and that researchers in other disciplines, such as lawyers, political scientists, sociologists, and anthropologists, can be encouraged to undertake comparative research on business environmental factors. In teaching as well as research, the research flow from comparative business studies and foreign business operations research will be utilized as it fits into the international business framework.

By following this approach, we in international business can concentrate our limited research resources on the problems of business activity across national boundaries, the phenomenon of the multinational firm and its problems of operating in more than one country, and governmental problems and policies relative to international business. The research teams will, of course, include functional specialists and experts in related disciplines, as required by the specific projects.

I might add that I include in the field of international business many activities other than trade and production. Substantial and growing international business activities also exist in the fields of transportation services; private banking, finance, insurance and investment; construction; services such as advertising, accounting, hotels, manpower, and travel arrangements; communications, news media, and publishing; and the sale of technology through licensing, consulting, and management contracts.

II

My second topic is that the absorptive capacity of our teachers and curriculum has lagged behind the availability of knowledge and materials on international business. In other words, available knowledge on international business is much better than what comes through in our classes. This is true for specialized international business courses as well as for the introduction of international content into traditional functional or core courses in the business curriculum. "We (in a generic sense) know better than we do."

2Stefan H. Robock and Lee C. Nehrt (Eds.), **Education in International Business**, Graduate School of Business, Indiana University, 1964, p. 8.

This lag phenomenon is due to the newness of the field and the fact that most of the present crop of international business professors (like myself) are "converts" from related fields, not having had the opportunity for formal training in international business. In addition, the spectacular growth in student demand for international business courses has prevented many professors from dedicating the necessary time to absorbing and integrating available knowledge and research into textbooks, course materials, and curriculum design.

To be sure, the needs for new and additional research are great. But we also need a deliberate and major effort to bring business education up to a level permitted by the present state of knowledge on the international dimension of business. And the need is greater for the traditional business courses than for the specialized international business courses. Such an effort requires the better preparation of both professors and teaching materials. And the challenge may be similar to that faced by business schools in absorbing mathematics and quantitative analysis into business education.

III

My third and final topic is research needs, priorities, and approaches. And here I will be able only to introduce the subject.

One of the top priority needs is for comprehensive statistical reporting by national and international agencies on the international dimension of business. Most of the statistical data currently available comes out of a narrow international trade concept of international business and the balance of payments interests of national governments and international monetary agencies. Attention to international private investment is growing, but only limited data are available for most countries. And official information on the many types of international business activities other than trade and international production that were enumerated above is obscured or lumped into highly aggregated balance of payments accounts.

A worthy project for international business researchers, in cooperation with government officials, would be a task-force effort to develop concepts, a list of statistical series, and suggested operational techniques for providing comprehensive and current data on international business activities. The product of such an effort should then be presented for implementation to national governments and international agencies.

Another priority field of research is multinational business operations and business decision-making. Fortunately, several major projects are under way in this field. Professor Raymond Vernon has a pioneering venture in process to study changes in the patterns of production, marketing, finance, control, personnel, and organizational policies being made by multinational corporations. Professors Richard Farmer and Barry Richman have a major project to test through field research some of the relationships suggested in their theoretical work on comparative management.

A third priority field of research is the effect of government policies and decision-making on international business. The problem of international business statistics previously mentioned reflects the failure of governments to recognize specifically the international business phenomenon. Policies and programs are still emerging mainly from an international-trade or balance-of-payments type of concern.

Part of our task in international business teaching is to educate future business executives on the special problems of dealing with governments and adjusting to different governmental environments. An equally important part of our task should be to improve governmental decision-making and program formulation by examining international business activities from the standpoint of governmental goals, policies, and programs. An example of ad hoc governmental policy-making that suffers from a lack of knowledge on international business activities is the current voluntary, private foreign-investments restraint program of the United States.

Another field of needed research, which might be classified as a sub-topic in the category of governmental policies and decision-making, is a critical examination of the potential contribution that international business can make to the less-developed countries. For almost two decades, the U. S. foreign aid program has accepted the basic postulate that foreign private investment can play a *major* role in development assistance. Even though many types of aids to private investment in underdeveloped countries have been made available, the flows of private investment to the less-developed countries have not been increasing. Yet the government and much of the business community still cling to this optimistic but questionable postulate.

The final priority research field that I will mention is what I call environmental forecasting. (One of my colleagues has suggested that I call the subject "Environomics.") The international business firm operates in a multiplicity of national and supra-national environments, all of which are dynamic and in process of rapid change. Comparative studies of different institutions, cultures, legal systems, and policies toward business are helpful. But often such studies are snapshots at one point of time, or static pictures that are past history even when the studies are completed.

The international business firm making long-term investments or commitments needs both an understanding of the environments and a projection of the environmental changes that are likely to occur over a substantial period of time. Thus arises the need for environmental analysis and forecasting.

Environomics research requires attention to forecasting techniques; analysis of factors underlying specific policies, institutions or other features of different environments; identification of the dynamic forces influencing changes in components of the environment; determination of alternative paths over which the evolution of environments might travel; and, of course, best judgments as to the patterns which environmental changes are likely to follow. This may sound somewhat abstract and academic, but the idea of environmental forecasting can be illustrated concretely by many examples.

A general issue that I would like to mention before closing is the special need for contributions by disciplines other than economics in developing the field of international business. Even more so than in the case of domestic business, international business draws upon concepts, knowledge, and research from anthropology, geography, history, psychology, sociology, and political science. To some extent, our problem is to absorb existing knowledge from these disciplines. And in part, we need to better identify for scholars in these disciplines the kind of data and analyses that the international business field needs and that they can supply. But the most productive approach may be to get more teachers and researchers with professional training in the aforementioned basic disciplines involved in team or group research projects and in international business teaching.

I trust that I have given you a more than ample agenda for discussion in the limited time available.

Discussion Comments
Research in International Business

Panelists: Aliber and Robock

REPORTER: Hugh B. Carnes

Vernon initiated the discussion, pointing out the paucity of past research in the field now denominated International Business and the reliance on concepts and knowledge borrowed from disciplines such as economics and sociology. Such concepts tend to be peripheral and out of focus for international business, which cannot deal with the "ideal case."

There was some reaction to Aliber's comment that researchers whose backgrounds are in accounting, economics, behavioral sciences, or one of the functional fields will be the likely source of meaningful insights into the wide range of international problems. Some participants believed that this meant that international business researchers would be abdicating 80 percent of their responsibility. In response, it was suggested that some order of priority is imperative and that international business should first devote itself to those problems which are peculiarly within its purview. A proposed solution: bring social scientists into the research team.

Spier (Penn State) suggested that the basic problem is that of synthesis of social science and business.

It was suggested that international business should strive to be prescriptive first and then predictive. (Up to this point, the controversy seemed to be mainly over priorities.) Fayerweather (NYU) stated that wastage of resources through poorly organized and coordinated research activities is a serious problem, and better communication between schools is a solution.

Robock urged an attempt to obtain feed-in of research information from other countries, with particular effort in interesting some government agencies. Let's not make international research a national project, he suggested. The chairman (Vernon) posed the question of how one gets information, and illustrated the possibility of effective use of published sources, creating first a "critical mass" of data.

The question was put as to whether attempts to coordinate our research with that going on overseas are worthwhile. Several felt the "game was probably not worth the candle." Prins (The Netherlands) cited his own experience to indicate that while such coordination and cooperation are difficult, they are not impossible, and efforts in that direction should be made.

The opinion was advanced that shared research is a valuable approach to integration of interests.

The consensus seemed to be that involvement of people in other countries is essential to obtaining the international information which is one dimension of education for world business.

THOMAS A. GRAVES, JR.*

Harvard University

Technical Assistance on the Campus: Visiting
Students, Faculty and Businessmen Studying in
the United States—An Evaluation of Experience

The ICAME Program at Stanford

It is very difficult, and perhaps dangerous, to generalize about
technical assistance on the campus, for each situation is different from
the next. So I would like to focus on one particular experience at
ICAME, where I had the privilege of serving as Director from 1964
to 1967. This is number 30 of the 34 strategies discussed in the *EWA
Report,* concerning the development of a structured program with
a separate faculty to educate teachers from abroad.

ICAME is the International Center for the Advancement of Management Education. Under a seven-year grant from the Ford Foundation, its purpose has been to help build institutions and help develop
their teachers, working with schools of business in the developing
countries of Latin America, Asia, Africa, and Eastern Europe. ICAME
has focused its attention on some fifty of these schools from 25 countries, with its major emphasis being a nine-month training program
each year for faculty members of these schools, who came to the
campus of Stanford University for study.

I would like to concentrate first on the pitfalls and potential
problems with which a school may be faced in undertaking a major
effort in technical assistance on the campus, such as ICAME. And I
hope that our experience may be relevant to some of the decisions
with which you may be faced.

In contemplating such a venture, ask first whether this is a
program that your faculty really wants on its campus and at its school,
and ask whether your faculty is ready to give wholeheartedly to it
in time, effort, and resources. Such a program, to be successful, must

---

*[For biographical sketch, see p. 180. —Ed.]

be an integral part of the total educational thrust of the school. And the participants in such a program will take considerably more time, effort, and attention on the part of your faculty than do regular students. This suggests that your faculty, in order to undertake successfully this kind of a venture, must have a sense of service, must wish to make a contribution, and must recognize the very real rewards, feedback, and contribution which such a program may bring to the school.

Secondly, the feasibility of such a program should be looked at very hard before it is undertaken. Are its objectives realistic, is it do-able? For example, can you, as we tried to do with some success at ICAME, include all of the developing countries under one umbrella in a viable and integrated program? Also, remember that such a program requires relatively heavy faculty and administrative staffing by people who have some real interest and competence in this kind of work. Are the expertise and interests of your faculty really relevant to the needs of the faculty members' schools and countries represented in the program you hope to start? Are there sufficient funds and time to do the job, whatever its objectives? It will take more time and money than you think. Does the program really make sense — in terms of homogeneity or lack thereof of the participants, the institutions being served, the degree or certificate awarded at the end, the mix of countries? Let me urge you to have objective and realistic members of your faculty involved in the feasibility study, not advocates or proponents, for eventually your entire faculty will have to be involved.

Before you finally sign the contract to go ahead with this kind of a program, look at the contract very carefully. Is it flexible and workable, and can it really be administered with imagination? If you are working, as we have at ICAME, with the Ford Foundation, you are very fortunate. For when the Ford Foundation grants money to a school for such a program, it assumes that you know your business, and you are given a free hand to make decisions within very broad policy limits.

ICAME's success may be attributed in large part to the fact that from the very beginning the top people at the Stanford Business School were involved in it. Dean Ernest C. Arbuckle himself made the feasibility study, traveling around the world in the process. The most qualified man in the United States was searched out as the Center's first director, and Professor Ezra Solomon was the right choice. In the first program and each year thereafter the top Graduate School of Business faculty members were heavily involved in the teaching program. Just as important, it was accepted from the start that the program needed to be staffed administratively by sympathetic, skillful, and dedicated men and women.

ICAME has been unique as a teacher-training program in its emphasis on institutional relationships. The school from which the participant came, his relationship to it, its problems, needs, and potential were just as important as the man himself. ICAME's objective has been institution-building, of which teacher-training is a part. All this suggests very careful selection of the schools with which to develop a relationship — in terms of their stability, influence, and potential. And it suggests very careful selection of the faculty members who are nominated by these schools to come to your program. Then there is the job of follow-up on the man and his institution. Each of these steps requires time, money, and very considerable travel, expertise, and dedication on the part of your faculty. This particular approach is perhaps more than most schools can undertake, but I believe that it has been ICAME's greatest strength.

It is imperative that the program of study at a center such as ICAME be relevant, applicable, and useful to the needs, backgrounds, interests, and expectations of the men and institutions which it is trying to serve. This is not an easy goal to reach. It requires careful study of each of the institutions and interviews with each of the prospective participants on his home ground. And it requires extraordinary flexibility in the program itself, especially in the core, from year to year and man to man, to respond effectively to individual needs and interests. It is of course an impossible task for any one school in the United States to be an expert on all developing countries and their schools, but if you are to offer a useful teacher-training program you must do your best to develop at your school some real understanding in this area.

In this connection, expectations are important. In this kind of program you cannot expect State-side performance, and you are not in the business of selling the American way of life. The mores of the cultures from which these participants come are very real indeed, and you must be ready to adjust and respond to them. At the same time, your expectations of participants' performance will probably have to be higher than some of them would wish. And your high standards from the start are essential to the success of the program. Although the participants are probably very high-status faculty members in their home countries, the chances are good that you will have to treat them in some ways like students. This is a difficult tightrope to walk, especially when there is great heterogeneity among the participants, despite your best efforts for homogeneity. Their performance is more important than any certificate or degree they may obtain at the end of the program.

Also do everything you can to involve the participants in your program in the total work and life of your school, university, and community. The role of host families, the involvement of participants in your master's and doctoral programs in their elective courses beyond the core, and the relationships between the participants and your faculty and regular students are all matters which merit your careful attention.

Obviously, a program such as ICAME is a major undertaking. We at Stanford have been fortunate in having an advisory board made up of the deans of several of the leading business schools and representatives of key government and educational agencies. This cooperative base of support and counsel has been of very considerable value at key stages in ICAME's development and evolution.

Now I come to my final point. Be ready for change in a program such as ICAME. Mistakes will be made and you will learn from them, and the needs and interests of the schools you are serving will change. ICAME itself is now in the process of very major changes in basic character, objectives, and activities, which suggest only that it has been in part successful in meeting its early goals, and it is now time to turn ICAME's attention to some of the other more pressing new needs of the evolving institutions which it serves.

A recapitulation of some of the problem areas and pitfalls which your school may face as it embarks on a major program of technical assistance on campus suggests perhaps some of the factors for success of such an undertaking:

A faculty which is ready and willing for the program.
An objective and realistic feasibility study.
A flexible and workable contract.
The involvement in the program of the top people at your school, from the beginning.
Institution-building relationships.
A program of study that is relevant and applicable.
Reasonable, realistic, and high expectations and standards of performance.
Involvement of participants fully in your school, university, and community.
A cooperative and supporting advisory board.
Flexibility and readiness for major change.

ICAME at Stanford and the International Teachers Program at the Harvard Business School are unique in their depth and breadth. And obviously a major effort like these requires some more attention if it is to be successful, in comparison to a more modest undertaking. But I suggest that whenever a school is considering how best to respond to visiting students, faculty, and businessmen who wish to visit or study on its campus, most of these factors described above are relevant to a degree. Such programs and visits, if done well, are not only of great service and make a real contribution to those who come, but they are also of significant value to your school. As your school starts to undertake such a program, be selfish enough to consider what the program and the people who visit you will contribute to your faculty and your school. And then work hard to make sure that it is in fact a two-way stream. This is what education is all about.

VERNON K. ZIMMERMAN
University of Illinois

Technical Assistance on the Campus: Experience at the University of Illinois

The efforts in international education have had a long history at the University of Illinois. This institutional commitment to international education in general and international education for business in specific has gone on for many decades at the University.

The annals of the University of Illinois furnish documentation of a significant and continuing debt to both visiting and permanent international scholars. In addition, there has been a constructive history of international student attendance.

The size of the present commitment to international education at Illinois is approximately 1,700 students. The many and varied needs of these international students have been institutionalized in such University offices as the Foreign Student Office and the Foreign Graduate Admissions Office. In addition, there is a definite air of awareness and a sensitivity to the needs of the international student by the department heads and other administrative officers of the University. Quasi-University organizations, such as the YMCA and certain service clubs, have also assisted in the many vital social aspects of the short-run or permanent assimilation of people of various cultures into the Illinois community.

VERNON K. ZIMMERMAN is Professor of Accountancy, Acting Dean, and Director of the Center for International Education and Research in Accounting, University of Illinois. He has MS and PhD degrees from the University of Illinois, and is a Certified Public Accountant. He was a Fulbright Visiting Exchange Professor in 1960-61 at the Hochschule für Welthandel, Vienna, and Guggenheim Research Fellow in 1965-66 in Western Europe. In 1964, he was chairman of the Committee on International Accounting of the American Accounting Association. Presently, he is a member of the Ford Foundation Study Committee for the Internationalization of the Business Curriculum. He has written extensively on accounting subjects, including *Accounting Theory: Continuity and Change* (co-authored, Prentice-Hall, 1962).

THE DIMENSIONS OF COMMITMENT

The commitment of the College of Commerce and Business Administration to international education for business may be measured in several dimensions. Three are suggested by the full title of our panel session.

In terms of visiting students, the current international graduate students in business number approximately one hundred. These represent a wide spectrum of the countries of the world. In the Department of Accountancy, one of the major departments of the College, 35 foreign graduate students, representing 13 countries, are currently in residence for advanced graduate work.

The faculty of the College has also made a significant commitment both to international business programs and to the utilization of the talents of international scholars. More than ten percent of the present permanent faculty of the College have earned their terminal academic degree from institutions outside the United States. Some of the countries currently represented in this classification are: Austria, Germany, Switzerland, Venezuela, Canada, Denmark, Japan, Jamaica, Hungary, the Netherlands, and Israel. Significantly, none of these international staff members has been isolated from the mainstream of local academic effort, in the sense of aiming their contribution to specialized international business courses. Rather, the deliberate policy of the College has been to utilize these international staff members in the same teaching and research manner as for staff members of a domestic background.

The third category of international contact indicated by the title involves visiting businessmen. This has been an area of lesser attention at Illinois. Yet for periods as long as one year, the College has worked with visiting business leaders from other countries, such as Germany, England, Austria, Indonesia, Japan, and France. The absolute number of such contacts is quite large. Many visitors, however, only spend a day or two visiting the College to survey its total educational programs.

GOALS OF TECHNICAL ASSISTANCE ON THE CAMPUS

The College has attempted to achieve two primary goals in its technical assistance to visiting international students.

The first goal is to furnish as comprehensive and useful an educational program for business as possible in the total time available. The second goal is to attempt to integrate the visiting international student as completely as possible into the educational structure and system of this Midwestern university. In other words, there has been no attempt to isolate or to establish special sections or courses specifically designed for the visiting student. Rather, through such stipulations as a prescribed proficiency in the use of English and through a conscious attempt to minimize problems in social adjustments, the course of study for international students is basically the same as that of domestic students. In my opinion, the experience from this approach has been favorable.

An additional goal of the University's policy in relation to international students has been the encouragement of their return to their homeland, equipped with the new backgrounds and skills hopefully acquired during their university stay. In other words, the much publicized "brain drain" is consciously attempted to be avoided by the University. Obviously there are many temptations for the international student to stay at his American university or in the United States. These include the easier road to academic title and prestige available in the United States, the availability of a higher real salary than that which is available in his homeland, and the development of a certain cultural "gap" or social preferences. We can agree that these are significant temptations.

May I cite one case with which I am personally acquainted and ask you to attempt to appreciate the stress placed upon this particular student from Austria. As an engineering, post-doctoral student at Illinois, Hans earned approximately $350 per month. Upon his return to Austria, his position in industry, approximately the same as that which he had left two years before, commanded 4,000 Austrian schillings, or $160 per month. In addition, Hans found that there seemed to be little, if any, social or economic recognition of his United States interval. You can well imagine the long period of depression this shift of circumstances brought to him.

There are also temptations to the instructing school in relation to the international student graduate. Often there are new international programs for which his talents seem uniquely matched. He represents a known quantity and often an available quantity in a very tight market. In addition, the recruiting process of the local graduate is the most economical in terms of campus visits or entertainment efforts. Also to hire an international, as well as a domestic, graduate of your own university does presuppose that a significant degree of institutional loyalty is achieved by such an arrangement.

Many articles have been written concerning the impact of the "brain drain." For instance, *The Economist* often notes the impact on the English medical and social scene of the migration of English medical scholars to America. The American government, as well as individual universities, has attempted to discourage the stay of foreign scholars in American universities beyond their terms of study or visiting scholarships. This point has been of particular interest to me because of the opportunity to observe its impact in both the American and overseas environments. This interest prompted me to examine the history of 14 of the most recent graduates in Accountancy at the University of Illinois to determine whether a "brain drain" situation existed or not. Of the 14 people, one remained at the University. Only two other students stayed in the United States (both as college teachers) in a capacity which could be considered as contributing to an undesirable shifting of academic resources from the foreign country to the United States. Of the other 11, four returned to their native countries and assumed university teaching positions, one went to another country but remained in teaching, two assumed positions at the World Bank, and four entered professional accounting in their native countries.

VISITING STUDENTS

In terms of actual numbers, and immediate and potential impact, the academic programs of the visiting students are the most significant factor involving the international aspects of business education. The numbers involved in the case of the University of Illinois have already been noted. When one compares these international graduates with the total of all those having graduate degrees in business in the United States, or even with the total of such degrees internationally, the impact is significant.

One of the strongest impressions that I have received in my association with this on-going program at Illinois is the casualness with which the program continues. In other words, the presence of a substantial number of international students does not cause any undue excitement. More than a generation of significant contact has made their presence commonplace. The several areas in which problems could arise, such as language and customs, have been quite well anticipated because of the familiarity of both the institution and the professor with the special problems of the international student. The United States has standard tests, such as the Michigan Test for English, and their use in the case of admission to graduate study has helped achieve a standard of relative uniformity.

When one appraises such a program of commitment to international business education for visiting students, the advantages, certainly in the short run, seem to be to the student involved. In other words, participation in the American program, knowledge of the American theories and techniques, and exposure to a different economy and society, all seem to be opportunities for a significant intellectual advancement for the visiting scholar. This is not to say that this happy result always occurs. The earlier comments about the "brain drain" indicate one of the undesirable developments which may occur. In addition, certain foreign scholars (although they too have their domestic counterparts) drift into a state of seemingly perpetual graduate status.[1]

In summary, the experience of the College of Commerce and Business Administration at the University of Illinois with visiting students has been quite satisfactory. There have been no special classes, no segregation of topics or language sections, and the same package of educational ingredients offered the American graduate student has, in essence, been made available to his foreign colleagues. As one thinks of the positions and contributions made by those business graduates of his direct acquaintance, the program seems to work very well. The alternative of not having these individuals making their contribution in the capacities they now have would be a grim prospect indeed.

The University of Illinois program has attempted to integrate the visiting student into the existing program. In turn, the University has, when on the foreign scene, consistently attempted to work through the existing academic institutions of the host country. Experience indicates that the success of American educational inputs in the foreign academic setting is greatest when the American presence is channeled through the existing domestic institutions. In other words, our visiting faculty members have attempted to join the existing schools and programs of the host country. For a variety of reasons, our observations of those schools, well-intentioned as they may be, that are founded, financed, and molded in the American image, are that they do not offer the highest probabilities of long-run success.

VISITING FACULTY

The experience of the College in its continuing contacts with international members of the academic community has been one of

---

[1]One recent case, while perhaps extreme, indicates the length to which such foreign training can go. A recent applicant for the MBA listed as his background an undergraduate degree and a master's degree, both in his native country. This was followed by another master's degree in the United States, a master's in a related field, following which he applied for admission and financial aid to the University of Illinois in order to work on his fourth master's degree. His age was 37. This case has been repeated in less severe form by some students who have enrolled at the University. The formal program has in some cases been doubled in length, with a certain loss of man-years of contribution to the home country.

gradual evolution. While there were instances of visits by Americans, particularly to European universities earlier in this century, there does not seem to have been a significant degree of interchange until after World War II. In other words, these earlier travels of American business professors abroad seem to have been educationally beneficial only to the extent that travel is considered broadening and intellectually stimulating.

Official government encouragement of the exchange of scholars under the terms of such programs as the Fulbright Exchange Program significantly affected the University. In general, the business faculties have seemed to lag behind in their participation in exchange programs compared to the humanities or the scientific fields. But certain exchanges of visiting professors have occurred, and approximately ten percent of the present permanent Illinois business faculty has actually assumed teaching assignments in foreign universities.

To those of us who have been associated with the present faculty for a substantial number of years, a definite shift in attitude in their respect for foreign scholars and scholarship is noticeable. A certain sense of realism in international academic affairs is present now, and the appreciation of the opportunities for a truly international exchange of ideas is much more apparent.

The University's sabbatical policies have served to foster this sort of exchange. The economics of adequate payment while in an overseas setting have been facilitated by coordination with a grant from the government or a foundation. The cross-currents generated by these visits have been specifically manifested in the visits of colleagues and by friendships developed in the foreign setting, and also in the exchange of teaching assistants. The latter exchange, however, is usually only one way — to the United States.

To a limited degree, visiting scholars at the University of Illinois have been permitted to teach in an existing course with a rather prescribed subject matter content and method of presentation. Furthermore, in the new program of the Center for International Education and Research in Accounting, visiting professors are encouraged to develop a lecture series for graduate students in accounting which stresses the significant theories and practices of the professors' homeland. In addition, a specific invitation for research in the same area is given. In the main, lectures of this type have proven very beneficial to the home university. The mechanics of graduate student registration and participation offer certain problems but do not seem either insurmountable or too costly in relation to the possible benefits.

In two cases, this program has generated such an enthusiastic response from the foreign scholar as to lead to a discussion of a second visit. The opportunities to be derived from a second visit and the more effective use of time because of earlier knowledge are obvious.

VISITING BUSINESSMEN

In many respects the total University program for visiting business leaders has been the least organized and most diffused of the three educational emphases discussed in this paper. Explanations for this condition are, at least in part, derivatives of the often impromptu timing and nature of the visit. The lack of coordination and lead time, and the fact that the University's main business really concerns the regular semester-type of attendance and instruction instead of short visits by business leaders of varying local backgrounds and abilities are apparent factors. Yet the long-run impact of these visits, based on my observation at the University of Illinois, has been positive in two specific aspects.

The first involves the businessmen themselves, whether they are from the so-called developing areas or from more developed countries, such as Japan and Western Europe. We have been pleased to note an open appreciation on their part of American business education techniques. Anyone who has witnessed at first hand the operation of the tightly controlled and selective educational system of Europe, for instance, and compared this approach with the deliberately broad approach of American education cannot help but be impressed by the contrast in educational viewpoint.

Secondly, nearly every academic commentator admits that business education at the collegiate level is one of the academic areas in which the United States is a definite and genuine leader. The academic stature of business school faculties has reached its peak to date in the United States. The visiting businessmen have, I believe, observed the methods of instruction and educational approach in their visits to our University, and in certain cases have deliberately attempted to initiate similar ideas or modifications of them in their own environment.

Complementary benefits from these visits have been experienced by the University. That is, the faculty of the University, through this interchange with colleagues of other environments and cultures, has adopted certain strong points from the educational systems of the other cultures. These visits by businessmen allow the practical verification via first-hand experience of conditions in markets and other practices of other economies. This experience has afforded a valuable opportunity for intellectual interchange.

It is with this group, the itinerant visitor, that the problems of follow-up and meaningful long-run communication are most difficult. The lack of a regular and lengthy exposure to the local campus conditions cannot be totally bridged by correspondence, regardless of its timeliness and frequency. Yet for those visitors with an adequate degree of motivation for a continuing exchange of ideas, the mails and occasional visits by both parties have, in many cases, enabled meaningful exchanges concerning business practices and business education.

CONCLUDING REMARKS

In preparing this paper, I was repeatedly impressed by the significant number of deliberate program steps which had been taken by the University and which were noted in the range of levels of commitment by the *EWA Report*. For example, the listing of the activities constituting a program of international business which are helpfully outlined in 34 escalated steps by the *Report* in the instance of the University of Illinois are being followed in almost every respect by the College of Commerce and Business Administration. Also the order of commitment has followed historically in nearly the same order as that noted by the *Report*. Also it is my impression that the commitment at Illinois is on a firm footing. The involvement of faculty is widespread, and the interest is genuine. The interchange, on both a personal and professional basis, has created bonds which indicate a sustained and growing involvement in the area of international education for business. Recent events in terms of specific contracts for assistance overseas are adding a new dimension to education for business at the University. In conclusion, the program has been tried over a period of time and has been accepted with a feeling of accomplishment at least by this university.

Discussion Comments

Technical Assistance on the Campus

Panelists: Graves and Zimmerman

REPORTER: James T. Murphy

By and large, this discussion centered on a comparison of ICAME (Stanford) and International Teachers Program (Harvard), although several peripheral matters were discussed, relating to comments made in other discussion sessions:

1. Visiting professors do influence the development of an International Business program through their seminars with faculty and through a more subtle influence on faculty via the students.

2. There should be pressure on the foreign student to obtain financial assistance, aside from the normal amount of PhD aid. Many such students can get money if the pressure is on them. Be careful, however, of using grant money to build up a student body; the grant may be cut!

3. Teaching foreign nationals does take time and may justify a modification of a U.S. professor's load.

COMPARISON OF ICAME AND ITP

In the main, the objectives of these two programs are the same, namely, to train teachers. ICAME has tended to be more structured than ITP, but the latter now seems to be moving toward having more structure. Haynes (Harvard) thinks that unstructured programs are better for highly motivated students having clear objectives. A few poorly motivated students can spoil an image, however; so a shift to about 30-percent "structure" seems desirable. By 30-percent "structure," Haynes meant a set of specially designed core courses which cover the broad dimensions of business administration, to include integrative-type courses for which students have been, and are, reluctant to register. For the highly motivated student, such structure may be discouraging, and so ITP may lose a few potential students.

In other respects, ICAME more than ITP has emphasized institution-building. Teacher-training is only a partial objective of ICAME. ITP has drawn its students more generally from the world, while ICAME has generally limited participation to the so-called "developing countries."

Eventually an "ideal" middle ground will exist for both programs: a similar orientation to core courses will be required or will be open to all students; special courses will be available to suit the additional needs of participants; finally, there should be flexibility to adapt to changing conditions and inputs.

ICAME has thus far avoided the awarding of a degree, because foreign students tend to be much too degree-oriented, and this attitude should be discouraged. To the extent that a degree is desired, a good share of ICAME courses can be transferred to a degree program. As an environmental constraint, however, foreign institutions are more and more interested in sending students to degree programs; therefore it may be necessary in the future to make the relationships between non-degree and degree programs much more explicit.

Because foreign institutions, especially in Latin America, intend to offer their own PhD programs in Business Administration or International Business, it makes sense for them to want to send their future teachers to degree programs. There is some danger in this, however. PhDs may want to teach only the research-type courses and not the more mundane matters relating to the daily decision problems of a manager — working capital management, for example. Perhaps the PhDs should be used mainly in a research capacity or in writing cases where their advanced education and expanded resources will be used most efficiently.

Two final aspects: 1. Follow-up programs are usually a good thing, since many students do wish to maintain some sort of identification with the U.S. school. It is a prestige factor for them, and it may be beneficial for the U.S. institution to know who has moved into what influential position and where. 2. At both Stanford and Illinois, the student is greatly encouraged to stay in school to finish the advanced degree program; but the "all but dissertation" problem is not really a serious one.

ALAN B. COLEMAN
Stanford University

Technical Assistance Abroad:

FEEDBACK MUST BE PROGRAMMED

In this paper, summarizing my remarks at the Conference on Education for International Business, I should like to pose essentially three questions:

1. Does significant feedback at home occur in an organized way due to technical assistance projects abroad?
2. Where and how should such feedback occur?
3. How might universities achieve a higher and more consistent level of feedback in the future?

First, let me make clear my own bias. I believe that there is considerable potential for valuable feedback in the broadest sense to the university community from technical assistance programs abroad. I also believe that such feedback can prove a valuable contribution in helping to achieve our objectives of training managers for substantial responsibility and leadership in tomorrow's world community.

Let me also state a personal conclusion: I do not believe that in the university we are doing nearly as effective a job as we might

ALAN B. COLEMAN is Associate Professor of Business Administration, Graduate School of Business, Stanford University. He has MBA and PhD degrees from Stanford, his dissertation dealing with "Problems in the Financial Management of Foreign Operations." In 1957-58, he lectured at IMEDE, Lausanne, and from 1963-66 he served as the first Dean of the Escuela de Administración de Negocios para Graduados (ESAN), Lima. Prior to joining the Stanford faculty in 1962, he was at the Harvard Business School. For nine years, he worked for Parker Pen Company, San Francisco. He has co-edited three books of cases on commercial bank management, finance, and financial institutions. He is presently an advisor to the Ford Foundation on its Latin American programs.

in capturing for our own benefit the experiences we have gained in technical assistance abroad. That is, there remains much to be desired in terms of the feedback which now occurs on campus when faculty members return from overseas assignments. This is not to say that feedback does not occur: it does. I think that what does happen, however, results "informally" from the interests and efforts of individual faculty members and often does not reflect any conscious, organized effort on the part of the university or the business school to capitalize upon an important new asset: a returning faculty member who has enjoyed a significant exposure and experience abroad.

There are several reasons which might explain why we have not utilized fully the valuable experience and new resources available to us from faculty members who have acted abroad as teachers, researchers, or advisors. One of the principal reasons relates to the nature of the business school's international commitment in the first instance. Frequently this commitment is not expressly thought out as it relates to the total effort of the business school within the university community. International programs are often undertaken on an *ad hoc* basis without reference to any conscious or well-formulated policy as to the nature of international responsibility and activity as a part of the total business school effort. Such a policy might address itself to these kinds of questions: how much of our total capability should be committed to activities outside the United States; should we concentrate these efforts in limited geographic areas; should we restrict our efforts only to developing countries; should we undertake any international programs that may have major long-term staffing implications; and so forth. Perhaps it is inappropriate to ask for a very specific long-run policy to guide business schools in their international commitments and involvements, since the area itself is a relatively new one. Nonetheless, to the degree that programs are accepted without reference to some policy framework as a guide, the potential for capitalizing on the feedback at home which may result from these projects may be reduced.

The second point relating to my general conclusion (that a great deal more needs to be done to capitalize on campus feedback) involves the basic notion of cost-benefit analysis insofar as the undertaking of specific international programs is concerned. If in fact I am correct that many schools do not have a policy framework upon which to base program decisions, it clearly becomes difficult to analyze a proposed overseas program in terms of its cost (primarily investment of faculty and administrative time) and its benefits (to us, in large measure, the feedback we are discussing here). Naturally any cost-benefit analysis of an individual international program will be necessarily imprecise. We are dealing with both tangible and intangible values to the host country as well as to ourselves. Nonetheless, I am convinced that frequently there is but little effort made to undertake a cost-benefit analysis, with as much specificity as possible, on individual international project proposals. While this may be done informally or intuitively, I believe more emphasis should be stressed on assessing particular costs and benefits related to a specific proposal in order to increase the chances of beneficial and systematic feedback at home.

I would lay heavy stress upon the "enlightened self-interest" factor in decisions about technical assistance abroad, again to increase the chances of feedback. *Unless the U. S. institution can visualize clear and substantial benefits on the home campus, I believe a strong case should be made for not undertaking such commitments.* Since faculty and administrative resources are scarce, and since really qualified faculty who are available and interested in international assignments is extremely limited, the benefits to the home institution must be abundantly clear before the investment of these scarce resources is made. Presumably feedback on the home campus represents one of the greatest benefits to us from an international technical assistance project. Such feedback will more likely occur, if in fact the administrative decision to undertake a program assumes in advance that specific and concrete kinds of feedback will occur at some predictable time in the future.

Given my belief that many schools do not have a policy framework to guide them in their international involvements, and that any cost-benefit analysis on specific programs may frequently be done in a most informal way, it follows that faculty returning from overseas assignments may not be fully able to integrate their new experiences and interests into the several aspects of the United States business school life and work. The fact that much feedback does occur testifies to the interests of individual faculty members in sharing their experiences with colleagues and students, but the process is more random than I should like, and I believe it can be improved.

WHERE AND HOW SHOULD FEEDBACK OCCUR?

A. The Professor. Clearly the direct impact of overseas technical assistance falls squarely upon the individual faculty member. It will influence him in many ways: through exposure to a new cultural, political, and economic environment; frequently through the necessity to adapt himself and his family to a new foreign language; and professionally in providing him an opportunity to contrast and adjust his own area of competence to similar activities in new cultural circumstances. It is my own belief that the greater impact on the faculty member will occur due to his responses to new cultural and environmental factors rather than to the fundamental differences in the nature of the faculty member's professional area of competence. Perhaps the greatest benefit to the individual business school faculty member will result from a broader awareness of international affairs and their implications for the United States rather than of the processes of international business *per se*. The faculty member will also probably learn more about the United States through the perspective he gains on our country by living and working abroad. All of us will react differently to this kind of new awareness to international affairs, and many of us will use differing methods of drawing upon such experiences to enrich our teaching and research when we return to the United States.

We can all suggest, I am sure, various examples of the impact upon the individual faculty member which may occur due to overseas experience. I would like to cite only one example which illustrates, rather dramatically, the "feedback" which may occur due to a technical assistance program abroad.

The Graduate School of Business at Stanford has been involved since 1962 with a technical assistance program in Lima, Peru. This program, supported jointly by the governments of Peru and the United States, has involved the establishment of a Graduate School of Business Administration, called ESAN.[1] The school was initially staffed largely by Stanford faculty members; however, it now is operating primarily with a Peruvian faculty. One of the members of the original faculty team, Professor Frank Shallenberger, spent nearly 18 months in Peru and returned to the United States with a deep sense of the problems of that country and the opportunities for further cooperation between the United States and Peru. Specifically, Professor Shallenberger felt that many young men and women from the United States could themselves learn and benefit a great deal by working with small and medium-sized business enterprises in countries like Peru through trying to help such firms operate more effectively. As a direct result of his experience in South America, Professor Shallenberger proposed to the Peace Corps that a new program be established for a limited number of American MBA graduates. These

---

[1][For a discussion of ESAN, see the paper by Sterling D. Sessions, pp. 149-61. —Ed.]

graduates would complete the regular Peace Corps training, and the first "pilot project" group would go to Peru to spend the remainder of their two-year term working directly with several small and medium-sized business enterprises acting as advisors. In this way these graduates could utilize their administrative training, gain Peace Corps experience, and at the same time benefit from the enrichment of life in a foreign culture. This program, which began in July, 1967 with about 40 MBAs from some 20 universities (30 members in Peru and 10 in Colombia), represents a pilot model for what may become a similar application in several other developing countries.

Whether or not this Peace Corps pilot program succeeds or fails, the point remains: here is an example of strong "feedback" from an individual Stanford faculty member resulting from a technical assistance program abroad. This example could not have been anticipated in any "cost-benefit analysis" in advance of a decision to undertake the ESAN project. It does, however, provide an illustration of the feedback which may result from the individual professor who gains experience abroad. This example may have important multiplier effects upon both Americans and, in this case, Peruvian businessmen, segments of the Peruvian economy, and perhaps later, similar effects in other Latin American countries.

B. The curriculum content in teaching. Changes and adaptations in course content represent a major area where the returning faculty member may exercise his experience and knowledge gained abroad. He may simply encourage an "international awareness" on the part of students through his teaching, without making major course changes. He may prefer to add some additional new material, introducing an international dimension. Or he may in fact organize and teach a totally new course. These variations will depend upon the personality and interests of the individual faculty member, but they will also be guided to some extent by the nature of the business school's international commitment — a point which has already been discussed. If the international dimensions of business administration have been developed within a given school in a policy context, it may prove somewhat easier for returning faculty members to integrate their new experiences and interests into business school teaching and curricula.

One of the issues posed here relates to a matter much debated at this Conference: that is, does there exist in fact an international field of business apart from the fundamental curriculum, or does an international operation represent only a special case of the generalized principles we already attempt to teach our undergraduate and graduate students? Although I have personal views on this subject (i.e., that there is not a distinctly separate field of international business), nonetheless, the greatest potential for feedback due to foreign technical assistance may relate to the faculty members' attitude and interest in adapting curriculum content and teaching to encourage what I would call "an international awareness" or sensitivity to the significance of international political and economic events among students of business administration. That is, the student may, at the very least, be encouraged to place American business enterprise not within the context of our own geographic boundaries, but within the framework of world-wide enterprise and political and economic activity.

C. *Students, especially PhD candidates.* There is an opportunity for substantial feedback from technical assistance abroad into PhD programs for those men who may be attracted to this activity as a partial career interest. There now exist many opportunities in business school international programs for PhD candidates to participate, and in some cases to write dissertations overseas, based on international research problems. I doubt that this opportunity has yet been adequately exploited. Increasing numbers of PhD candidates are expressing interest in gaining international experience, and one important feedback from foreign technical assistance programs into the university community could involve PhD candidates undertaking overseas assignments, especially where they might combine such opportunities with dissertation research.

For example, at Stanford we specifically negotiated with the Agency for International Development (AID) to permit a limited number of Stanford PhD candidates to participate as research associates in the ESAN program in Lima in order to allow them a chance to live and work abroad while undertaking dissertation research as part of their overseas involvement. Two doctoral dissertations have been completed by PhD candidates who were research associates at ESAN[2], and we have been generally satisfied with this phase of the program.

D. *Faculty research.* There are numerous opportunities for feedback on the home campus relating to faculty research, either undertaken abroad or at home. There are innumerable areas for

---

2"A Business Investment Decision-Making Method for Developing Countries," by Harold Wyman, and "A Comparison of the Impact of Executive Development Programs upon Owner-Entrepreneurs and Employee-Managers," by Lawrence McKibbin.

comparative disciplinary research and especially for interdisciplinary research abroad when faculty members from differing academic disciplines are working together on a common program. This represents one area (as does the PhD participation described in C above) in which cost-benefit analysis might be applied in advance of negotiating an international agreement.

It is also frequently feasible to negotiate research agreements in university contracts such that a specific benefit to the university and particular faculty members may occur due to the advance provision for funds to undertake research in connection with foreign programs. Indeed, advance provision for and encouragement of research opportunities abroad and/or at home may make the recruitment of capable faculty for overseas assignment somewhat easier. And, if the home institution has an on-going commitment to international business education, there may be continuing opportunities for further research into international business problems after the faculty member has completed his tour abroad and returned home.

In summary, then, feedback can and should occur starting with the individual faculty member and, through him, extending into curriculum content and teaching, encouragement of PhD participation, and in research both abroad and in the United States.

RECOMMENDATIONS

How might the university community achieve a higher and more consistent level of feedback from technical assistance programs in the future?

Based on the above observations, I would make several specific recommendations.

1.   There is a greater possibility of higher and more consistent feedback occurring on campus if a statement of policy has been prepared defining the international scope and dimensions of a particular business school's effort. Accordingly, as a first important step towards encouraging feedback, greater emphasis should be placed on clarifying and communicating to the faculty the business school's sense of commitment and responsibility towards assisting in the progress of business education abroad. From this policy framework, faculty members should then be able to perceive how they individually could capitalize on foreign experience and how they could integrate that experience into various business school programs upon returning to the United States.

2.   An attempt should be made to make as express as possible

(perhaps in written form) a concrete cost-benefit analysis relating any proposed international program to the business school's overall philosophical commitment to the international dimensions of business education. In such a cost-benefit analysis, heavy stress should be placed on "enlightened self-interest" — i.e., specifically how can our institutions benefit from a particular international proposal. If significant potential benefits (feedback) are not quite clear, such a proposal should become considerably less attractive. This should result since those proposals whose benefits are high will stand the greatest chance of receiving continuing and active faculty and administrative support, thereby enhancing the probability of success for a particular program. Without such continuing broad support by faculty and administration, the possibility of reduced effectiveness or outright failure may rise sharply.

3. There is, however, one further area which clearly will encourage consistently higher and better feedback from technical assistance abroad: that is, the reward structure. It is unfortunately true that the reward structure in the academic world, at least in many institutions, does not usually encourage even a moderate amount of time dedicated to international experience, particularly on the part of junior faculty members. There are many reasons for this which are familiar to all of us. Geographic remoteness from campus for a significant period may have its hazards; it becomes more difficult to undertake research and publication when abroad for a wide variety of reasons; it is much more difficult to measure individual performance abroad in the total business school evaluation structure; such experience is not considered by many senior faculty members to be significant in career development; and so forth. Since many, indeed most, junior faculty members perceive a value system which operates to discourage international involvement, it becomes difficult to find individuals who are willing to make a commitment to gain this added element of professional competence. I am convinced that a much greater interest on the part of individual faculty members, particularly junior ones, would become evident if they could be persuaded that good performance abroad and utilization of such experience at home would prove both personally and professionally meaningful to them. I am not convinced, however, that most business schools and universities are yet prepared to modify their reward structure in order to encourage younger faculty members to seek overseas commitments as an integral part of their professional career. In this I think we define the desirable professional qualifications of a business school faculty member in today's world too nar-

rowly, and we may therefore deny him the opportunity of experiences which will enrich both himself, his family, and his students for many years to come.

I would hope in the years ahead, as the international aspects of American enterprise and American business education expand, as I am convinced they will, that we may as a university community gradually revise our definition of faculty competence such that significant overseas experience may be considered an important and indeed vital part of professional development. If and when that time occurs, I am equally convinced that more orderly and effective feedback in our universities from technical assistance abroad will in fact be achieved.

LEO G. ERICKSON
Michigan State University

Feedback from Overseas Projects

On page 24 of the *EWA Report* the statement is made that:

It is the central theme of this report that professional schools of business and public administration have failed to face fully the international aspects of their professional responsibilities.

My remarks are addressed to this central theme, within the context of technical assistance and institution-building projects in business administration. Moreover, I have been asked by Professor Zeff to make some reference to our activities at Michigan State. I suspect I would have done so anyhow.

We start out on a point of agreement that, in large part, we at Michigan State, as well as business schools in general, have not done as much in providing feedback from our overseas projects as we could have done, or perhaps should have done.

We at Michigan State have indeed done a considerable amount in the field of international business. For example, using the tests on pp. 30-31 of the *EWA Report,* we think we rank in the highest category—i. e., "schools which wish to develop a special international

LEO G. ERICKSON is Professor of Marketing and Director of the Bureau of Business and Economic Research, Graduate School of Business Administration, Michigan State University. He has MA and PhD degrees from the University of Iowa. From 1960 to 1962, he was technical advisor on MSU's Brazil Project, in São Paulo, where he helped establish the research and publication center of the São Paulo School of Business Administration and organized and directed the School's graduate program. From 1957 to 1960, he was Director of Marketing Services, Grain Processing Corporation, in charge of the company's market research. He has written several articles, including "Analyzing Brazilian Consumer Markets" (MSU *Business Topics,* Summer, 1963), and a section on marketing in Mc Millan and Gonzalez, *International Enterprise in a Developing Economy* (MSU, 1964).

competence in the world affairs aspects of their profession"—we can tick off those attributes which characterize such a school and apply them to our Graduate School of Business Administration.

Yet we frequently hear that we have not done enough in capitalizing on the competence of our faculty who have been on overseas projects. And I believe a very good case can be made for such criticism.

Of importance to us in this meeting is to try to analyze why we have not done more in feeding-back on campus, so that we can decide if we want to do more; and, if so, how we might accomplish it.

First, let us briefly examine what we at MSU have done and are doing, taking up curriculum initially.

CURRICULUM

The statement was made in the *EWA Report* that at Michigan State we try to embody international business into our existing courses wherever possible, and that, further, we believe the best preparation for international business is through the regular curriculum. Both statements are correct, even though necessarily incomplete.

Outside of economics, which is a part of our business school and which has a number of international courses, we have one course in international business in our undergraduate curriculum and three in our graduate curriculum, and none of these is required. All four of these courses are taught in the Department of Marketing and Transportation Administration. There probably is little content in these courses which results directly from our overseas projects. But—and this is important—it is no accident that these courses are taught in the Marketing and Transportation Department. Most of the regular faculty in the department have been overseas on long-term project assignments. It is from this department that we have had chiefs of party of both our Brazil and Turkey projects as well as the Dean of the School of Business in Nigeria.

From having had a part in designing these courses, I know that adding them to our curriculum was a direct result of our faculty's interest in international aspects, triggered by their experience in technical assistance projects. Thus, even though the course titles, and even the course content, don't evidence it, the very existence of these courses is a result of our overseas projects.

POSSIBILITY OF COURSE ADDITIONS

We have given formal consideration on several occasions both to offering a degree in international business and to requiring courses in this area. Thus far, we have rejected both proposals. There are a number of reasons for this action, but I think the major one is the trend against fragmentation of the curriculum into additional specialized courses.

There are some aspects of this basic reason of not fragmenting curriculum which are worth mentioning specifically. One of these is in the area of opportunity costs. Our programs are so tight that it is extremely difficult to squeeze in additional courses. For example, at MSU an undergraduate in the business school can get his bachelor's degree with as few as 12 quarter hours in his major department. He cannot count over 20 hours. At the MBA level he takes a maximum of 20 hours in his major—4 or 5 courses. Nor are we likely to increase the total number of hours required for a bachelor's degree. Such a change would be counter to the trend we see at other schools. We might very well increase the number of hours required for the MBA. If we do so, we might add additional courses in international business. But make no mistake about it. If we do add to the required hours for the MBA, we will not be doing so in order to introduce courses in international business. We will be doing it because we have decided we need the additional hours to accomplish the task we set out to do—i. e., to prepare our students for careers in business administration by educating them in those subjects which we believe will stand them in good stead in any environment.

Personally, I believe that there should be a required course in international business at each level. But I'm as reluctant as anyone else to add the requirement at the expense of the major.

Thus, I think the sensible approach is to do what we are trying to do — incorporate the international dimension into our existing courses. However, I'm not too sure how well such a policy works. Obviously it varies with the course and the instructor. But I think as a general statement that as we are currently teaching our courses, we could add specialized courses in international business without much risk of duplicating the international material in our existing courses. I can readily understand why some schools have established international departments as a sort of temporary stewardship of the subject until the regular departments really integrate the material into their existing curriculum.

RESEARCH ACTIVITIES

Turning to research activities, within our Division of Research we have the Institute for International Business Management and Economic Development Studies. The broad but basic purpose of this Institute is to assist our faculty in any way we can in their research projects. We are aided in these activities by a very small grant of Ford Foundation money through our University's Center for International Programs.

Many of our faculty are perfectly willing and able to formulate their own research projects, find their own financing, and arrange for publication of the results. In those cases the Institute is not involved. In other instances the Institute does assist in one or more of the stages of the research. Thus, we have a somewhat limited contact with what our faculty is doing in research in international business and an even more limited control over such activities. My remarks about research stem from such a perspective.

How much research activity has there been in international business at our school? Measuring it in the only terms that I know—output in the form of publication—there has been a considerable amount of activity in the two short years that the Institute has been in existence. For example, our Division of Research has published nine books on International Business in our series on this subject, with two more presently in the process of being published. Further, our faculty has written a substantial number of articles on international business.

Of this number, how many have resulted from our technical assistance programs? Two books resulted directly from our Brazilian program. Additionally, there have been several articles based on our research there. One doctoral dissertation has also directly resulted from this program.

We have had four texts by our professors written in Turkish for our Turkey program. Our first group of faculty has just returned to the States from Turkey. We expect some additional publication based on their research. Again, there has been one doctoral dissertation which has been connected with the Turkey project.

Add to these studies the cases which our professors have worked up, and that is about the extent of the observable research results.

We are currently involved in a program which has some technical assistance aspects. The research output of this activity is already starting to materialize, and it will be substantial. But this program is primarily research-based and probably should not be included in the present description.

How much indirect effect have our technical assistance projects had on research? I really don't know, but I doubt that it has been very great.

Therefore, we come back to the original statement that we have done quite a bit in international business. However, we fall into the category of not having done as much as an outside observer might expect, based on the considerable competence in international business that our faculty has acquired from overseas projects.

Let us turn to an examination of why this is so. And in this explanation, I believe we will be dealing with a general situation, rather than one which is unique to Michigan State.

REASONS FOR LIMITED FEEDBACK

Based on conversations with fellow faculty members as well as personal impressions and opinion, I think there are some substantial reasons why we have not made more on-campus use of our overseas experience. Primarily, I think the reasons can be classified under the broad heading of faculty attitude—or as our behaviorally-oriented brethren would say, they stem from a role conflict which is not being resolved in favor of either curriculum or research in international business.

Many of the things I'm about to say have been mentioned in the *EWA Report*. But they have only been mentioned and usually in the form of questions. I think these points merit considerably greater attention.

Subject Matter and Its Dimensions

When it comes to formalizing the feedback from overseas projects into specialized courses, we must recognize that the faculty member as an academician thinks of himself in connection with his functional specialty. True, he is aware of himself as many things—he is in his social role a member of a number of communities at different levels of abstraction. He is, toward the top of this abstraction, a member of both a national and worldwide community and is perfectly willing to exercise his membership responsibilities at both levels. I am convinced that it is a recognition of this responsibility that motivates more of our faculty to engage in overseas projects than it is the adventure of living abroad or even the expansion of the individual's professional competence.

But once back on campus, it's a different story. He now identifies himself with his professional reference group. He is now primarily a professor of marketing, a professor of accounting, or whatever he professes to be as an academician or member of a professional body of educators. To expect him to identify as a member of an international group here is to expect him to think of himself on an entirely different plane from that of his role in his office or classroom.

In this connection, I think it is a mistake to conclude that he therefore neglects the international dimension of his discipline in order to concentrate on the domestic. What he is really doing is viewing his own discipline in terms that transcend any geographic environment. Thus, for example, he is concerned with arriving at a generalized statement concerning the relationship between length of the channel of distribution and the costs of doing business. And if in progressing toward such a generalization he contrasts his experience in observing the operation of a local market in Nigeria with that of a supermarket in Chicago, he is doing so as means to an end— not because there is any academic, or professional, virtue *per se* in introducing the international dimension into his consideration. If similar conditions of demand and supply exist on the corner of State and Madison as exist in Nigeria, he would be willing to include that empirical observation in his study.

If he recognizes that similar economic conditions do not prevail, he will introduce his overseas experience in his research and his exposition to his classes. But to expect him to emphasize such experience and to formalize it into a course of study is to expect him to organize his efforts around a branch of his interest tree rather than the tree itself.

Course titles or the titles placed on journal articles will not necessarily reflect his having introduced the results of his overseas experience into his campus activities. Thus the cry goes out that we are not getting the feedback from our overseas projects into our research and curriculum. The feedback is there, but it is both unfortunate and unrealistic to expect our faculty to emphasize a single dimension of a broader concern which is virtually n-dimensional.

Not incidentally, it is this ordering of interest that leads to a situation in which the institution's own central administration of international programs may be firmly convinced that there is no real feedback into courses or research. It is also such a priority of interest that might cause a clash between a functionally organized department and the School's international Institute regarding the housing, and administration, of particular international projects—should the functional or the international aspect be emphasized?

Faculty View of Disciplines

Closely allied is the question of how far we can fractionalize a discipline. For example, a faculty member may be first of all a marketing man who is particularly interested in one or more commodity groups, institutions, functions, or some combination thereof. In treating his particular interest within his specialty, he may also emphasize quantitative tools or consumer behavior. To introduce the additional dimension of international focus may lead to an untenably narrow scope of a field of study which is still lacking in good working generalizations in its basic subject matter.

I recognize that one could reason completely in reverse. That is, that the very method of working toward a science of marketing, or anything else, is to start with very particular, isolated types of activity, analyze and classify these types, and thereby draw progressively higher orders of generalizations. But the question still remains as to what one observes, how he analyzes, and on what basis he classifies, without first having a body of generalizations as a frame of reference.

I think it is futile here, as elsewhere, to argue for a position of either induction or deduction coming first in developing a discipline. The point that is important to us here is explaining a considerable body of faculty attitude—an attitude which holds that to emphasize the international aspect is to emphasize differences rather than similarities, which runs contrary to attempts to establish a uniform body of knowledge.

Further, the same faculty members are aware that the thing that has made them attractive as sources of supply for overseas projects has been their knowledge of their own functional areas, not that they are international specialists. They view this also as being consistent with the notion that in business administration there is a core of knowledge which can be viewed as normative in nature, that this core of knowledge can be transferred, and that environmental differences are important though still special cases of generalized situations. They are important qualifiers which can, however, be rather quickly learned and embodied into the basic generalizations by a reasonably good logician who *knows* these generalizations. Such persons are the first to make the point that there are environmental differences of a social, cultural, and ethical nature. But such differences are not the things to be stressed. Similarities in basic objectives are more numerous and more important than differences. The differences we observe in many social systems are more likely to be functions of time and development rather than functions of needs, aspirations, or values.

Faculty Attributes

It is important also to examine the type of faculty member who engages in overseas projects. We do not (and probably should not) send on overseas projects those persons whose sole interest is their own personal scholarship. Generally speaking, on technical-assistance or institution-building projects we all require individuals who are capable of administering, advising, adjusting quickly, establishing rapport, and working effectively with both host-country and U. S. personnel of diverse backgrounds. Such attributes are less likely to be possessed by the eminent scholar than by our administrators or by those professors who are characterized as good teachers, who work well with students, with colleagues, and with the administration, and who do an average job in research and publication.

At MSU, we have had on long-term overseas assignment associate deans, department chairmen, and directors of research, as well as those professors who are known for doing a well-rounded job. Our experience has been that such persons perform uniformly well on overseas projects.

The point is that, upon his return from an overseas assignment, such a person will probably continue to participate in a manner indicated by those attributes which he possessed on the campus and those abilities he exercised overseas. If he was average in research and publication before, he probably will continue to be average upon his return. To expect anything else is to expect the individual to be even more of a chameleon than he had to be in order to be successful overseas.

SUGGESTED ATTITUDE

Finally, what should be our attitude toward overseas projects? Can't we reason that since the University has contracted for these projects, there should be a substantial direct and observable academic payoff? And if we're not getting it, we should not engage in such projects? I don't believe such is necessarily the case.

Every school attempts, in varying degree, to fulfill its obligation in the area of public service. And I am sure that a land-grant university such as ours is particularly aware of this obligation. There are faculty members who liken participation in overseas projects to participating in executive development programs, in the sense that there should be—and there is—some academic feedback into research and curriculum. But such feedback is probably incidental. Certainly it is not the primary purpose of either activity.

Making Projects More Productive Academically

I would not argue that we should back away from overseas projects. Rather, we should accept them as useful contributions to the educational process and try to see how we can make them more so. In doing so, there are several things we should insist on before undertaking a particular project:

1. *Selection*—Is it the sort of project which has an appeal to the academic or professional interests of our faculty? Or does it rest exclusively on a base of service to our national or international community? Further, are we learning something substantial from undertaking this project, or are we primarily plowing familiar ground by applying knowledge and techniques which we have perfected elsewhere? I think we should prefer relatively "high risk" projects.

2. *Built-in research component*—(we now have this in all our contracts at MSU). Permit the person who has solely a scholarly interest in the subject to exercise that interest.

3. *Provision for overstaffing*—so that the on-campus program doesn't suffer because of the overseas project.

4. *Provision for a multiplier effect through graduate studies and dissertations.*

5. *Provision for released time* upon return to campus in order for the faculty member to write up the results of his experience, to introduce his experience into course work, where appropriate, and to disseminate his new knowledge and understanding through seminars and workshops.

6. *Provision for publication*—a specific allotment of funds for this purpose. This is particularly important to an operation such as ours, where we have our own publication program.

At Michigan State, we are currently trying to assure that all of these components are present. In doing so we are being given considerable assistance through the Midwest Universities Consortium for International Activities and through the Inter-University Research Program in Institution Building, both of which are supported by Ford Foundation funds.

Even with all these provisions, we still won't get the feedback unless the faculty member is convinced of the need for devoting attention to the international aspect. Such a program, however, will encourage the feedback from those of our faculty who are interested in providing such feedback through research and curriculum. And as I have described our faculty participant in overseas projects, he is perfectly capable of contributing in these areas, given the proper encouragement.

I think there is a real danger of overcorrecting in response to the present reaction and attitude of many observers (and participants) toward technical-assistance and institution-building projects.

It has been through such projects that many of our universities have increased, or even started, their interest in international affairs. There has been an academic feedback, albeit limited and indirect to a large extent. It seems to me that our attitude should be the same as that of the entire *EWA Report*—i. e., how can we make such activities more productive in feeding back into curriculum and research? At the same time, however, we must keep sight of the basic purposes for which these projects are intended—public service.

Discussion Comments
The Problem of Feedback

Panelists: Coleman and Erickson

REPORTER: James J. Linn

Lombard (Harvard) reported that his school is now beginning to get explicit statements from a faculty member before he goes overseas. These cover such things as the research he expects to perform and what output he contemplates while overseas and upon his return. Originally, Harvard had not done this, but they now find it very useful in evaluating overseas requests. The expected research and publication are not always fulfilled, but having estimates is in itself an improvement over prior practice.

The discussion then turned to the subject of staffing the overseas project. One participant complained that staffing an overseas project places a severe strain on any school that is also trying to increase its size and faculty at home. Another participant pointed out that overseas projects could be used to obtain staff by hiring them for a year's work overseas, until they are needed at the home institution.

Overman (Arizona State) said that his school was in a unique situation, being in a city (Phoenix) which has an international program (American Institute for Foreign Trade); thus, it does not seem useful, in the school's opinion, to start its own international program when such a good one already exists in the city.

Miller (Nebraska) asked whether any other participants have become involved in overseas programs that did not originate in the area of business. At Nebraska, he said, the department of agriculture has an AID contract, and it is trying to get the business school involved extensively in the project.

In response to a question about the participants' experience in graduate and undergraduate programs abroad, Coleman stated that until five or six years ago, no graduate work abroad was being done.

Hill (MIT) mentioned that there is no undergraduate work at present at Ahmedabad.

In referring to feedback, Hill quoted Carmichael, who had recommended in his talk that overseas projects should go beyond the development of an educational program: they should introduce a research program and orientation. In subsequent discussion of this point, it was mentioned that this endeavor would require a different mix of effort and resources than would a purely educational project.

WILLIAM S. LINDSAY

Corn Products Company

Prerequisites for Effective Management of International Business Today

My remarks will be from the point of view of a customer who uses the products produced in your institutions. Through this manner, we will lead into the subject, "Prerequisites for Effective Management of International Business Today."

U. S. educational institutions are to be complimented on the success of their products, particularly in recent years. The success can best be measured by the evidence which describes the growth of American business investment and profitability outside of the United States. You are certainly entitled to take your share of credit for the accomplishments.

Dealing with the future, it is best to point out certain benchmarks, and I will describe those with which I am most familiar, reflecting the experience over the years of the Corn Products Company outside the United States.

Our first equity investment was made just prior to World War I. Today we are operating with equity investment in 32 countries. Operations abroad account for about one half of the total corporate sales and earnings.

Outside the United States, we employ approximately 24,000 people. Of these, approximately 140 are classified as international

WILLIAM S. LINDSAY is Administrative Vice President for Corn Products International, a division of Corn Products Company. He joined the manufacturing department of Corn Products Company in 1934, and later served in managerial positions in various processing plants and at the home office in New York City. In 1951, he joined the company's Brazilian subsidiary, Refiniações de Milho, which he served for eight years, rising to the position of managing director. He became a Vice President of Corn Products International in 1960, accountable for operations in the Western Hemisphere, and was named to his present position in 1965.

employees. Our definition of an international person is one who has been moved by the corporation from one country to work in another. In this group are about 45 Americans.

I call your attention to a very excellent publication of Business International, Inc. Its title is *1985 Corporate Planning Today for Tomorrow's World Market.* This summary gives an indication of the personnel and management needs in the immediate future.

Personnel needs are accelerating. The fact that Corn Products employs so few Americans overseas should by no means indicate that this is typical and that the need is not increasing rapidly.

Further, the fact that products from the educational institutions have been so successful in the past does not allow us to assume automatically that present methods are adequate to fill the coming needs. Previous panel meetings at this Conference have indicated a need for research in order to more adequately determine the specifications of the products required to meet future needs. The following are some suggested specifications.

> Individual desire—a real burn to engage in international business. (It is necessary to determine the source of the desires and reasons therefor.)

> Knowledge and awareness of international economics.

> An alertness for the benchmarks of business opportunities. Alertness to economic pressures and cultural change—an ability to cope profitably with changing conditions.

The need is for creativity and entrepreneurship at all management levels, regardless of the nature of one's function as compared to top-level decision-making.

People must be *simpático*, tolerant and understanding of differences in ways of life.

It is not necessary to adapt to a different way of life, but have respect and understanding for it.

The U. S. education system is drastically in arrears through lack of foreign language in the curriculum. This is needed very early in an individual's education, probably best at the elementary school level. It is grossly incompatible that a foreign language is required of candidates for PhD degrees but not for graduate degrees in international business.

FRANK PACE, JR.

International Executive Service Corps

Role of the International Executive Service Corps in Education for International Business

My first responsibility to this distinguished group is to explain very briefly the nature and function of the International Executive Service Corps (IESC), and then I will undertake to relate our efforts to the theme of Education for International Business.

IESC is a non-profit organization supported partially by government funds and partially by private funds, but from an operational point of view is conducted on a purely private basis. The thesis of IESC is that the great requirement of the developing countries is management, not money. Given competent management, all of the private and public capital that is needed can be attracted, but in its absence no amount of money will provide a solution.

To meet this challenge, David Rockefeller suggested that the private sector should call upon its managerial talents and undertake the difficult problem of translating our managerial and technical advances into terms that are meaningful and valuable to the develop-

FRANK PACE, JR., is President of the International Executive Service Corps, New York City. He has an MA from Princeton University and an LLB from Harvard University. From 1936 to 1942, he practiced law in Arkansas. In 1946, he was special assistant to the Attorney General (taxation division), and in 1946 he became executive assistant to the Postmaster General. He was assistant director, Bureau of the Budget, 1948-49, and Director, 1949-50. From 1950 to 1953, he was Secretary of the Army. In 1953, he was named executive vice president and a director of General Dynamics Corporation, becoming Chairman of the Board in 1957. In 1964, two years after leaving General Dynamics, he became President of the International Executive Service Corps, a non-profit organization having the purpose of exporting managerial talent to industrially developing nations. He is presently a director of several companies, including Time, Inc., Eurofund, Inc., and Continental Oil Co.

ing countries. One of the first precepts of our operation was that we would charge a fee, and a relatively demanding one, on the theory that the only services that are truly appreciated and used are those that are paid for. A great many of our clients have emphasized the importance of this approach in rendering effective services. We also decided that the executives who went out for us should be volunteers. We felt that this brought them a measure of acceptance abroad and guaranteed the validity of their interest in the program. The latter decision has proven to be eminently sound, because we have almost 4,000 pre-screened businessmen on our volunteer list, and we hope to eventually increase that to 6,000.

The success of our program has been in large measure due to the patience, judgment, and even the wisdom of our volunteers, as well as to their technical competence. It is our belief that the success of an assignment abroad is 60 per cent psychological and 40 per cent technical. Possibly the most interesting feature of our operation is that we have found that the average tour measures about three months. I had originally assumed that it would take a year to do an effective job, but we found in our early experience that three months was adequate. I questioned the first fifteen men who returned, and every one of them said, "Mr. Pace, never send a man for more than six months." When I inquired as to the reason, they said that if a man stays longer than six months, he will inevitably end up running the business, and IESC's purpose should be to help businesses abroad to help themselves, not assume the responsibility. With that thesis we all agree thoroughly, and now as we approach our 500th project, the average tour still stands at three months.

We have some twenty-one resident representatives abroad who are dedicated, competent men, many of them serving as volunteers. We are in forty-two countries around the world, and in over 90 per cent of the cases we have definitive evidence of client satisfaction. It is fair to say that we are now in a position to carry out substantial numbers of projects with a high level of success in the years ahead. Our major problem is how do we, because of our small size, maximize the impact of our work in the developing countries? To do this we must find a means of extending the value of each project we undertake.

What can all of this mean to education for international business? First, there is, I believe, a very valuable set of quite modern case histories available to the business schools and schools of public administration to use in the educational processes. It is my hope that there can be established a multi-university team that might assess these cases and determine those that carry real implications for education. Then it might be possible for business school professors to study in depth a certain number of cases and reduce them to the form that would be most valuable in the business-school process. We also hope to encourage professors in the schools of business administration to undertake a tour abroad of about two months, working with our country representatives and pursuing certain case studies that are going on in the country to which they have been assigned. We also hope to invite some five or six outstanding students in the business schools to undertake similar tours with our country representatives. It is hoped that these students might be in their junior year, so that their experiences might be a subject of discussion in the business school. They might also invite one or two of the executives whom they would meet on their tour to come to the business school for practical discussion with the students themselves.

All in all, we feel that we are pioneering new ground that provides a fascinating opportunity for observation and understanding in the schools of business administration around this country and abroad. This is the first time that Americans have been able to sit on the same side of the desk with their counterparts in the developing countries, and to understand problems as they are seen through the eyes of local business executives. A whole new order of magnitude of understanding is available if we have the wisdom to take full advantage of it. The decision as to whether it should be done and, if so, how, rests with you.

Discussion Comments

Prerequisites for Effective Management of International Business Today; Educational Role of IESC

Panelists: Lindsay and Pace

REPORTER: Eric W. Vetter

Five separate topics received attention during this session. Most of the discussion was directed at Lindsay and Pace in order to learn the experience of their organizations that would be helpful to international business educators.

1. CAREER PATTERNS OF INTERNATIONAL BUSINESS EXECUTIVES

Although empirical studies of the career patterns of executives currently involved in international business were not presented, strong interest was shown in how men progressed in international business organizations. It was suggested that to date, most men in responsible international business positions have first demonstrated competence in a functional field (e. g., marketing, production) before being given an international assignment. Who, specifically, is selected for overseas work was not discussed, and so the problem of determining selection criteria was not examined. It was noted, however, that a number of large U. S. corporations now recruit men directly from colleges for international business assignments, either for abroad or home-desk duties. The typical future career pattern is thus in doubt, but it seems clear that the past career patterns may not be duplicated in the future, at least in a number of organizations.

2. CONTINUING EDUCATION FOR EXECUTIVES IN INTERNATIONAL BUSINESS

Because many executives receive overseas assignments after several years with an organization, a need exists for programs in international business for these persons. Several such programs appear to have been successful, but the nature, content, and length of the programs have apparently not yet been resolved satisfactorily by all parties. The Executive Program for International Managers, at Columbia University, has been substantially over-subscribed by companies. It has drawn executives from throughout the world, with as many as 20 different nations represented at one program offering.

3. U. S. BUSINESS ASSISTANCE TO FOREIGN BUSINESS SCHOOLS

Increased support and participation by business in the operations of emerging schools of business around the world appear to be needed. Currently, this support is given by a number of companies, but the need for assistance is considerable.

Company support now is seen in the financing of students, in the use of overseas executives on advisory boards and boards of trustees, and in the use of company personnel as part-time instructors. Pace indicated that International Executive Service Corps (IESC) personnel might be able to lend assistance in this field through the use of their overseas executives in temporary part-time instructional capacities.

4. LANGUAGE ABILITY

Substantial agreement existed among the participants that knowledge of the language of a country is vital to a business executive's successful performance in that country. An ability to "get by" initially in the country was suggested as perhaps the minimum requirement, with a high level of fluency and depth in grammar skills not required at this stage. Dependence on interpreters for everyday affairs is a major disadvantage to a businessman abroad.

Disagreement was substantial, however, as to where and when language skills should be acquired. Only four schools represented in the session require some level of language proficiency by their students.

Opposition to requiring a language proficiency of students centers on the allocation of perhaps substantial time during one's business education to the study of a language, when it is uncertain whether the student will ever need to use that particular language. Furthermore, if overseas assignments are delayed some length of time after the study of a language (as suggested by the career patterns discussed earlier), one's proficiency might become very low in the interim, making the previous language study very uneconomical. Finally, it is felt that modern instruction in foreign languages makes it possible for companies to equip their personnel, in a relatively short period of time, with the basic conversational skills in the language of the specific country to which they will be assigned.

Advocates of a foreign language proficiency emphasize its central role in overseas performance. They minimize the problem of assignment to "third countries" because of the modern personnel management procedures in use today. Even if this occurs, they contend that knowledge of two languages facilitates communications nearly anywhere in the world.

It was also felt that the skills developed in learning a second language are generally transferable when studying a third language, in addition to any similarities between the languages (e. g., between French and Spanish). It was also questioned whether students should be allowed to devote a major portion of their business education to international business if they do not have a proficiency (or at least an aptitude) in language. The usefulness of major educational efforts in international business by students who might never function successfully abroad was thus challenged. A comparison was drawn between doctoral programs which require language proficiency and international business programs which do not.

5. PREPARING FOR CULTURAL SHOCK

The preparation of an executive or professor for possible cultural shock on going abroad currently appears to be less than fully satisfactory. Some programs in this area have been disappointing. IESC has found it highly desirable to have an executive intending to go abroad talk with an executive who has recently returned from the specific country or region of the world. In addition, written reports of returned executives on their encounters with social and cultural problems are used. IESC has found that a strong sense of "humility" on the part of the executive is an important factor in overseas success. Cooperation between IESC and business schools (through the AACSB) in helping to prepare professors going abroad, by arranging interviews with returned IESC executives, is possible. Pace invited the AACSB to pursue this matter, and indicated that IESC would be willing to assist business schools in this area.

COURTNEY C. BROWN
Columbia University

The Next Ten Years in Education for International Business

Your program chairman, Dean Grayson, asked me to do two things. He gave me the title, "The Next Ten Years in Education for International Business." But he also asked me to provide something of a wrap-up of the discussions that we have shared for the last two days.

WHERE WE HAVE BEEN

I think I shall try to do that by starting a little back of the present to get a sight on where we have been and where we are now, as a preface for prognosticating where we might be going. I'm reminded of the story of the Irish gang boss who always had the crew that got the straightest rails. They asked him how he did it. Well, he said, I just back up about a hundred yards from where I am, I take a squint at where we've been, and then I push it on out a little bit further, and he said, you never miss. So let's look at this matter of the factors of education for international business, using the Irish gang-boss' squint-eye method.

I'll start with a very brief description of where we were ten years ago. Perhaps we might start with what the situation was ten years ago abroad. I had the privilege of an Eisenhower Fellowship study tour at that time. It was for the purpose of looking at business education as it was then being conducted, or aspired to be conducted,

COURTNEY C. BROWN is Dean of the Graduate School of Business, Columbia University. He has a PhD from Columbia. Prior to coming to Columbia as dean in 1954, he spent 10 years in investment management work, 3½ years during the War with the Department of State and Commodity Credit Corporation, and several years in different staff and line capacities with Standard Oil Company of New Jersey. He is director of several large corporations, including The Borden Company and Union Pacific Railroad Company. From 1959 to 1962, he was a public Governor of the New York Stock Exchange.

in 17 of the lesser-developed countries of the Eastern Hemisphere. There was a great interest in education for business in the business communities. There was some interest in the academic institutions, but primarily among the administrators. It was regarded with some disdain by the faculties, it seemed to me; the kind of a real "dug-in" resistance all of you would recognize. However, in some places, such unexpected places as Chulalongkorn in Bangkok and even out in Kandy, Ceylon, there were schools of commerce in the universities. Their programs were not business education in the sense that we know it. But they were teaching some of the basic skills of business. They were thinking of business almost entirely, not as a management matter, but as a small shopkeeper's concerns – that kind of thing. That's what business was, and to an extent still is, in those communities.

There were some early assistance programs. Unfortunately, they were not prospering too well in most cases. If one characteristic probably explained this, it was that too many of us sent over people whom we didn't quite know what to do with here. Those who went felt a sense of frustration. They were asked to teach student classes. The practices of foreign universities in that part of the world, then and now, include the giving of external examinations prepared in London. These examinations had very little to do with what went on in the classroom. The students attended the first class, but attendance dropped off very quickly, and by the end of the term, these teachers had very few students. They felt that they were not being used adequately.

Management as a subject of interest, when approached at all, was pretty much handled as an extension of economics or public administration. There was a somewhat critical undertone of complaint that the U.S. parties were transplanting U.S. curricula, materials, and teaching methods. This might have been in part because of the inadequacies of the institutions themselves, but there nevertheless was that complaint. All in all, it was not a very encouraging picture, except in the sense that there was a strong desire, other than in the traditional faculties, to develop this activity.

What was the situation in the United States ten years ago? I think all of us will recall vividly that we were in a state of ferment regarding the total business curriculum. There were a number of international business courses, although only a scattering of programs contained concentrated study in the field of international business. Those that did exist had only recently been inaugurated. There was uncertainty as to whether there really was a field of international

— 285 —

business. Perhaps the way to do it was to inject some foreign considerations into our traditional fields of study. That's an issue, as you know, that hasn't been resolved to this day.

Ten years ago, faculty with high qualifications were hard to come by and difficult to spare, a condition that still exists today. Opportunities for material reward in a foreign assignment were sometimes less than at home. The academic ladder itself militated against people going abroad. How could one spare a year or two out of his professional progress? The question of whether, in an exchange program, you would send people abroad and insert them in existing academic faculties or create a new institution was very much up in the air. In an atmosphere of quasi-hostility in the host-university faculty, the decision frequently was to create a new institution. This was done in Brazil, it was done in Peru, it was done elsewhere. The idea of bringing members of foreign faculties to the United States, not as teachers but as degree candidates or scholars, had not been developed very far.

This was the situation in the United States, and it stood alongside the situation abroad which I've briefly described. All that you could say ten years ago was that here was an awakening to the existence and to the potentials of international business study, but it didn't have a very promising future when you looked at it realistically.

What has occurred during the past decade in business education in the United States? There has been a large increase, but not as much as many of us would desire, in the development of course materials dealing with international business. We had a Friday morning session on this subject and I will not try to take your time to review it. There has been a large number of experimental exchange programs extending over the full range of possibilities, from independent hires by foreign universities and colleges to the establishment of new plants and new faculties abroad. There has been some increase in the number of foreign students studying business in the United States. And some new programs in the U.S. have been designed specifically for foreign students, such as ICAME, at Stanford.[1] Still more have studied as degree candidates in regular programs.

A large amount of time, talent, and money has been allocated to research in the field of international business. All of this, of course, has been experimental. We have tried various ideas and approaches, and I think it's constructive that we all have felt that we wanted —

1[For a discussion of the ICAME program, see the paper by Thomas A. Graves, Jr., pp. 240-44. —Ed.]

within the limits of our own resources, our own faculties, our own associations and contacts — to do things that we thought would maximize our efforts. As a result, the heterogeneity of the effort has tested many different kinds of programs. This is good.

Yet much more has occurred, it seems to me, in the world of international business itself than has occurred in the field of education for international business. Though the decade of development has been vigorously pursued, it has been disappointing. The polemic that we all felt so vividly a decade ago between capitalism and socialism seems to have diminished in intensity, even to the point of business becoming the instrument for breaching the iron curtain in a number of cases. Perhaps one of the most important and significant developments within the last decade has been the appearance of the multinational corporation, which has created an inter-woven network of inter-communication throughout the world. We have seen the development of a set of corporate relationships that penetrate national borders which begins to require a theory of international production to replace or stand alongside the theory of international trade. Comparative advantage is no longer a matter of raw materials; it is much more a matter of organizing ability, technical knowledge, and the capacity to serve.

A GLANCE AHEAD

So much for the squint-eye method, standing ten years back and looking forward to today. Now for the squint forward to the next ten years. More specifically, how will our past experience, together with these environmental changes that have occurred in the field of international business, affect education for world business during the next decade? First, let me make several observations regarding curriculum, and then I will refer to what seems to me to be some of the prospects in the field of exchange programs. It's much easier to talk about what may occur ten years from now, or what the situation may be ten years from now, than to describe what might happen next year.

In regard to curriculum — and here I know I'm probably going to say some things that will sound controversial — of the several ways available for organizing the study of world business, I'm inclined to feel that, first, injecting foreign considerations into traditional business materials will be progressively more used. Why? Because all of our faculties are becoming much more aware that business is a global thing. Whatever may have been heretofore valid in a domestic setting will be valid henceforth only if it is thought about and analyzed in the light of its action and reaction in the world setting. Faculties tend to deal with those materials with which they are most familiar. And for reasons that I'll describe later, I think faculties are going to become more and more familiar with the world scene.

Second, the building of an international business curriculum as an extension of and elaboration of the economics department's materials of international trade and finance will be found to be less than satisfactory. I agree with some of the things that have been said in the last couple of days, that we must, of course, use the materials that are available to us from the field of international economics. But simply to build on them, I think, is likely to be less than satisfactory. Today, business and its management are rooted in far more than economics. And the attempt to understand business, either domestically or internationally, exclusively in terms of economics, leaves one short of full comprehension.

Third, I believe that regional studies will have only limited acceptability in the business curriculum. I think this is so for the same reason that was advanced this morning in discussing why we do not require foreign language. Business is global, and it's becoming more global daily, and while there may be opportunities to do some work in regional studies, my hunch is that we will find it appearing more frequently in the faculties of political science, and in other faculties, rather than in the faculties of business.

Fourth, I believe the great rewards of world business study will derive from an area of work that has not been sufficiently emphasized in our discussions during the past two days. I refer to the fascinating problems of managing in different cultures, and particularly of managing the world corporation and the challenge it offers of reconciling national interests on the one hand and world interests on the other. National interests are usually constricted to inward-looking concerns for security, sovereignty, and preferment. The global corporation has a more expansive dimension of services. You are all familiar with the classic comment of the British foreign office, "We have no friends, only interests."

In contrast, the global corporation could not live without friends. It gets its sanction from acceptance. It relies not on might and compulsion for its security but on competitive advantage that wins voluntary approval from the people of all nations.

In many respects, the global business is basically incompatible with the nation-state. To the extent that we concern ourselves in international business with this kind of organization, whether we realize it or not, or whether we like it or not, we will be quite radical. Indeed, I am beginning to see this expressed by people where you would least expect it. May I throw this in as a commercial: In the November-December, 1967 issue of the *Columbia Journal of World Business*, George Ball has an article in which he says if the multi-national business is to be multi-national it must be multi-national in ownership, in management, and indeed in charter, perhaps issued by the United Nations. The extent to which business will intervene across national boundaries and national interests is, I submit, going to provide one of the most challenging, exciting bodies of academic material that we can inject into our curriculum. The management of a world business involves not a physical change from the management of a domestic business, but a chemical one, with so many different variables that we seldom comprehend them until we really begin to think deeply about it.

There is another thing that I think will find its way into the curriculum, and this is going to be harder to come by and perhaps somewhat more subtle. The program of education in international business, I think, will slowly awaken to the reality that it is world business that we are studying, not international business *per se*. By that I mean a shifting of the incidence of competition among nations to competition among world-wide industries and among world-wide firms. Indeed, I hope that in the course of time we will drop the term "international business" completely and adopt the term "world business," because this is the real subject of our concern.

Now, let us turn to the next ten years in our exchange programs. Despite many frustrations, disappointments, and doubts, all of which have been very intelligently and effectively presented at this meeting, it's my judgment that this is an activity that will increase in the coming decade. That is true for a number of reasons. First, there is a growing awareness abroad of the need for management talent, and there is a growing awareness in this country that the world is going to be made a good place to live with some degree of stability only if the rest of the world can manage its affairs and seek its own opulence with some capability. Second, I think I see evidence, among those I meet and talk to from foreign universities, of a far greater readiness to accept business as a field of study in their universities than I would have believed possible ten years ago. Finally, this activity should increase because we may once again, perhaps for only an interim period, begin to develop some surpluses of faculty. That will depend in part upon the administrative rulings that Mr. Hershey makes in the draft. But irrespective of the draft, I believe we may find ourselves in a somewhat more comfortable position with regard to faculty availability.

On the matter of "professors for export," it has seemed to me that if this world is going to move in the directions that we've all been discussing, it should become in the course of time a definite part of the academic ladder that every man on a faculty of business spend at least some time in foreign service. I have, at times, felt a sense of undesirable constrictiveness about the academic ladder. A man gets his PhD, obtains a faculty appointment, and is told by his senior colleagues, "Get the journal article written as fast as you can, and don't leave the campus. You're wasting time, and you'll lose your place in the progression." This is not doing the man a service, in my judgment. It provides him with a limited range of personal experience that will reflect in his professional development throughout his career, whereas if we could build into this academic ladder an expectation that an academic career in a faculty of business would carry with it a year or two abroad, working with other cultures, I think we would find that that man, a decade hence, would be a far more useful citizen – to himself, to his students, and to his institution.

How should the faculty members that do go abroad be used? Should we think of the assignment as participation in course construction, in total curriculum development, in the conduct of faculty seminars, in student instruction? These are questions that I shall not try to answer. But I think that only when the universities in the other parts of the world begin to develop practices that make direct contacts with students more productive and more fruitful, should our export faculty be used in the classroom.

Another aspect of this exchange program will, I think, be a large expansion in the enrollments of foreign students in this country. In this I think we have a very definite feedback, just as we would have a feedback in sending many of our young men to foreign posts for visitations, and some of our older ones as well. The feedback is that, in the classroom, the discussion will be from the background of different cultures, different attitudes, and different ideas.

We must, in developing this expanding enrollment of foreign students, be very careful of the financial assistance arrangements that are made available. We must do everything we can to induce them to return to their home countries, where they will be far more useful to themselves and to the world than they would be to us. I know the temptations of a first-rate man coming out of a PhD program: you want him. We have all been guilty. We take them, too, but I feel a little guilty, frankly, every time we do. In making assistance available to foreign students while they are here, we ought to find some imaginative ways in which the result would be an inducement for them to return to their home countries on completing their work.

In addition to exporting individual professors on various kinds of exchange programs, the idea of the consortium is coming into play, in which teams of from three to as many as fifteen professors, recruited from a variety of university campuses in this country, would go abroad. Here again, I think we must be careful that their assignments are of maximum usefulness, including research assignments. One of the great deficiencies in the foreign university, as you all know better than I, is its lack of research habit.

Whether these exchange programs in the future will, as some of them have heretofore, take the form of creating a new campus outside of the university framework, is doubtful in my mind. The costs are high, and there is a lack of access to the basic disciplines of the social sciences, the behavioral sciences, mathematics, and economics; there is some question of prestige when not attached to a university; and finally, the universities themselves are beginning to become much more ready to accept the idea of a faculty of business.

I would like to close by asking two or three debatable questions. We talk about these exchange programs as though we had the United States "here" and the foreign community "there." But there are many different foreign communities, and they differ by degrees from place to place. For purposes of illustration, I'll present the matter in terms of the Northern Hemisphere and the Southern Hemisphere. In the Northern Hemisphere, we hear much of the technological gap. It really translates itself, it seems to me, into a managerial gap. The organizations are there, the basic skills are there, already in place, and the solution might be some form of long-range preparation and planning, involving programs of management education, to bring those countries of the Northern Hemisphere up to parity with the United States. In the Southern Hemisphere — I'm simply generalizing with full knowledge that I'm doing violence to many of the more advanced countries in the Southern Hemisphere — there doesn't seem to me to be great value in teaching sophisticated management skills, when there is only a limited number of business organizations to manage. The first job in much of this part of the world is organization-building and the teaching of basic skills to make these organizations function. The time for them is now; long-term planning is less relevant.

Perhaps the point might be vividly illustrated if I cite the need for electric energy. The creation of a sales organization, knowing what it is doing in selling ten-horsepower diesel generators to villagers, would be much more meaningful, much more significant, than helping to develop an engineering or contracting firm to design a 600,000-KW hydro-electric generator that might be available ten or fifteen years from now. The job is different in different parts of the world, and this is one of the things, it seems to me, that we have failed to fully appreciate, to fully understand, in setting up our programs of business education in different parts of the world.

One last thought: I have seen some reports of survey teams that urge limited business education programs, fearing that no ready job market would exist for graduates of such a program. Let me ask a question in an imperative manner: When will we learn that it is the task of business education to develop job creators, not just job takers? Creators of new business organizations, yes, but also creators of new activities in existing organizations. Unless we find ways to give substantive expression and vivid visibility to the responsibilities of business education in their full range, both domestically and globally, we shall not make our full contribution to the achievement of the Great Society to which we aspire for this world.

As Alfred North Whitehead so truthfully stated, "A great society is a society in which its men of business think greatly of their functions." And that's true whether we're talking about world business, domestic business, local business, or education for business.